When the rest of the world is confused and torn, it is more important than ever before for the young adults of the LDS Church to stand up and proudly proclaim their commitment to eternal principles. These principles will keep them steadfast and immovable. This book wonderfully presents solutions to key life challenges through the lens of eternal principles.

—Hyrum W. Smith, author of *The 10 Natural Laws* and
What Matters Most

Shawn Moon is bursting with sound advice and inspiring guidance for young adults standing at so many of life's most critical crossroads.

—Richard and Linda Eyre, New York Times #1 Bestselling Authors

I see young adults from all walks of life take the important steps toward independence. Whether on the football field, in the classroom, or in other aspects of life, the principles taught in this book are critical to creating a winning game plan.

—Kyle Whittingham, Head Football Coach, University of Utah

Congratulations to anyone who reads this because they will be that much closer to discovering who they really are. Young adults will relate to On Your Own, as it gives comfort in knowing we are not on this path alone. This book gave me courage to step up, and provided me with essential tools to face the unknown.

—Jill Stevens, Miss Utah 2007, Afghanistan War Veteran,
Army Combat Medic

On Your Own

On Your Own

A Young Adults' Guide to Making Smart Decisions

By

Shawn D. Moon

CFI
Springville, Utah

ISBN 13: 978-1-59955-260-6

Published by CFI, an imprint of Cedar Fort, Inc., 2373 W. 700 S., Springville, UT 84663
Distributed by Cedar Fort, Inc. www.cedarfort.com

Library of Congress Cataloging-in-Publication Data

Moon, Shawn D. (Shawn Daniel), 1967-
  On your own : a young adults' guide to making smart decisions / Shawn D.
Moon.
     p. cm.
  ISBN 978-1-59955-260-6
  1. Decision making--Religious aspects--Church of Jesus Christ of
Latter-day Saints. 2. Young adults--Conduct of life. I. Title.

  BX8656.M662 2009
  248.8'30882893--dc22

2009002828

Cover design by Angela D. Olsen
Cover design © 2009 by Lyle Mortimer
Edited and typeset by Natalie A. Hepworth

Printed in the United States of America

10 9 8 7 6 5 4 3 2 1

Printed on acid-free paper

To Michele, the love of my life.

CONTENTS

Acknowledgments

While a project of this sort is intensely personal, it is never accomplished by just one person. This book represents a combination of efforts from many people to whom I am deeply grateful. Among those who helped me, I wish to acknowledge the many young adults I have been privileged to know work with. Their faith, determination, curiosity, and commitment serve as continual sources of inspiration for me. I also express gratitude to the following for edits, ideas, candid feedback, and other help: David Covey, the Brimhall Bunch, Von Orgill, Mark Josie, Bill Bennett, William Shupe, Sam Bracken, Debra Lund, Greg Link, Tammy Morgan, Todd Davis, Preston Luke, Karen Hahne, Stephen M. R. Covey, Matt Murdoch, Kevin Miller, my nieces Leslie and Kyra, Stephen Mongie, Steve Chudleigh, Rob and Gretta, Curtis Garbett, Steve Smith, Brady Whittingham, Brad Norton, Nate Bexfield, Ryan Richardson, Catherine Sagers, Tanna Gledhill, and Elaine Bateman.

A special thanks goes to Annie Oswald for her generous help at every turn of this project; Stephanie Calton, who served as my research assistant and contributed energy and enthusiasm for the project and devoted many hours to its completion; Sean Covey, whose vision and encouragement helped prod me into action; Natalie Hepworth and the team at Cedar Fort for their many efforts in assembling the final product; Mayva Moon for her lifelong example of goodness and Christlike love; Harold Kay Moon for his wisdom, confidence, and editing (I want to be just like him when I grow up!); My wife, Michele, for her love, patience, and constant encouragement; and to my children, Cameron, Ryan, Mallory, and Matthew, for subjecting themselves as guinea pigs to my various stories and ideas and for their regular examples of choosing wisely. I watch the decisions they make with awe and wonder. Finally, I express deepest gratitude to my Savior, whom I love and whose love I feel.

Foreword

By Sean Covey

Here you are. You've survived your tumultuous teen years and you're now on your own. At last. Welcome to adulthood! If you're like I was, you're probably eager to be leaving the nest, distancing yourself from your parents to some degree, and becoming your own person. You can go to bed and get up when you want, do your homework if you want, and eat what you want. What a world!

As you look to the future, I hope that you're as excited about it as I am. I realize there are lots of problems in the world. Each day in the news we read about war, terror, and violence. We hear stories about child, spouse, and drug abuse. And when we go to the movies we are reminded how messed up Hollywood really is.

Yet, despite all those challenges, I would argue, that this is the single greatest time to be alive! There is more freedom, wealth, resources, information, choice, and opportunity upon the earth today than ever before. When I was a young adult I used to have to go to a library and search for some obscure book or magazine to do my research, for crying out loud! Now, you can just Google it. With the Internet, cell phones, and iPods, the world and all its information is literally at your finger tips.

Because things are changing so fast there is never a dull moment. Communism collapsed almost overnight. China and India, once obscure countries, are fast becoming global economic powers. Who knows what exciting change will come next.

It is also a day of great contribution and a time to spread your influence. For example, who would have guessed that Oprah Winfrey, abused as a child and raised in poverty, would become one of the most influential women in the world, positively impacting millions from all over the world? Or think about Nobel Peace Prize winner Muhammad Yunus who started the global microfinance movement wherein the poor around the globe have been given small loans, resulting in hundreds of millions being brought out of poverty. Together, we could recount numerous other stories of everyday people who have made great contributions to society at large or within their own families. Such is our time. As President Spencer W. Kimball said about these last days, "[our] influence today can be tenfold what it might be in more tranquil times" (*New Era*, Jan. 1979, 42).

So how can we avoid the pitfalls and make the most of these tremendous opportunities? It all comes down to making smart choices. As you look around, you'll see some people who are happily married and some who aren't; some are people drowning in debt while others are happily debt-free; some people are prospering in their careers while some are floundering. The difference is usually the result of a few key decisions that were made when these people were young adults. Some chose poorly and others wisely.

Truly, the stakes are high.

Over the past many years I have written several books directed to teens. My goal in writing these books was to help teens around the world make smart choices about school, friends, dating, parents, addictions, and life's other big decisions.

Now, at last, comes a book that was not written for high school students, but for young adults, to help them manage the toughest decisions they face: What should I study in school? What career should I go into? Who should I date? Who should I marry and when? What if I make a big mistake? How can I truly make a difference in the world?

Shawn Moon, a close friend of mine, has knocked it out of the park with this book, *On Your Own*. I can't wait to have all of my kids read it when they become young adults! It is the perfect solution for the recent high school graduate, the new college student, the recently returned missionary, or for anyone who is trying to figure out the whole dating and marriage scene.

I wish you every good wish as you live out your young adult years. Make them extraordinary! I believe that you are destined for great things; you were born to lead families, businesses, schools, churches, communities, and governments. This is your responsibility . . . and your privilege.

Good Luck!

—Sean Covey

Sean Covey is the author of *Fourth Down and Life To Go, The 7 Habits of Highly Effective Teens, The 6 Most Important Decisions You'll Ever Make,* and *The 7 Habits of Happy Kids.*

INTRODUCTION

Choice and Responsibility

Oh, the Places You'll Go!
Today is your day.
You're off to Great Places!
You're off and away! You have brains in your head.
You have feet in your shoes.
You can steer yourself
Any direction you choose.[1]

—Dr. Suess

Freedom is only part of the story and half the truth. . . . That is why I recommend that the Statue of Liberty on the East Coast be supplanted by a Statue of Responsibility on the West Coast.[2]

—Viktor Frankl

So you're on your own! Congratulations! Many of you have been anticipating this event for what seems like eternity. For others, it has loomed like a brooding storm. You knew it was coming, and that perhaps it would bring a bit of excitement and possibly even chaos, but you never worried about it too much because it was so far in the future. Well, now it is here, and you need to deal with it. In a sense, you are your own boss for the first time. You can sleep as long as you want, you can go to class if you choose—you set your own schedule. If you want to make your bed, then go for it; if you don't, that is your prerogative. Some of you will find work and start to earn a little cash. While you will probably not make millions right away, you will get a regular paycheck and begin to establish a little financial independence. At some point you will acquire a car, if you don't already have one. You will develop friendships that will last a lifetime, go on road trips, live in an apartment, and provide your own food. It is a time for spontaneity, taking risks, and exploring new vistas. Of course you love your family and are grateful for all they have done. You are, at least in part, who you are because of them. But independence beckons with insistence! Here is what some of you have said regarding this exciting time in your life:

> Living on my own forces me to be independent, free of my parents; this is a stretching yet fulfilling way to live.
>
> —Eric, 22

> I really like the feeling of being independent. My family has done a lot for me in my life, but it feels really nice to live as I want and make choices that are not dependent upon anyone else. I also love the social aspect of living with roommates in a student ward . . . it's a lot of fun.
>
> —John, 23

> I like being in charge of my own schedule and priorities. It gives me the opportunity to learn from my mistakes without the safety net of parents. The rate of growth is much quicker when living on your own.
>
> —Stephen, 24

> I enjoy living on my own, because it makes me completely responsible for my life. I have to decide when to eat, sleep, do my laundry, study, and shop for food. I have to make decisions about my life spiritually, emotionally, physically, socially, and academically. I love having this independence; I think it is a necessary experience for all young single adults.
>
> —Stacie, 20.

> I think the most exciting thing about living on your own is the scariest thing as well: you're free to make *all* of your own decisions, but you're also on your own to suffer all of those consequences, without your parents to bail you out.
>
> —Rob, 21

> I've found that the most exciting part of all this is the opportunity to learn to live with people other than my family. I have to get along with all sorts of personality types, and I find that pretty exciting. I also find it exciting that I can eat wherever or whatever I want and, while my roommates might look at me funny, they can't tell me it's against

the rules, so I can. I'm learning how to fend for myself.

—Leslie, 19

Notice that running through these comments, either directly or by intimation, is the recognition of responsibility, greater than ever before. Parents are no longer standing by to prompt you, nudge you, or urge you toward proper choices. No longer are high school associates providing ballast or offering approval. New surroundings and social pressures invade your familiar comfort zone. There's laundry to do and groceries to buy. Doubts arise, causing you to question your maturity. Are you ready for this? The stakes are high. Consider the following: If an airplane leaving New York bound for Cairo is off just one degree on its flight plan, it will end up in Copenhagen. Similarly, little deviations in our life's course can also have the impact of arriving at an unplanned destination. A lot of weight is placed on the key decisions at this time in your life. In his book, *Standing for Something*, President Gordon B. Hinckley writes about the consequence of choice:

> Many years ago, I worked in a Denver railroad office. . . . One day I received a telephone call from my counterpart on another railroad in Newark, New Jersey, who said that a passenger train had arrived without its baggage car. Three hundred patrons were angry, as well they had a right to be. We discovered that the train had been properly made up in Oakland, California, and had subsequently traveled, intact, to Salt Lake City, then to Denver, and on to St. Louis, from which station it was to depart to its destination in the East Coast. But in the St. Louis railroad yard, a switchman had mistakenly moved a piece of steel just three inches. That piece of steel was a switch point, and the baggage car that should have been in Newark was in New Orleans, fourteen hundred miles away.[3]

Often, small decisions have astonishing impact on our ultimate destination. I posed the following question to several young adults: "As you consider your independence, what concerns do you have about the next few years and the decisions you are required to make?" Below are some of the responses I received:

> One of the biggest concerns I have is the financial burden of school. My husband and I are trying hard to save now so maybe we will not have to borrow quite so much, but that is hard to do! It blows my mind how people actually get out of this kind of debt while having a family,

buying a house, buying cars, and living in general. I know it will just take time, but it is still scary!

—Amy, 22

The biggest fear I have is not meeting my own expectations, and not living the life that I dream of living. At this age, it feels as though I'm standing on the edge of eternity and everything I do will shape it.

—Stephen, 24

I am concerned about getting married and where my career will take me. Will I be able to realistically provide for a family (given I can convince some beautiful young woman to go to the temple with me)? I fear being single and 30 years old.

—Tom, 24

School is the big one for me at this point. I've been a full-time student for many years now and know how to do it, but I know that each year gets successively more challenging and time consuming. I am concerned about keeping the balance I need between school, church, and a social life. I also have financial concerns (the one causes the other). I lose sleep about how much my education is costing me and how much debt I have been forced to accept in order to gain my education. I worry about being a slave to my student loans for the rest of my professional life. Finally, there is of course, the constant ulcerating worry about still being in the dating pool and if, how, and when it will culminate in marriage.

In moments of introspection, I worry that I am totally unprepared for such a responsibility and yet it's what I desire more than anything else. I worry about how my feeling of unpreparedness for marriage affects my efforts at dating now—do I put a lack-luster effort into dating because subconsciously I don't believe I am ready to be a husband and father? Do I let the bad marriage experiences I've seen in some families or in my friends affect my dating efforts? In my head I know these are lousy reasons for not trying very hard to date, but I still find it hard not to be influenced by them, and it concerns me.

—Jae, 23

I am concerned about a mission. I deeply want to serve, and I know that my Heavenly Father is aware of this and has given me the choice between a mission and marriage at this time in my life. I need to prioritize my life according to the gospel principles I have been taught and I need to have trust in myself that I will make the right decision.

—Kyara, 21

Many things have plagued my mind concerning the next few years. Being able to provide for a family has always been on my mind, but lately even having a family has occupied my thoughts. I think the desire to be a spouse and parent comes into everyone's life at some point.

—Alex, 22

Marriage and my future career are the biggest. I am in the pre-med program and am looking at Physician's Assistant programs across the country right now. But it's hard because I know that I want to get married, and the opportunity to get married is very real and right in front of me. I need to figure out if I want PA school that badly, and, if I do, will my husband be willing to go with me wherever I happen to be accepted?

—Melissa, 21

I have fears about the responsibility of growing up. It's terrifying to think of finding someone you love more than anything else in the world (including yourself), and having that person loving you that much back. And THEN to know that you are then responsible for her and your future children! What if I chose the wrong profession? What if I'm not a good dad? What if? What if?

—Robert, 24

There are the obvious concerns about growing up: buying your own food, clothing, and shelter; buying a car (a big girl car that actually runs) and taking proper care of it; getting a good job. But now that I have moved away from home, I find the most difficult responsibility is time management—not in balancing the time I spend working versus playing, but the time I spend working versus working. Not only do I have to go to work from 9–6 everyday, but I have to set up my own utilities, clean my own house, do my own shopping, and spend hours on the phone with customer service when everything goes wrong—which it almost always does.

—Karen, 24

I'm concerned about school right now. And a mission. I really want to do what's right for me but I'm not always sure what that is. It worries me that I have all these opportunities in my life and I don't know what I'm going to end up doing. I still feel so much like a child; anything that requires me to act like an adult is terrifying to me. How am I supposed to make it?

—Diana, 19

Do their responses resemble your own? Clearly, this is a vulnerable time in your lives, when patterns are set and habits established that will either bless or curse the years to come. Every choice you make, either good or bad, carries natural consequences. Society recognizes this vulnerability, and has even given your generation its own unique classifications, including the "Millennials," "Echo-Boomers," the "Youthhood Generation," "Gen-Y," "Boomerang Kids," "Creative Connecteds," "Net Geners," "Emerging Adults," and "Thresholders." This is a time for a new and heightened level of responsibility, and some of you may feel you are not ready to grow up and assume all the responsibilities associated with your age. Time magazine highlighted a growing trend of indecision among young adults regarding employment and starting a family, and gave yet other names for this stage of life: "Permanent adolescents, . . . twenty-something Peter Pans" who never grow up. The article noted:

> Social scientists are starting to realize that a permanent shift has taken place in the way we live our lives. In the past, people moved from childhood to adolescence and from adolescence to adulthood, but today there is a new, intermediate phase along the way. The years from 18 until 25 and even beyond have become a distinct and separate life stage, a strange, transitional never-never land between adolescence and adulthood in which people stall for a few extra years, putting off the iron cage of adult responsibility that constantly threatens to crash down on them. They're betwixt and between. You could call them twixters.[4]

In a commencement address to university graduates, Elder Earl C. Tingey offered this response to that article:

> You know better. You have been better trained. You have an eternal view of life that helps you see beyond and through the shallowness and emptiness of allowing a self-centered adolescent period following college graduation. We expect more from you. We have faith in you. You have developed faith in yourself.
>
> You are now entering the real life of family, employment, increasing Church service, and even more significant responsibility.[5]

As you weigh the decisions to be made, don't lose sight of the incredible opportunities you will have in the next few years, some of which come around only once. Don't create a future of regret for not taking advantage of these opportunities. Don't let fear of the unknown govern your life and make decisions for you. Build regular, daily habits for spiritual growth.

Do things that will enable you to have personal religious experiences. Take your concerns, problems, insecurities to the Lord and let Him help you. Be involved in your ward—look and ask for opportunities to serve. Until you push and stretch yourself you won't know all your strengths. If you only do what is easy, you will never realize your full potential.

Over the next few years, you will determine what type of person, parent, spouse, and Church member you are going to be. You will be required to set the direction for your education and career. You will decide if you are going to serve a mission and what type of missionary you will be. Then all too soon, you will have the unique challenges associated with returning home from your mission. For many, that is a far greater and more difficult adjustment than beginning your full-time service. As scary as it sounds, you will soon be making decisions about marriage. How do you know when it is the right time and who the right person is for this very crucial decision? You have been told for years that you are the next generation of Church leaders, that you have been prepared to come at this point in the history of the world to lead the Church through the perils of our time. Well, that time has arrived. And what about finances? You quickly learn how much life costs and what a short distance a dollar will carry you. On top of these and other crucial challenges, you might struggle with identity and crises of confidence.

In writing this book, I have relied on wise friends, family members, colleagues, mentors, and leaders who provided valuable and inspired insight. I have received hundreds of letters and email responses from young adults across the world about the issues and challenges of young adult life. You will see many of their thoughts, concerns, and experiences throughout this book (though I have changed the names and ages of many to preserve anonymity). And I have drawn on my own experience as I worked my way through these crucial years—something that doesn't feel too far distant (a matter of perspective, I realize). I have also had the privilege of serving and working closely with hundreds of youth and young adults over the years in formal Church callings and have spent untold hours listening, counseling, and seeking to understand the issues and pressures heaped upon you at this time in your lives. I have learned of your hopes and dreams, your fears and challenges, your shortcomings and successes. Occasionally, I have grieved with you as I have witnessed the hardships many of you experience—sometimes self-imposed, but often thrust upon you. I have also watched in awe and wonder as you have faced these daunting challenges, met them squarely, and risen above them.

Benjamin Zander is the conductor of the Boston Philharmonic Orchestra. He also works with various business leaders and other groups demonstrating methods of producing beautiful music—methods that have application to other aspects of living. At one point, he was invited to meet with a certain orchestra to help them focus on and improve their technique. In preparation for this meeting, Benjamin sent members of the orchestra copies of Beethoven's magnificent 9th Symphony, "Ode to Joy." This is a jubilant, innovative, and dramatic piece of music with stirring melodies and beautiful rhythms that, when presented well, truly projects a sense of wondrous celebration.

Knowing Benjamin's reputation, the orchestra diligently practiced the symphony and when the conductor arrived, they were prepared to perform. When he approached the orchestra, he asked them, "Do you really need a leader?"

Having rehearsed the music extensively, they confidently replied, "No. We can do it without one."

So Benjamin joined the audience and listened to the performance. It went quite well. The musicians knew their parts, and they were anxious to demonstrate their expertise. When they were finished, they received warm applause from the audience. That was when Benjamin got to work. He spoke with the orchestra, saying, "Now, let me tell you about Beethoven, his life, his philosophy. Let me share with you some information about who he was."

Benjamin's intent was to help the orchestra obtain a vision of Beethoven's motivations and values. He then went to the violin section and told them: "You are capable of reaching a level you have never reached!" The audience and musicians alike were taken aback—after all, these were professional musicians who performed at the highest levels every day. Nonetheless, Benjamin persisted. He asked them to play a note, and while they were playing he told them a little more about Beethoven. He had them play certain parts of the music softer and other parts louder. In doing this he was accomplishing two things.

First, he wanted the musicians to be mindful of the composer's vision for the music. Second, he wanted the musicians to gain a deeper understanding of their own capabilities. To the amazement of both the musicians and the audience, their sound improved. Benjamin then moved to the brass section and did the same. Then to the winds. Section by section, he worked with the entire orchestra helping to create a vision, a sense of achieving their highest potential, and forcing them to reach new and higher levels.

At the conclusion of this process, the entire group, orchestra and audience alike, felt the music more deeply, with insights into the composer's life and his vision for this particular symphony. This understanding helped them translate their performance into something beyond their initial attempt, bringing greater focus, discipline, feeling, and authenticity to their performance. After working with each section, Benjamin brought the entire orchestra back together to play Beethoven's 9th once again, this time with him as the leader. The difference was startling, and at the conclusion of the piece, the audience erupted in thunderous applause. Benjamin concluded his coaching with the orchestra by telling them, "I don't care how you feel or about your opinions. All I care about is what I know you are capable of achieving. And you have achieved that! Now, how do you feel?"

In a sense, Benjamin Zander's message to the orchestra is the message I hope to convey in this book. Like the musicians, you each bring marvelous talent, dedication, and training to this crucial point in your lives. You are also capable of reaching significant levels beyond where you currently stand. This time of your life is a time for decisions and great learning, important transitions and new challenges, and for establishing firm foundations and patterns of effectiveness.

Remember the saying: "Sow a thought, reap an action; sow an action, reap a habit; sow a habit, reap a character; sow a character, reap a destiny." The good habits you sow now will reap tremendous rewards down the road. You will make mistakes, as everyone does, but you will also learn from these mistakes. You will build the framework for future successes and begin to discover what your unique contributions will be. You will create growth opportunities for yourself and will be the means of blessing others' lives at the same time. Experience gives you new feelings, and a leader can give you new experience. Sometimes that leader is someone else, and sometimes that leader is you.

The following chapters share ideas on spiritual matters, career matters, financial matters, leadership matters, and matters of the heart. My intention is to provide hope and guidance, advice and wisdom you will need to make good choices.

Sounds exciting, doesn't it? Are you ready for the coming years and your great new adventures? You will be. Just remember, there are two types of people: those who go through the motions and just get by, and those who have vision, passion, and discipline, who make their lives and contributions extraordinary. And the small and seemingly simple choices we make help determine significant outcomes.

Notes

1. Dr. Suess, *Oh the Places You'll Go!* (New York: Random House, 1990), 1–48.

2. Viktor E. Frankl, *Man's Search for Meaning* (Boston: Beacon Press, 2006), 132.

3. Gordon B. Hinckley, *Standing For Something* (New York: Times Books, 2000), 37.

4. Lev Grossman, "Grow Up? Not So Fast," *Time,* 24 January 2005, 44.

5. Earl C. Tingey, *BYU Spring 2005 Commencement*, BYU, April 21, 2005, 2.

1
YRULDS?

The Testimony Choice

I believe in Christianity as I believe the sun has risen, not because
I see it, but because by it I see everything else.[1]

—C. S. Lewis

Several years, ago my wife, our two small children, and I moved from
Utah to the Washington D.C. area. We loved living there. We knew my
work assignment would only require us to be there for a few years, so we
made a concerted effort to take in the area's rich history and culture. We
enjoyed the museums, historical sites, and the battlefields. We loved the
hustle and pulse of the nation's capital and the proximity to New York,
Philadelphia, Baltimore, Williamsburg, North Carolina's Outer Banks,
and the Delaware beaches. We made wonderful friends who, after many
years, are still an important part of our lives. Yet, despite all the rich and
amazing experiences we enjoyed, we found ourselves feeling homesick for
our family and the familiar surroundings of the West.

On a trip back to Utah for business, I was in the Salt Lake airport
where I saw a gentleman wearing a T-shirt with a huge block "Y" on it in
the same style and format used by Brigham Young University. I remember
thinking how nice it was to see people wearing "Y" shirts again, and had
to restrain myself from running up and talking with him. Frankly, my
feelings of homesickness kicked in and I wanted to embrace him. As I got
nearer, however, I noticed this was not the average BYU shirt. To the left of
the block "Y" I saw a large "?" and to the right of the "Y" were the letters,
RULDS, and the words "my Mormon friend." The entire message became

clear: "YRULDS—why are you LDS—my Mormon friend?" The back of his shirt revealed his motivation: "Ex-Mormons for a more glorious hope."

I was immediately taken aback, but then smiled to myself. Just like the numerous BYU shirts and paraphernalia, this man's message is not an unfamiliar one in the state that houses the Church's headquarters. And while I was left to wonder about the man's story and experience, the message on his T-shirt struck a chord: Why was I LDS? Of all the choices I could make, why would I choose to devote such a significant part of my life to the Church?

As members of the Church, we are asked to give 10 percent of our income to the Lord. We choose to live a strict standard of health, abstaining from coffee, tobacco, tea, and alcohol. For many outside the Church, parties with alcohol have become synonymous with college—even a rite of passage. Yet we as members of the Church forego this. Similarly, we choose not to date until we are sixteen, and live a strict moral standard as it relates to sex—specifically, that we do not engage in premarital sex of any form. From the world's view, this is limiting, even unnatural.

We interrupt school, scholarships, relationships, athletic careers, and jobs to serve missions—at our own or our family's expense. During our missionary service, we live far below the poverty level, eat unfamiliar food, knock on thousands of doors, suffer both extreme heat and intense cold, and struggle with illness and language barriers.

When we return, we look to marry—often while we are still in school and before we are financially established. We devote a significant portion of our time to callings in the Church. We are asked to avoid R-rated movies. We are also asked to devote Monday evenings to family teaching instead of NFL football, another night for youth activities, and yet other nights throughout the weeks and months for temple worship, service projects, and Relief Society meetings. We are expected to do home teaching or visiting teaching at least monthly. We have scout camp and girls' camp that take significant time, Klondike and pinewood derbies, youth conferences, and Primary activities. And on top of all this, we go to Church for *three hours* every Sunday!

Why do we do all of this? It is a question we each need to answer, because a straightforward answer brings clarity to so many aspects of our lives. As a young adult, you are at a crucial "point of choice"—and only you can make the choice.

My friend Lindsay, 24, shared the following experience with me:

There was a time not very long ago when I considered becoming inactive in the Church. Not really going out with a bang in some huge apostasy, but quietly becoming inactive and "hiding out" for a while.

I moved from one of the largest cities in the nation where I grew up in a large family, to a town of 14,000 where I didn't know anyone, and was living alone for the first time in my life. I moved into my own apartment one afternoon and started my first post-college job the next day. I also went from a life of strong, full-sized, and great college wards to a struggling branch with 120 people on the rolls, but only about half of that actually attending sacrament meeting (on a good week).

I had been in the branch about a month and still didn't have a calling, let alone even a conversation with my branch president, so I figured they either didn't need me or didn't care. That Sunday, the first counselor in the Branch Presidency pulled me aside and extended a calling as a counselor in the Primary Presidency. We were both in a hurry, with people waiting on us, so I immediately said okay and didn't think much about it. I really had no idea what I was getting myself into until my first meeting with the Primary president. After going over everything the calling entailed, how important it was, and what all my responsibilities were, I was barely able to hold back my tears back until I got home.

At the side of my bed, I sobbed to my Heavenly Father how inadequate I was and that I had never wanted a calling in the Primary; I didn't really even like children that much in the first place. After praying, I was filled with some measure of peace. But after hours and hours of meetings several nights a week for the first few weeks and time spent working on, thinking about, and talking about primary and a calling I never wanted to begin with, I quickly became really discouraged and lost that initial feeling of peace. I thought of every excuse to not be where I should be and not fulfill my calling. I thought of all the other things I wanted to be doing since moving there, like serving in the community, joining clubs, developing new talents, and traveling. All these were good and worthy things that I could be doing if my calling didn't take so much time.

Because the branch was so small and everyone knows everyone else's business, I knew there was no way to just not do anything or ask to be released without a million questions. So eventually, I came to the point in my mind where I either had to just do it, or give up and walk away. I had watched my sister go inactive for a few years and then come back so I thought it wasn't that big of a deal. Somewhere in the middle of all this, I kept thinking of a story I heard in general conference where a man said about the Church, "It's true, isn't it? Then what else matters?" and I kept coming up with the answer that I knew the Church was true and I couldn't deny it. Slowly, as I kept hearing that phrase, it changed to: "It's true, isn't it? Then what am I going to do about it?" And I knew that as long as I knew it was true, there wasn't really a choice except to do what the Lord asked of me.

I don't pretend to be perfect Primary leader now. I still struggle a lot and have a long way to go, but I've found peace and comfort in the Primary theme for this year: "I'll Follow Him in Faith." I have decided that's all I can do at this point. I don't know why the Lord led me to this tiny town or gave me this calling, but if I give up now, I'll never know. I don't know what else He has in store for me, but I can follow Him in faith, because now I know without a doubt that it's true, so what else matters?

Consider the message our Church sends to the world: We claim that in the spring of 1820, a young, uneducated farm boy from rural America, who was curious about which church to join, went to pray and received a visit from heaven, specifically from God the Father and His Son, Jesus Christ. These two divine beings then instructed this sparsely educated lad of only fourteen years that no church contained the fulness of the gospel and that the gospel as it had been in the meridian of time would be restored to the earth through him. Subsequent to this, the boy, whose name was Joseph Smith, received numerous other heavenly visitors, including a significant one from Moroni, a theretofore unknown "American continent" prophet. John the Baptist, Peter, James, John, Paul, Moses, Elias, and Elijah, among others, also visited him. This boy was instructed by Moroni as to the location of an ancient record inscribed on plates of gold. This record was deposited in the hills of upstate New York and later translated through Joseph by the power of God, as the Book of Mormon. Consider further the subsequent organization of the Church—the restored Church of Jesus Christ—led today by prophets of God, just as Noah, Enoch, Moses, Isaiah, and Jeremiah were prophets of God. Quite a staggering declaration!

In his book, *What do Mormons Believe*, Rex Lee discusses this story and the response to it of many people as one of incredulity: how can anyone possibly believe this could happen in our day? He writes:

> To this response, I make two comments.
> First, I not only believe, but I know that it happened. No, I was

not there in 1820 when Joseph Smith saw the Father and the Son. . . .
Instead, I know through the power of the Holy Ghost, which the Lord
has promised will teach the truth to his disciples and testify of him
(John 14:16–17, 26; 15:26; 16:7–14).

Second, these contemporary revelations are no more unusual than
the accounts of angelic visitations contained in both the Old and New
Testaments. If you accept those as true, then does not the possibility of
modern-day revelation follow as a matter of course?

Is there any reason to assume any lesser need in today's world
for prophets and direct revelation than in millennia already [passed]?
Indeed, can there be any serious doubt that if comparisons were to be
made, the need today for direct guidance is greater than it has ever been
in the past?

Claims of angelic visitations and divine revelation are not outrageous unless one regards the Bible itself as outrageous. And think of
the consequences if it really is true. It means that once again, in these
modern times, our Heavenly Father has reestablished contact between
the heavens and the earth. It means that we need not guess concerning his will for his people. It means that Jesus Christ, in whom we
believe, is no mythic figure but truly is the living God and Savior of
this world.[2]

This message is either the most preposterous ever conceived, or one of
the most profound ever given.

On one level, the answer to the question, "Why are we LDS?" is a
pragmatic one. Through the Church, we gain access to a community.
Whether we are in Provo or Paraguay, New York or New Zealand, the
Church provides an established support system, a built-in social structure
that offers common ground and common experience. One can grow up in
Boise, Idaho, move to Bern, Switzerland, and, despite whatever language
barriers that might exist, feel at home in the Church. Of course, there
are unique cultural aspects to the Church in its various countries, and
the experience level in Salt Lake will be different from that in countries
where the Church has recently been established, but the Spirit remains
the same wherever you go. Going to church in an unfamiliar place is, in
many ways, like going home.

On another level, we may participate in Church activities because
they are part of a familiar pattern. We may have grown up in the Church,
attended Primary, and participated in youth programs. Our parents
believed and went to Church and served faithfully, and therefore, so do

we. We do it because that is what we have always done. We do it because it is familiar and comfortable. My friend Adam, 24, relates this experience from his youth:

> When I was about ten or eleven years old, my whole family stopped going to church—but, because I knew it was the right thing to do, I kept going. I found it hard to call people in the ward to ask for rides and was even a little embarrassed to do so; but I did it. One of the things that kept me going was the feeling of love and peace that I felt as I walked into the chapel. Going to church was a way for me (even as an eleven-year-old) to break away from all the pain and other things that I was feeling at that time.

Ultimately, however, we are members of The Church of Jesus Christ of Latter-day Saints for a far deeper and significant, though not entirely unrelated, reason. Once, while I was meeting with my stake president, he said to those in the room, "Remember, this is real." Meaning, the Church and all it requires is not just something we do because we have to. It is something we do because the gospel is true, because we have a Heavenly Father who loves and knows us, because He sent His Son to overcome both sin and death, because He has restored the fulness of the gospel in our day, and because Jesus Christ stands at the head of our Church and guides it through a living prophet. It is where we have access to priesthood power. It is where we receive saving ordinances. It is where, through restored priesthood keys, we have power to bind in heaven that which is bound on earth. It is where we learn about the plan of salvation and our roles in that plan. It is the organization the Lord himself established, through which we can claim the full saving power of the Atonement and prepare to return to His presence.

Do you believe that? Have you had the experience described by Alma of pouring your heart out to your Heavenly Father and feeling yourself wrapped "in the arms of [His] safety?" (Alma 34:16). Have you felt washed clean through the power of the Atonement? Do you feel the Spirit touching and teaching you as you immerse yourself in the scriptures? If not, begin the process immediately. If you have felt this in the past but don't feel so now (Alma 5:26), start doing the things that will invite, once again, the Spirit into your life.

Spencer, 24, shared this experience with me:

> On my twentieth birthday, I took time to evaluate my life, and as

I did I felt terrible dissatisfaction. At this age, I had gradually slipped into inactivity. Through introspection I traced this feeling of emptiness that persisted to the time when I began high school—when I consciously chose to make righteous living a second priority so I could find social acceptance. Upon this realization, I promised myself that I would never again look back on my life with regret. I immediately severed relationships with those impeding my goals—including a girlfriend of two years—quit a high paying job that put me in a spiritually-dark environment, and moved back home to attend school and save for a mission.

As I prepared for my mission, I drove to the mountains to seek confirmation from the Lord. I asked him to confirm to me that all these sacrifices were necessary. After pouring my heart out to him, seeking forgiveness, and expressing gratitude for the discipline he blessed me with to leave it all behind, I felt the showering of the spirit in divine affirmation that I was on the correct path, and I felt the promise that he would light my way. And he has. It has been four years since that day, and I have had the privilege of serving as a gospel principles teacher, ward missionary, full-time missionary, and in the Elders Quorum Presidency. I'm currently studying at the university, and have developed hundreds of meaningful friendships since the day I left the world behind. That terrible feeling of emptiness I once felt is all I have to remember whenever temptation crosses my path, and I feel that I will never go that way again.

This testimony-gaining process requires sustained effort. Like an aspiring athlete who begins his workouts only to find himself sore and struggling after the first few days, you might find yourself feeling confused by and disinterested in the scriptures. You may feel disconnected from your Heavenly Father and your Savior, and wondering if your prayers hit the ceiling but go no further. Stay with it. Don't give up. Again, like the determined athlete who sticks with his workout regime and finds himself getting stronger, faster, and more responsive in just a few weeks, you will begin to experience some wonderful things in your life as you engage in your "spiritual workout process." You will begin to feel peace, an inward tranquility. You will begin to feel connected to your Heavenly Father in a more substantial way. You will begin to rekindle embers of testimony that have not warmed your heart in some time.

A testimony comes by doing the things that invite the Spirit and by eliminating the things that repel it. Consider the following pattern from

Moroni as a guide in your efforts to strengthen your testimony. This particular scripture is one of the most-often quoted scriptures in our entire canon, and for good reason. It outlines the essential steps in gaining a testimony of the Book of Mormon, the Savior's divine mission, and His Church.

> Behold, I would exhort you that when ye shall *read* these things, if it be wisdom in God that ye should read them, that ye would *remember* how merciful the Lord hath been unto the children of men, from the creation of Adam even down until the time that ye shall receive these things, and *ponder* it in your hearts.
>
> And when you shall receive these things, I would exhort you that ye would *ask God, the Eternal Father*, in the name of Christ, if these things are not true; and if ye shall ask with a sincere heart, with real intent, having faith in Christ, he will manifest the truth of it unto you, by the power of the Holy Ghost.
>
> And by the power of the Holy Ghost ye may know the truth of all things (Moroni 10: 3–5, emphasis added).

Let's briefly explore Moroni's pattern for gaining answers in our search for truth.

Read. This doesn't mean we have to spend hours each day reading the scriptures. It does, however, mean putting more effort into your scripture study than a token verse or two once in a while. Be willing to pay the price. Make a point to have a meaningful experience with the scriptures each day. Begin your scripture study with a prayer, telling Heavenly Father your intentions, and ask for His help in the process. Tell Him your desire to gain insight from the scriptures and ask Him to bless you with the Spirit so you can learn what you need to learn. If you find yourself struggling to focus or even stay awake during your reading, stop and pray again. Do this as many times as you need to. What begins as a task on your "to do" list (as daily scripture reading often is) will soon become something meaningful and powerful. Young adults Emily and Alex offer the following insights:

> When I have regular scripture study, I truly feel the spirit in my life. He becomes my constant companion and I learn and know my Father in Heaven. When I don't have regular scripture study, I can tell something is missing in my life. I am neither happy nor fulfilled. Scripture study allows me to receive personal revelation. It guides my life today.
>
> —Emily, 24

Just like a car needs gas to run, the spiritual side of anyone needs spiritual fuel. Scripture study is that clean-burning fuel that reminds me of the presence of God in my life.

—Alex, 27

In a general conference address, Elder Keith K. Hilbig addressed the power associated with studying the scriptures, and the impact it will have in our quest for strengthened testimony. He admonishes us to "immerse ourselves more consistently in the words of Christ and of the prophets. When our study efforts expand, so will the influence of the Holy Ghost in our lives increase. Let us search the scriptures with pen in hand, making note of new insights and recording spiritual promptings. Thereafter, let us strive to apply what has been learned to our personal lives. The Spirit will quicken our inner selves; new understanding will come precept upon precept."[3]

Remember. Think deeply and carefully about the Lord and how merciful He has been to you personally. Approach this process with an attitude of gratitude and sincerely acknowledge Him in all things. Despite the significant challenges we face, each of us has been abundantly blessed in ways we can't begin to quantify. Remember the price He paid for you personally in the garden and on Golgotha. Remember that all we have and enjoy comes from Him. Remember we came from His presence, and even though we have had a veil of forgetfulness placed upon us, we have not been sent to mortality without significant assistance—assistance which comes from heaven. The word "remember" is used 275 times in the scriptures. President Henry B. Eyring urged each of us to "find ways to recognize and remember God's kindness." He promised as we do so, "it will build our testimonies."[4]

Ponder. This means to think deeply about what you are reading. Consider the relevance of the scriptures to our day, and specifically in your life. Think about your desire to grow closer to your Heavenly Father. Think about your goals, your problems, and potential solutions. Think about your love for Jesus Christ, and think about His love for you and His desire for your ultimate success and happiness. His work and glory is for you to return home to Him, and ultimately achieve your fullest potential—eternal life.

Pray. Could there be a correlation between how frequently and effectively you are praying and your feelings of "connectedness" with the Spirit? For those who have served missions, think back on your mission's morning routine: how many times did you pray? You likely had personal prayer when you awoke; you prayed silently as you studied your scriptures, language, and lessons; you had prayer with your companion as you studied together; you offered a blessing on your breakfast; and you knelt with your companion in prayer before you left your apartment for the day. Think about it—you most likely prayed five or more times before you even opened your front door! Your prayers were targeted, specific, and efficacious. But when this pattern of prayer changes, and daily morning prayer is lost in the shuffle of other activities, it is natural to expect a diminished spiritual sensitivity.

Whether you are a returned missionary or otherwise, take a lesson from this and make the commitment to begin each day on your knees in prayer. Don't let a day go by without doing this. Plan your day with Heavenly Father, and tell him your worries and concerns, your hopes and aspirations. Pray vocally when possible. This can be a very powerful and wonderful experience. It will help clarify thoughts and feelings. As mentioned, pray before and during your scripture study. Conclude your day back on your knees—not lying in bed—and report your day to your Heavenly Father. Tell Him what worked throughout the day, what didn't work, and thank Him for His guidance and for your safety. Ask Him specifically about the Church, the scriptures, and if the things you have been reading and studying are true.

Moroni counsels us not just to pray, but to pray with real intent. This has reference both to your attitude while praying as well as your intentions once you receive your answer. When I read that counsel, I think of Mormon's description of praying to gain charity. He said: "Pray unto the Father *with all the energy of heart*" (Moroni 7:48, emphasis added). Make this your mantra as you search to discover your own testimony—"with all the energy of heart." Make this pursuit the most important thing in your life. As you prayerfully seek guidance about your testimony (or whatever you are seeking), tell the Lord specifically what you intend to do when you receive your answer. Prayer is not a passive step—it is very active. For example, when you receive an answer about the Book of Mormon, and therefore about the Restoration of the Church, discuss with your Heavenly Father what actions you will take. For those investigating the Church, this would likely include committing to baptism. For those already in the Church, this could include rededicated focus on and commitment to building the kingdom;

perhaps the resolution to serve a mission. Do this sincerely and repeatedly.

These four steps—read, remember, ponder, and pray—combine to create a powerful and proven testimony-building process. Remember what you are considering as you engage in this process: Did Jesus atone for my sins and break the bonds of death for me and all mankind? Where can I turn for peace in my life? Is the Book of Mormon true? Did Joseph Smith really experience what he said he did? Is there a living prophet? Is the plan of salvation really available for me? Does my Heavenly Father love me enough to answers my prayers? I promise as you pay the price to get answers to these questions, you will receive answers. Your Heavenly Father knows you and loves you. He will not leave you alone in your search for truth.

Through the Prophet Joseph Smith, the Lord revealed His formula for success. He said, "Search diligently, pray always, and be believing, and all things shall work together for your good" (D&C 90:24). If we want answers, we must be diligent in our efforts . . . we must do the work. We must be prayerful, and have faith we will receive an answer.

Here are a few more steps to consider as you go about this process:

Fast. This can be a tough step, especially if you are out of the habit. If you are anything like me, you love to eat. We need to eat to live, but sometimes we live to eat. Eating is good; our bodies like and need nourishment. But there is something very powerful about putting aside our own temporal needs and wants in favor of higher priorities. A little sacrifice can go a long way. Do this in conjunction with the other steps. A friend of mine shared this experience with fasting:

> I was struggling with an important decision regarding a work opportunity. I enjoyed my job, but I was being recruited rather aggressively by another firm. I had been praying about this situation for some time, and determined I needed to make this decision a matter of both prayer and fasting. Shortly after fasting about it, I got a call out of the blue from my father, who knew nothing about this situation—in fact, he lives nearly two thousand miles away and I hadn't had a single conversation with him about this. My dad mentioned to me that he felt impressed during his morning prayers to call me and suggested I talk with my boss. He told me, "You need to stay with your current employer." The call from my father was an unusual answer to prayer, but it was a specific answer to the problem I had been wrestling with. And it came after fasting.

Elder Joseph B. Wirthlin emphasized the need for fasting to be combined with prayer. He wrote:

> Without prayer, fasting is not complete fasting; it's simply going hungry. If we want our fasting to be more than just going without eating, we must lift our hearts, our minds, and our voices in communion with our Heavenly father. Fasting, coupled with mighty prayer, is powerful. It can fill our minds with the revelations of the Spirit. It can strengthen us against times of temptation. . . . It can help develop within us courage and confidence. It can strengthen our character and build self-restraint and discipline. Often when we fast, our righteous prayers and petitions have greater power. Testimonies grow. We mature spiritually and emotionally and sanctify our souls."[5]

Service. Focusing on the needs of others creates some wonderful magic and brings perspective about our own circumstances. As you serve others, the significance of your own problems all but diminishes. By serving others, you are emulating the Savior, and this brings great spiritual power. It is easy to be consumed by our own troubles, and when we focus on them, they seem to multiply. One of the surest ways to combat discouragement is to get over yourself and bless the lives of others. I can guarantee the Lord will answer your prayers when you ask Him sincerely who needs your help. N. Eldon Tanner once said, "Service is the rent we pay for living on this earth."[6] This statement is true. Serving others is also one of the best ways to gain a testimony of the Savior's love for us. Make it a point to perform at least one act of service per day. This is prayer in action!

Keeping a journal. My mission president once recommended I keep a record in my journal of how and when the Lord blessed me with miracles. As I began to write of my experiences, I became astonished at the frequency of these miracles; I began to look for them and expect them. Interestingly, I began to more fully recognize specific and direct answers to prayers. This exercise heightened my awareness of the richness of my blessings, and I found myself more appreciative of Him and His love for me. I have since made an effort to keep what I call a "tender mercies" log, where I record the little events that remind me the Lord is involved in the details of my life.

President Henry B. Eyring shared an experience he had when his children were small. He returned home one evening just in time to see his father-in-law carrying a load of pipes as part of a service project for his family. President Eyring was touched, and as he was walking toward his house, he heard the following inspiration from the Spirit:

"I'm not giving you these experiences for yourself. Write them down."

I went inside. I didn't go to bed. Although I was tired, I took out some paper and began to write. And as I did, I understood the message I had heard in my mind. I was supposed to record for my children to read, someday in the future, how I had seen the hand of God blessing our family. Grandpa didn't have to do what he was doing for us. He could have had someone else do it or not have done it at all. But he was serving us, his family, in the way covenant disciples of Jesus Christ always do. I knew that was true. And so I wrote it down, so that my children could have the memory someday when they would need it.

I wrote down a few lines every day for years. I never missed a day no matter how tired I was or how early I would have to start the next day. Before I would write, I would ponder this question: "Have I seen the hand of God reaching out to touch us or our children or our family today?" As I kept at it, something began to happen. As I would cast my mind over the day, I would see evidence of what God had done for one of us that I had not recognized in the busy moments of the day. As that happened, and it happened often, I realized that trying to remember had allowed God to show me what He had done.

More than gratitude began to grow in my heart. Testimony grew. I became ever more certain that our Heavenly Father hears and answers prayers. I felt more gratitude for the softening and refining that come because of the Atonement of the Savior Jesus Christ. And I grew more confident that the Holy Ghost can bring all things to our remembrance—even things we did not notice or pay attention to when they happened.

The years have gone by. My boys are grown men. And now and then one of them will surprise me by saying, "Dad, I was reading in my copy of the journal about when . . ." and then he will tell me about how reading of what happened long ago helped him notice something God had done in his day.[7]

Eliminate activities that repel the spirit. In the *Enoch Letters*, Elder Neal A. Maxwell writes, "Each of us must not only renounce evil, disengaging from doing wrong, but we must also engage anxiously in doing much good. Only then can a mighty change occur. Even then, our moral appetites seem to persist, for perfection is a direction to be pursued in the process of time."[8]

We are bombarded every day with worldly influences—things that are offensive to the Spirit. Some of these are thrust on us simply because we live in a wicked world. Others are brought on through our own actions. Be conscious of the music you embrace and the movies you watch. Be cautious of the amount of time you spend watching mindless TV, and avoid the easily-accessible but destructive influences of pornography.

Once, while working with a group of young adults, we received a challenge from our priesthood leaders to go a full month without participating with the media in any form—we called it a "media fast." This was tough work. It meant no popular music, movies, video games, television or DVDs, and no Internet unless specifically required by a school assignment—for a full thirty days.

For the first week or so, those who participated in this challenge struggled to find things to do. Media is such a pervasive part of our lives and has become the default activity for many of us. But after a very short time, the participants in the challenge began to lose their desire for these influences. More time was spent with friends. More attention was given to scripture study. Individuals who were struggling with the addictive pull of pornography simply cut off their access to this vile practice. Some of these individuals had been struggling for years to eliminate this temptation, and just after a few weeks, gained a new hope that pornography did not have to rule them. It was an amazing experiment as we learned how much we are influenced by the media. Don't fool yourselves into thinking that what you listen to or watch has no impact on your spiritual sensitivity.

Know your place in the race. My grandmother passed away when she was ninety-nine years old. She had been a monumental part of my life and a nurturing influence for which I will be eternally grateful.

In preparation to speak at her funeral, I reflected on her life, and was struck by all that she had experienced. The year she was born, Henry Ford sold the first Model A for 850 dollars. Theodore Roosevelt was president, the Wright brothers' plane first took flight at Kitty Hawk, and her family had the only telephone in town. She lived through the great San Francisco earthquake, World War I, the Great Depression, World War II, the Korean War, Vietnam, and space travel. By her fortieth birthday, there was still no sign of television, penicillin, polio shots, or frozen food. There was no radar, there were no credit cards, laser beams, or ball point pens. Man had not invented panty hose, air conditioners, dishwashers, or clothes dryers. Five- and ten-cent stores were places where she could actually buy things for five or ten cents.

As I thought about all that transpired in her lifetime, I was struck with the pace and excitement, and the pressures and prominence of the times in which we now live. Marvels of technology, once imagined only in science fiction novels, are now a part of our daily experience, and yet because things are moving so fast, the technology we enjoy today is obsolete before it even hits the market.

Sheri Dew describes our day this way:

> The last days are not for the faint of heart or the spiritually out of shape. There will be days when you feel defeated, exhausted, and plain old beat-up by life's whiplash. People you love will disappoint you—and you will disappoint them. You'll probably struggle with some kind of mortal appetite. Some days it will feel as though the veil between heaven and earth is made of reinforced concrete. And you may even face a crisis of faith. In fact, you can count on trials that test your testimony and your faith.
>
> Aren't you glad I came bearing such optimistic news? Actually, I am nothing if not optimistic about you, for everything about your lives is an indicator of our Father's remarkable respect for you. He recommended you for now, when the stakes are so high. Now is the day when His kingdom is being established once and for all, never again to be taken from the earth. This is the last leg of the relay. This is when He needs His strongest runners.
>
> The simple fact is that our Father did not recommend Eve or Moses or Nephi or countless other magnificent exemplars for this dispensation—He recommended you and me. Do you think God would have left the last days to chance by sending men and women He couldn't count on? A common theme of patriarchal blessings given to men and women your age is that you were sent now because our Father's most trustworthy children would be needed in the final, decisive battle for righteousness. That is who you are, and it is who you have always been.[9]

Much about the times in which we live can cause great fear and trembling, but there is also so much to be grateful for. And you are equal to the challenge. Gaining an understanding of your role and expectations in building the kingdom of God brings great perspective to the testimony-building process.

President Ezra Taft Benson reminded us:

For nearly six thousand years, God has held you in reserve to make your appearance in the final days before the second coming of the Lord. Some individuals will fall away; but the kingdom of God will remain intact to welcome the return of its head—even Jesus Christ. While our generation will be comparable in wickedness to the days of Noah, when the Lord cleansed the earth by flood, there was a major difference this time. It is that God has saved for the final inning some of His strongest children, who will help bear off the kingdom triumphantly. That is where you come in, for you are the generation that must be prepared to meet your God.[10]

Share testimony. Bearing your testimony is one of the post powerful ways to strengthen your convictions. This is tied to the principle that the more you give, the more you receive. Alma taught, "For the which ye do send out shall return unto you again" (Alma 41:15). On this point, President Boyd K. Packer writes:

> Oh, if I could teach you this one principle. A testimony is to be found in the bearing of it! Somewhere in your quest for spiritual knowledge, there is that leap of faith, as the philosophers call it. It is the moment when you have gone to the edge of the light and stepped into the darkness to discover that the way is lighted ahead for just a footstep or two. The spirit of man, is as the scripture says, indeed the candle of the Lord. (Proverbs 20:27)
>
> It is one thing to receive a witness from what you have read or what another has said; and it is a necessary beginning. It is quite another to have the Spirit confirm to you in your bosom that what you have testified is true. Can you not see that it will be supplied as you share it? As you give that which you have, there is a replacement, with increase.
>
> Bear testimony of the things that you hope are true, as an act of faith. It is something of an experiment that the prophet Alma proposed to his followers. We begin with faith—not with a perfect knowledge of things. That sermon in the thirty-second chapter of Alma is one of the greatest messages in holy writ, for it is addressed to the beginner, to the novice, to the humble seeker. And it holds a key to a witness of the truth.
>
> The Spirit and testimony of Christ will come to you for the most part when, and remain with you only, if you share it. In that process is the very essence of the gospel.
>
> Is not this a perfect demonstration of Christianity? You cannot find it, nor keep it, nor enlarge it unless and until you are willing to share it. It is by giving it away freely that it becomes yours.[11]

Act "as if." This means to behave as if you had already received your answer that the Church is true. Alma taught the Zoramites that if they wanted to increase their faith and ultimately gain knowledge (aka a testimony), they needed to start planting the seeds of faith and give the seeds a place to grow. He admonished them to not cast it out by their unbelief. If they would test it out, in other words act "as if," the seed of faith would "begin to swell within [their] breasts," and begin to "enlarge" the soul and begin to "enlighten" understanding (see Alma 32:28). If you want a testimony of the truthfulness of the Church, give the seed a place to grow by being active in the Church and attending all your meetings. Be where you are supposed to be when you are supposed to be there. Expect an answer and demonstrate this expectation by your actions. Acting "as if" is to be anxiously engaged in helping to build the kingdom through accepting and magnifying callings and striving to be faithful in living the principles of the gospel.

Each of the four Gospels contains an account of the Savior's miracle with the loaves and the fishes. Jesus was with a vast multitude; there were "about five thousand men, beside women and children" (Matthew 14: 21). The people were hungry, but all they could pull together were five loaves and two fishes. Jesus blessed the food, and then had his disciples distribute it. Everyone ate until they were full, after which twelve baskets of food remained. Imagine what it would have been like to have participated in something like this! The account in John, however, provides a unique data point that is particularly relevant to our discussion. Andrew, Simon Peter's brother and one of Jesus's disciples, mentions to Jesus, "There is a lad here, which hath five barley loaves, and two small fishes" (John 6:9). It was the young man who provided the food. This young man was privileged to participate in one of the great miracles of Jesus, because he was present—he was in the right place, at the right time, doing what he was supposed to be doing. And he was willing to share what he had with those who lacked. That is what it means to act "as if."

On occasion, I have counseled with young people who are struggling to come to terms with their testimony. They have reached a crossroad in their lives, with pressures to either follow the tenets of the Church or pursue the world's path. Not surprisingly, many of these individuals had not spent a meaningful amount of time studying the scriptures in past years. Nor had they developed the habit of regular, earnest personal prayer. Yet some were spending substantial time reading material intended to expose the Church for a particular doctrine or historical inconsistency, and they wondered why they were not feeling the fruits of the Spirit. Remember, we must "give the seed a place to grow."

The testimony-gaining process may take some time, but it will be worth the effort. In the scriptures we learn of miraculous conversions through the visiting of angels and other dramatic experiences. The accounts of Alma and the sons of Mosiah, Nephi, Paul, and many others teach us that the Lord is powerful and that heaven is close. No less powerful, however, are the conversions of people who feel the magnificence of the still small voice penetrating their souls and affirming the truth of the Gospel.

For me, this is how I gained my testimony. Growing up I had faith in the Savior and believed the things I heard at Church. I had felt the Spirit, but lacked confidence in my testimony. I had read the scriptures—hit-and-miss—and even made an effort to pray about them. But initially my effort was half-hearted. It was only when I sincerely applied Moroni's counsel and began to read the scriptures prayerfully and carefully and with intent, and remembered the Lord's goodness in my life, that I began to feel, at profound levels, the poignancy of the Lord's love for me.

My testimony-gaining process required real effort, including sincere fasting and intense service. While I have had many sacred experiences in my life, I can't point to a single moment when the visions of heaven opened to me and I was given full knowledge. My testimony was built line upon line, grace for grace, as I have diligently read, prayed, and worked. What emerged from this process, however, established a vital foundation for the remainder of my life. I learned of the reality of the Atonement, of the Lord's great plan of happiness, and of the joy and contentment that comes from aligning one's life with the Savior's teachings. I learned that I mattered to the Lord and that He had things for me to accomplish. I learned that I wanted to contribute.

If you are fortunate enough to have had exposure to the gospel and Church doctrines for most of your life, but still don't have a burning testimony of its truthfulness, take heart. Others have had a similar experience. President David O. McKay described such a scenario that happened when he was a young man. He was convinced that a confirmation of his testimony would come through a powerful, heavenly manifestation similar to what the Prophet Joseph experienced. He wrote:

> I realized in youth that the most precious thing a man could

obtain in this life was a testimony of the divinity of this work. . . . But somehow I got an idea in youth that we could not get a testimony unless we had some manifestation. . . . I remember riding over the hills one afternoon, thinking of these things, and concluded there in the silence of the hills was the best place to get that testimony. I stopped my horse, threw the reigns over his head, and withdrew just a few steps and knelt by the side of a tree. . . . I knelt down and with all the fervor of my heart poured out my soul to God, and asked him for a testimony of this gospel. I had in mind that there would be some manifestation, that I would receive some transformation that would leave me absolutely without doubt. I got up, mounted my horse, and as he started over the trail, I remember rather introspectively searching myself, and involuntarily shaking my head, said to myself, "No, sir, there is no change; I am just the same boy I was before I knelt down." The anticipated manifestation had not come. Nor was that the only occasion. However, it did come, but not in the way I had anticipated. Even the manifestation of God's power and the presence of his angels came, but when it did come it was simply a confirmation; it was not the testimony.[12]

That has been my experience as well. My testimony was built and has been reinforced time and again through the soft, yet often overwhelming confirmation of the still small voice. And I have also been blessed to witness and even participate in miracles that demonstrate the hand of the Lord in our everyday lives. I testify that you too will have these experiences, but know that they come as you make the daily effort to listen to the subtle promptings of the Spirit. The gospel is a gospel of miracles. You can expect them in your life, but you must prepare for them.

Harvard professor and Area Authority Clayton Christensen shared his testimony-gaining experience to the students at BYU—Idaho. He described how he had served a faithful mission to Korea, but even after that (and having read the Book of Mormon seven times), he couldn't say he had his own testimony. His reading had always come as an assignment from either his parents, a BYU instructor, or his mission president. He relied on the testimonies of others whom he trusted, but ultimately came to a point in his life where he desperately needed to know. He received a scholarship from the Rhodes Scholarship Trust to study at Oxford University in England, and was working on a very demanding and rigorous academic schedule. Due to his busy schedule, he had to make a choice about his service in the Church. He simply didn't have any time to waste. He said:

I decided that I would commit every evening from 11 to 12 o'clock to reading the Book of Mormon to find out if it was true. I wondered if I dared spend that much time, because I was in a very demanding academic program, studying applied econometrics, and I was going to try to finish the program in two years, whereas most of the people in the program finished it in three, and I just didn't know if I could afford allocating an hour a day to this effort. But nonetheless I did, and I began at 11:00 by kneeling in prayer by the chair and I prayed out loud. I told God how desperate I was to find out if this was a true book, and I told Him that if He would reveal to me that it was true, I would dedicate my life to building this kingdom. And I told Him if it wasn't true that I needed to know that for certain, too, because then I would dedicate my life to finding out what was true. Then I would sit in a chair, and I read the first page of the Book of Mormon, and when I got down to the bottom of the page, I stopped, and I thought about what I had read on that page, and I asked myself, "Could this have been written by a charlatan who was trying to deceive people, or was this really written by a prophet of God? And what did it mean for me in my life?" And then I put the book down and knelt in prayer and verbally asked God again, "Please tell me if this is a true book." Then I would sit in the chair and pick up the book and turn the page and read another page, pause at the bottom, and do the same thing. I did this for an hour every night, night after night in the cold, damp room, at the Queen's College Oxford.

By the time I got to the chapters at the end of 2 Nephi, one evening when I said my prayer and sat in my chair and opened the book, all of a sudden there came into that room a beautiful, warm, loving spirit that just surrounded me and permeated my soul, and enveloped me in a feeling of love that I just had not imagined I could feel. And I began to cry, and I didn't want to stop crying because as I looked through my tears at the words in the Book of Mormon, I could see truth in those words that I never imagined I could comprehend before. And I could see the glories of eternity and I could see what God had in store for me as one of his sons. And I didn't want to stop crying. That spirit stayed with me for the whole hour, and then every evening as I prayed with the Book of Mormon by the fireplace in my room, that same spirit returned and it changed my heart and my life forever.

I look back on the conflict that I experienced, wondering whether I could afford to spend an hour everyday apart from the study of applied econometrics to find if the Book of Mormon was true, and you know, I use applied econometrics maybe once a year, but I use my knowledge that the Book of Mormon is the word of God many times every day of my life. In all of the education that I have pursued, that is the single most useful piece of knowledge that I ever gained.[13]

Ultimately, as you are faithful to a similar process, you will begin to feel a certain strength and power grow within your heart, and you will sense more direction in your life. You will also begin to feel the Savior's love permeate every aspect of your being and you will gain a greater appreciation for the Restoration of the Gospel and what it means to you personally. You will see and participate in the blessings of the priesthood. As you nurture and act on the feelings and promptings you receive, including having "faith unto repentance," (Alma 34:17), you will gain confidence in the Lord and His purposes for you. In short, you will feel the power of the Lord's love in your life in very personal and important ways.

I love Elder Bednar's discussion about tender mercies, which are described as the "very personal and individual blessings, strength, protection, assurances, guidance, loving kindnesses, consolation, support, and spiritual gifts which we receive from and because of and through the Lord Jesus Christ."[14] As you faithfully, diligently, and persistently strive to both gain and strengthen your testimony, you will experience the tender mercies Elder Bednar talks about. You will come to know repeatedly how God is involved in your individual lives.

Recently, I was speaking with a friend about patriarchal blessings. As a convert of several years, he mentioned he was initially quite taken with the concept that he could receive this blessing in his life. Throughout the years, his blessing has been a source of tremendous strength to him. For him, it is sacred and personal scripture, and is not something he has shared with anyone other than his wife. One passage of his blessing in particular provides him with affirmation and encouragement. Recently this friend was struggling with a host of issues, including pressures at work and general feelings of discouragement. One evening, his fifteen-year-old daughter came into his room and shared with her father the love she had for him and other thoughts she had about him. Unbeknownst to her, she quoted word for word this particular passage in his patriarchal blessing. He was overcome with the confirmation that the Lord knew him and cared about his struggles. Later, he wrote his daughter a letter, thanking her for her kindness, and shared with her that she had quoted his blessing verbatim. She, in turn, came to him with tears of gratitude as she shared her recent concerns about her place in the family and if she made a difference or even mattered. Both were blessed with tender mercies.

Another friend, who happened to be serving as a bishop of a singles ward, shared this experience with me. He was praying one evening about the members of his ward. Quite out of the blue, but very distinctly and directly, he felt one sister needed to serve a mission. Now this sister had experienced some serious struggles but had made tremendous progress of late. He wrote in his planner the note: "Sister _____ is supposed to go on a mission." A couple of weeks later, this good sister came to his office and asked if, given her background, there was any way she could serve a mission. He opened his planner, showed her the note, and said, "Yes, the Lord expects you to go. He has told me."

I too have had similar experiences as I have worked with the young adults of the Church. I have personally experienced a portion of the Lord's love for His children and seen His tender mercies manifest in both my life and the lives of others (in great abundance). I have shed tears with young adults as they have shared their troubles and burdens with me. I have rejoiced as they overcame these burdens and became new (or renewed) men and women of Christ, filled with confidence and light. I have seen countenances brighten and testimonies' fires rekindled. Young adults deal with difficult, real-life stuff, and I have marveled at their strength as they face life with courage, determination, and faith.

In times of discouragement, disappointment, or even despair, remember that you are not alone. When you are making important decisions or struggling with your place in the world, remember you are not here by accident. You were not sent to live in the time of Enoch or Moses or Nephi or Columbus because you are needed here and now—in the last days—to be part of the Lord's work in the most exciting time in history. Remember, the Lord is concerned about your success, and always remember the love your Savior has for you, for it is through Him that all good things are possible.

So this is "YRULDS" . . . why you are a member of the Church of Jesus Christ—because it is true. Through the Church, you will come to know the Lord and His goodness and love. You have a role to play in the building up of His kingdom.

Notes

1. C. S. Lewis, *The Weight of Glory and Other Addresses* (New York: Macmillam Publishing Co., 1980), 92.

2. Rex E. Lee, *What Do Mormons Believe* (Salt lake City: Deseret Book, 1992), 8–9.

3. In Conference Report, Oct. 2007.

4. Ibid.

5. In Conference Report, Apr. 2001.

6. As quoted in Stephen R. Covey, *The Seven Habits of Highly Effective People* (New York: Free Press, 1989), 299.

7. In Conference Report, Oct. 2007.

8. Neal A. Maxwell, *The Enoch Letters* (Salt Lake City: Deseret Book, 2006).

9. Sheri L. Dew, "You Were Born to Lead, You Were Born For Glory," BYU Devotional, 9 December 2003.

10. Ezra Taft Benson, "In His Steps," BYU Devotional, 4 March 1979.

11. Boyd K. Packer, "The Candle of the Lord," *Ensign*, Jan. 1983, 54–55.

12. In Conference Report, Oct. 1919, 181–82.

13. Clayton Christensen, "Decisions for Which I have Been Grateful," BYU-I Devotional, 8 June 2004.

14. In Conference Report, Apr. 2005.

2
Getting *a* Job

The Career Choice

> Find something you love to do and you'll never have to work a day
> in your life.[1]
>
> —Harvey Mackay

For many youth in the Church—young men in particular—life's goal
is to serve a mission. As members of the Church, we prepare for a mission
from our earliest days in Primary, continuing on through Young Men's
and Young Women's, Sunday School, seminary, family home evening,
institute, and so forth. And for good reason. A mission is an extraordinary
time in one's life. It is a time for concentrated service and focused study.
It is when you learn to pray with real intent and rely fully on the Lord. It
is a time to strengthen testimonies—yours and others'. You learn to work
with the Spirit, and you see the hand of God in the lives of His children.
You learn valuable leadership, language, and communication skills. You
learn to manage money, run effective meetings, cook, do your own laundry, and shop for groceries. You learn how to work, and you develop the
skills of a "self-starter," even when it is unbearably hot or bitterly cold. It
is a time of growth and personal magnification. No other experiences rep-
licate the experience of serving a full-time mission. We enter the mission
field as eager, committed, idealistic, but often naïve youth, and return
tried, tested, and true adults, with a mature understanding of life's purpose and the Lord's love.

Returning home from a mission is also a unique experience. Your
mission provided leadership opportunities, where the mantle of your

calling brought purpose and clarity, where the guidelines for success were crystal clear. I loved my mission. In so many ways it defined me—as a member of the Church, as a husband and father, and as a professional. But I distinctly remember my feelings as I left the stake president's office following my release. On one hand, I felt a significant sense of loss. On the other hand, I felt excited (but overwhelmed) about the million and one choices that were presented to me. I felt like I traded a very structured environment in which my entire focus had been on serving others for a very unstructured environment in which I was required to focus on more selfish, individual needs. I was forced to face the rest of my life, and I realized I had not really given it much consideration. To that point, my entire life's focus and emphasis had been on preparing for and then serving my mission.

Have you felt like that? For a few, the education and career decision is simple. You may have developed a clear picture of your aptitudes and talents, knowing exactly what you want to do and be when you grow up. The path forward is clear. I congratulate you and wish you good luck and Godspeed. Study hard and work hard, and good things will happen. But if you find yourself struggling with the career dilemma—realizing that what you study and where you work are colossal choices and that what you do now will impact the rest of your life—but you really don't know where or how to proceed, then read on. Often the hardest choices we have to make are between multiple good things. When faced with a choice between right or wrong, the decision is simple—choose the right (familiar phrase)—even if the choice requires sacrifice. But when the choice is unclear, with multiple good options, such as the choices of education and career, the dilemma can be daunting. Do any of the following quotes from young adults reflect your own questions and angst about your career?

> I have chosen a career that statistically has one of the most polar earning potentials, meaning that I could be very well-off, or very poor. It's *terrifying*! I work in the entertainment industry and every day I worry that I'm going to get stuck here and become the kind of person who thinks Hollywood is important.
>
> —Rob, 24

> I'm concerned about the kind of hours my chosen profession often requires. I can see how demanding work schedules could interfere with family time or, if I am still single at that point, how work

schedules could interfere with time spent dating and looking for a wife.

—Eric, 23

I am concerned I will not be able to support my family. Also, I fear that I will get into at job that I don't like, but I will continue to do it because it supports my family.

—John, 23

I have concerns about my future career. I want to make sufficient money at my job to be able to support my wife and children. I don't have to be rich, but I want to make enough money so I don't have to always think about how I am going to pay my next bill. I hate spending my time thinking about money. There are so many other things that I would rather spend my time thinking about. I also want to love my work. I want to help others and make a difference. If I enjoy going to work, I know that I will be a much better husband and father.

—Jacob, 24

As a general assignment reporter, I worry that I won't live up to my potential as a writer. (Or the potential that my dad tells me I have.)

—Gretta, 24

I'm strongly considering doing research in the field of genetics. As you may know, this is an area that has some ethical issues, such as cloning, engineering, and even embryonic stem cell research. I wonder sometimes what my stand will be on these issues and if I'll be able to work through my differences and find a way to better mankind without compromising my values.

—Leslie, 19

I'm considering teaching. I worry what impression I'll make on the students, because I know one good or bad teacher can entirely change the student's view on a subject.

—Halli, 19

How can you gain clarity on the course your career should take? I posed that question to various professionals, including medical doctors, dentists, CEOs of major corporations, authors, farmers, university professors, attorneys, business executives, educators, CPAs, engineers, and entrepreneurs. Their advice is summarized in the paragraphs below, and organized into what I call, "The 10 Points to a Successful Career."

1. Seek first the kingdom of God.

Regarding career success, Elder Packer taught:

> There is a formula. The Lord said, "Verily I say unto you, that every man who is obliged to provide for his own family, let him provide, and he shall in nowise lose his crown; and let him labor in the church." (D&C 75:28)
>
> The gospel of Jesus Christ is the formula for success. Every principle of the gospel, when lived, has a positive influence over your choice of an occupation and on what you will achieve. The counsel to labor in the Church has great value. Living the gospel will give you a perspective and an inspiration that will see you successful however ordinary your work may be or however ordinary your life may seem to others.[2]

I love the maxim, "seek to bless and not impress." There is great power in pure motives. If we make service to the Lord and His kingdom a priority, we will find that all other aspects of our lives will be blessed. Remember the Savior's council to the people in the land Bountiful: "Seek ye first the kingdom of God and his righteousness, and all these things shall be added unto you" (3 Ne 13:33). Having faith that the Lord will guide you if you put Him first can be tough. Sometimes we have to wait for His answers, and we don't know why. One young adult shared this experience with me as he sought confirmation about his career choice:

> I always wanted to be a doctor. I prayed and prayed that things would come together in my academic and personal life that would allow me to fulfill this dream. The time came for me to decide whether I would apply to medical school or not. For some reason I felt I should wait. Instead of medical school, I went on to work toward a master's degree. In the time that I worked on my degree I was able to serve in callings that instructed me in church administration. I made friends that I will always consider family. I became better prepared for my future. After obtaining my master's degree, I felt it was now time to apply for medical school. A few months before school was to begin, I received a call from the administration. They informed me that I would be receiving a scholarship that would pay for at least half of my medical school. They also informed me that this scholarship had been in the works for a few years now and it just became available that year. Money is not the driving force of my testimony, but the fact that the Lord provides a way when you are doing your best is a powerful lesson I have learned.

2. Broaden your perspectives.

A friend of mine considered entering public service, with the intent of eventually running for Congress. However, after an internship in Washington D.C., he discovered that although he had a tremendous respect for our nation's elected officials, he did not want to be one. He determined that his contributions and community involvement would come through different means. Another friend of mine had a goal to become an attorney. He selected an undergraduate program that emphasized writing and communication, and taught him to think critically and analytically. It was good preparation for law school. He entered law school and did well in his studies, but he quickly discovered that he couldn't see himself working as an attorney for the rest of his life. He has since found success in business. As you weigh your career options, make a concerted effort to broaden your perspectives as much as possible. Consider doing an internship or two. If you are thinking of becoming an attorney, spend some time with one. Volunteer to work at a law firm and see what attorneys do and how they spend their time. Talk with a lot of people who are established in their careers. If you think you might enjoy teaching, volunteer in a classroom or get a job as a teacher's assistant.

My friend Samuel, 24, shared with me this advice for his fellow young adults:

> Take a lot of different classes and try to find internships that are diverse. You often won't know what you are passionate about until you actually do something. Classes are a great way of seeing what you love, but internships are better. It will really show you a lot about what you love and, perhaps just as important, what you don't love.
>
> If you are considering business, you may want to flex your entrepreneurial muscles. Start a small business. The experience can be both tremendously rewarding and educational. You will learn valuable lessons in finance, sales, information technology, operations, marketing, product development, and leadership.

Another way to gain a deeper understanding of what's out there for you is to travel internationally. This experience generally requires some sacrifice, but it can help you to gain a perspective beyond the safe confines of home. You may discover opportunities that had not previously occurred to you, and you may discover you have a passion and aptitude for certain things that you otherwise might miss. If your situation allows for it, go on a semester abroad or find another way to travel.

It is okay to take time to discover where you want to make your career contributions. My father reminded me while I was in college that my education was not a race. He acknowledged the tension I was feeling to get on with my life and establish my career, but he encouraged me to take enough time to learn what I needed to learn and to study a wide range of subjects. Consider his advice. Take a variety of general education courses so that you can gain exposure to several different disciplines. Be curious and read outside your chosen field or course of study.

Eric, 24, shared with me his experience of selecting a major:

> I took a bunch of classes, a wide spectrum of different disciplines, and then started asking myself what intrigued me the most—what could I see myself doing with this information thirty years from now? If I couldn't see myself using and enjoying the information from the class as part of a career, I simply chalked up the class as experience and didn't take any more classes in that discipline. If I could see myself using and enjoying the information from the class, I investigated further. This funneling of what interested me eventually lead me to a very *totally* unexpected decision: that I liked chemistry and the biological sciences (a totally unexpected outcome). I made a 180-degree turn from being a journalism major and became a chemistry/biochemistry major.

As you explore your own options and abilities, think of five professional people whom you admire. Talk with them and learn what they do and what they like and don't like about their careers. If you take the time to interview people who have gained professional success later in life, many will reveal that they would never have predicted their ultimate destination. Many end up in careers that bear little resemblance to what they initially intended. Opportunities came to them as they worked tirelessly, stretched their skill sets, took calculated risks, studied and learned new ideas, and pushed themselves to add value to all their activities. Serendipity is defined as making fortunate discoveries by accident, and this what often happens as careers develop. As you broaden your view of the world and explore your options for contribution, you will be amazed at what presents itself.

Of course, you need to use discretion as you follow the advice to take your time. This point does not give you the excuse to become a perpetual student—one who is ever learning but never able to come to a knowledge of how to provide for a family. Elder M. Russell Ballard advised, "There are those who become professional thinkers. I don't want to encourage that. . . . I have met men who should really be out producing who are still studying. I think that there is a point at which you graduate and go on to the things that you have in mind that you want to try to accomplish in life."[3]

3. Pay the price.

Learning to pay the price is important when considering the direction of your education and subsequent career. Be prepared to work in a couple of different jobs to gain valuable experience. You should worry less about the specific job function right out of the gate. In fact, you shouldn't expect to find the perfect job opportunity on your first try. Make gaining experience a priority, and always be willing to learn. You might not love every job you have, but learn from every job you have. Tyler, a recently returned missionary, shared his insights with me about his current job: "My job is helping me narrow some things down with my career decision and is giving me opportunities to lead in the business world. I know that with the help of the Lord, as I stay close to the gospel, and finish school, I will find a career where I can excel."

I am impressed with the story of Chris Gardner, which surfaced in the film *Pursuit of Happyness*. Chris was a struggling salesman who, though he didn't love his job, learned he had a gift for working with people. One day he had a chance encounter with a stock broker, and he became intrigued with that profession; although he knew he had much to learn, he pursued making this career change. With intense persistence, he gains an interview and is granted an unpaid, highly competitive internship with a prestigious San Francisco brokerage firm. The internship was really an audition for full-time employment; only one in twenty interns would be offered a full-time job at the internship's conclusion six months later. To Chris, this was literally the opportunity of a lifetime. While he had less formal training than the other candidates, he determined to contribute more drive and dedication than others were willing to bring.

Unfortunately, events in his personal life made taking this internship difficult—he was going through a difficult breakup and he had custody of his young son. Accepting the unpaid internship made it nearly impossible to make financial ends meet. He couldn't pay rent, and he was consequently evicted from his home and struggled to provide food for his small family. Now his situation with his son's school schedule was such that he was unable to spend as much time at the office as the other candidates. Chris felt he had one chance to make this important career change work. So he approached his internship with the attitude that he couldn't waste a single second. His job was to call prospective investors and sell them on the services of his brokerage. In the process, he discovered that if he didn't physically hang up the phone between calls (instead keeping the receiver in his hands and accessing a new line by simply pushing a button), he would gain an additional eight minutes per day, resulting in several additional calls. He used this same ethic with every phase of his work. He didn't engage in wasteful office banter or gossip-mongering. He lowered his head, focused his vision, and made great things happen. After six months, he was one of two people selected to remain with the firm, and used past experience to create a very successful career. This movie might well be required viewing for all who are seeking to make their mark in the world.[4]

In Sam Parker and Mac Anderson's wonderful little book, *212: The Extra Degree*, they use the metaphor of raising the temperature of water from 211 degrees to 212 degrees. They write, "At 211 degrees, water is hot. At 212 degrees, it boils. And with boiling water comes steam. And steam can power a locomotive."[5] Their point is very powerful. To heat water to 211 degrees requires time and effort. But the real strength and power in the water comes with the final nudge. It is with the last unit of effort where transformation occurs, the magic happens, and the cumulative effort of all that went before bears fruit. Consider these interesting facts from their book:

- In the past 25 years, the average margin of victory in all of the Professional Golf Association's major tournaments (the U.S. Open, the British Open, the PGA Championship, and the Masters) was less than three strokes. That is less than one stroke per day. And yet, the winner of these tournaments took home on average 76 percent more prize money than the second-place finisher.[6]
- During the 2004 Summer Olympic Games, the margin of victory between the gold medal winner and getting no medal at all for the men's 200 meter Freestyle (swimming) was 1.42 seconds. For the women's 200 meter Freestyle, it was .59 seconds. In the men's 800 meter race (running), the victory margin was .71 seconds. In the women's 800 meter, it was only .13 seconds. For the men's long jump, it was 28 centimeters; for the women's long jump it was 11 centimeters. Every Olympic athlete has remarkable talent

and works incredibly hard. However, those who go the extra degree, push it just a little further, are the ones who ultimately prevail.[7]

I have a friend who started her career as an administrative assistant for a small, start-up firm. The particular organization had literally been operating out of the principal owner's garage and had just obtained its first real office space. Soon the organization began to grow, and with this growth came increased organizational complexities and operational difficulties. My friend was willing to learn and stretch beyond her comfort zone and was willing to work outside her official job responsibilities, demonstrating a desire to add value wherever she could. Over time, the processes she created became institutionalized, and she was awarded additional responsibilities. In a relatively short period of time, my friend became a trusted executive, running with distinction a major division of a large company. She has enjoyed success for many years and continues to bring leadership and sound judgment to her organization and clients. She did not begin her initial assignment with the clear picture of her ultimate responsibilities, but she did bring a determination to do her best every day and to go beyond expectations. And her career soared.

Author Jim Collins writes about Dave Scott, a six-time Hawaii Ironman Triathlon champion:

> In training, Scott would ride his bike 75 miles, swim 20,000 meters, and run 17 miles—on average every single day. Dave Scott did not have a weight problem! Yet he believed that a low-fat, high-carbohydrate diet would give him an extra edge. So, Dave Scott—a man who burned at least 5,000 calories a day in training—would literally rinse his cottage cheese to get the extra fat off. Now, there is no evidence that he absolutely needed to rinse his cottage cheese to win the Ironman; that's not the point of the story. The point is that rinsing his cottage cheese was simply one more small step that he believed would make him just that much better, one more small step added to all the other small steps to create a consistent program of superdiscipline. I've always pictured Dave Scott running the 26 miles of the marathon—hammering away in hundred-degree heat on the black, baked lava fields of the Kona coast after swimming 2.4 miles on the ocean and cycling 112 miles against ferocious crosswinds—and thinking to himself: "Compared to rinsing my cottage cheese every day, this just isn't that bad."[8]

So much of our success is tied to our willingness to bring discipline to our efforts, to do whatever it takes to do our best. As Collins writes, "it's really just that simple. And it's really just that difficult."[9]

4. Be passionate.

As I mentioned, you should not worry about finding the perfect job on your first try, but rather seek experience that will help you better understand the course your career should take. Ultimately, however, you need to do work that is meaningful to you. It is not good policy to pursue a career solely based on earning potential. There are plenty of unhappy, unfulfilled rich people. The staggering measure of your waking life spent in working deserves your passionate commitment. Your pursuit of excellence in work you love as you seek to contribute will bless your associates and bring personal satisfaction, and time will reward you with financial competence. Elder Boyd K. Packer counseled, "There is great dignity and worth in any honest occupation."[10]

Sam, 25, a college graduate and new entrant into the business world, advises:

> I thought choosing the "right" major was very important . . . and I do think we need to ask the Lord about it, but now that I am working, I realize that the specific major was not as important as I thought. If you are going into accounting or engineering, the major matters . . . but it is better to just choose something you are passionate about and minor in business. I know everyone tells you that but it is true. Sure, you probably won't work for Goldman Sachs with a Public Relations degree, but to a large extent, your major is more about what you are passionate about than what other people are passionate about.

Nathan, 25, another college graduate, suggests, "Find something that interests you. I am amazed at the wide variety of careers available in, what I thought, were very narrow fields. You want to be involved with something about which you feel passionate. You should love what you will do the rest of your life."

And a young man from Tahiti said this: "To be successful, you must be passionate in all you. Because of this passion, you will give your best effort—from the smallest, most insignificant task to the greatest."

Jack Welch worked for several years as the Chairman and CEO of General Electric, the second largest organization on the Fortune 500 list. During his tenure, GE market value grew from 13 billion dollars to 400 billion dollars. In 2005, he was voted Most Admired CEO of the past twenty years by *Chief Executive* magazine readers and as the World's Greatest Leader Today in a *Fast Company* magazine survey. When asked for his advice to those selecting their education and making career decisions, Jack said, "Do something that 'turns your crank.' Do what you enjoy doing. You will be better doing work you love." He also advised, speaking directly to the next generation of workers, "Over-deliver! If your boss asks for two things, deliver four!"[11]

Here is a little more from Jim Collins beyond "rinsing the cottage cheese." In his book, *Good to Great*, Collins and his research team examine the differences between merely "good" companies and the truly "great" companies (companies with superior financial performance that was sustained for at least fifteen years). One of the success factors is that great organizations are filled with people who are passionate about their work. One of the great organizations he highlights is Kimberly-Clark, a leading paper-based consumer-products company. He learned that the great companies did not say, " 'Okay, folks, let's get passionate about what we do.' Sensibly, they went the other way: We should only do those things that we can get passionate about. Kimberly-Clark executives made the shift to paper-based consumer products in large part because they could get more passionate about them. As one executive put it, the traditional paper products are okay, 'but they just don't have the charisma of a diaper.' "[12]

Regarding Gillette, another one of his "great" companies, Collins quotes a Wall Street Journal reporter, who described Gillette's hiring process: "People who aren't passionate about Gillette need not apply." The Journal reporter goes on to describe how a top business school graduate wasn't hired "because she didn't show enough passion for deodorant."[13]

Collins concludes, "Perhaps you can't get passionate about deodorant either. Perhaps you might find it hard to imagine being passionate about pharmacies, grocery stores . . . or postage meters. You might wonder about what type of person gets all jazzed up about making a bank as efficient as McDonald's, or who considers a diaper charismatic. In the end, it doesn't really matter. The point is that they felt passionate about what they were doing and the passion was deep and genuine."[14]

> Perhaps Robert Frost said it best in his poem, *The Tramps in Mudtime*. Frost's narrator discusses the virtues of work, and the need to combine passion with effort:
> *My object in living is to unite*
> *My avocation and my vocation*

As my two eyes make one in sight.
Only where love and need are one,
And the work is play for mortal stakes,
Is the deed ever really done
For Heaven and the future's sakes.

Your avocation—what you love to do—should combine blissfully with your vocation—your work.[15]

5. Know your values.

The year is AD 1140. The place: Weibertreu Castle in Germany. Janet Scharman writes:

> These were not easy times to be living. The thick castle walls, deep moats, and heavy gates were built for a reason. The battles fought during that time were probably not too different than those we read about in the Book of Mormon, where men fought hand to hand and eye to eye with their attackers and the occupation of the victors was most often devastating. King Konrad III and his powerful army attacked the castle of Weibertreu in a powerful siege. He knew his trade well, and those within the walls were unable to defend themselves. As the castle inhabitants were on the verge of surrender, Konrad, in a moment of kindness, said the women could leave the crumbling fortress, taking with them all they could carry on their backs. The gates opened, and the women staggered out, struggling under the heavy loads they carried. Konrad and his men were caught off guard, shocked and surprised by what they saw, for on the back of each woman was one of the men. They knew where their treasures were, and they chose to take what was very most important, even at the risk of stirring the anger of the soldiers. Konrad, touched by this tender display of love and loyalty, remained true to his word, and although his troops leveled the buildings, not a life was lost that day.
>
> Those must have been among the most harsh and brutal times to live, and yet the people of Weibertreu were able to reach beyond that to some degree and hang on to what was most dear to them. They understood the importance of their relationships and were able to summon the strength and courage from within to preserve that which was needed for their survival. Although there is little in the way of physical remains of the castle [today], the story of the "Castle of the Loyal Wives" lives on and is still an inspiring reminder to young and old alike more than 850 years later.
>
> Understanding who we are and what is truly important in this life is a vital element in letting the Lord help us through this journey on earth.[16]

Long-term, sustainable success will never come if you violate your core values. Taking time to clarify these values will be among the most important things you can do as you prepare for your career.

Too frequently, our very busy lives are complicated by outside influences that are unimportant. For example, you may have discovered that relationships are important to you, yet on close inspection, you realize that much of what you do pushes people away. Or you place high value on accomplishment and contribution, but an assessment of your daily activities shows you are spending pointless hours in front of the TV. In fact, a recent study showed that the average adult spends more than twenty hours each week watching TV. Twenty hours! That's enough time to fill a part-time job, or the equivalent of twenty-six forty-hour work weeks. Think of all you could accomplish if that time was spend in a way that coincided with your priorities.

Do you ever find yourself doing things contrary to your values? Of course you do; we all do. But focusing on what is important to you will help you correct your course and will guide you toward a life of contribution consistent with your talents and unique abilities.

Living true to your values stirs great energy and can awaken your passion, bringing amazing results. I had the privilege of meeting Dr. Muhammad Yunus, a world-renowned economist and the father of the microcredit movement. He lives in Bangladesh, a geographically small country about the size of Ohio; however, it is the seventh largest country in the world in terms of population, with approximately 160 million people. Poverty rages, and most of the modern conveniences like electricity, medicine, and adequate shelter are largely unavailable.

Muhammad Yunus was a sought-after teacher and expert in his field, but one day in 1974, he realized that all he was doing was talking about how to improve the economic conditions of the world while his own country languished in squalor. The women of his country, traditionally relegated to second-class citizenry, aroused his particular concern. When a baby girl is born in Bangladesh, the birth is viewed as "bad news." When women reach adult status, they are considered "burdens for their families." These women have little available means of improving their situation. One woman he encountered made about two cents per day making bamboo stools. She did beautiful work and made a marketable product, but couldn't improve her situation because she had to rely on a bamboo provider who also purchased her finished stools at fixed prices which did not provide her with any margin. Muhammad Yunus realized all this woman needed was a small amount of working capital to establish her businesses, but his attempts to secure this for her and other impoverished women through traditional loans were met with skepticism and ultimate denial from bank officials. These women, he was told, had no credit history and were not considered worthy candidates for financing, even for small amounts.

As though pursuing Grover Cleveland's great advice: "You can't do everything at once, but you can do something at once," Muhammad Yunus loaned the woman just $6, which in turn enabled her to earn $1.25 per day, immediately moving her to middle-class status.

Based on this success, Yunus began the Grameen Bank, which helps individuals in similar financial straits. More than just providing a little cash to relieve a short-term financial need, Yunus's microcredit initiative promotes self-sufficiency among these destitute people, 95 percent of whom are women who have no other place to turn. Starting with just $27, he has built an entity worth some 4 billion dollars in assets that now provides loans to over 2,400,000 customers. These women require very little capital to start businesses. In some cases it is $2, in others it is $10. Some buy pigs and re-sell them. Others sell milk. It starts small, but has lead to the elevation of literally millions of women, many of whom have gone on to higher education in engineering, medical school, and other fields. Today, the Grameen Bank has nearly a 100 percent repayment rate, far higher than traditional banks. In October 2006, Muhammad Yunus was awarded the Nobel Peace Prize.[17]

Muhammad Yunus has literally changed the world. He started small, as changes often do, stayed the course despite obstacles, and established a process that has improved the lives of millions. It's an amazing and inspiring story, and would never have happened if he hadn't examined his life and decided to act according to his values.

There will be occasions in both your education and throughout your career where your integrity will be tested. I love the story Stephen M. R. Covey tells in his book *The Speed of Trust*, originally written by the wife of a man who was in medical school.

> Getting into medical school is pretty competitive, and the desire to do well and be successful puts a great deal of pressure on the new freshmen. My husband had worked hard on his studies and went to attend his first examination. The honor system was expected behavior

at the medical school. The professor passed out the examination and left the room. Within a short time, students started to pull little cheat papers out from under their papers or from their pockets. My husband recalled his heart beginning to pound as he realized it is pretty hard to compete against cheaters. About that time a tall, lanky student stood up in the back of the room and stated, "I left my hometown and put my wife and three babies in an upstairs apartment and worked very hard to get into medical school. And I'll turn in the first one of you who cheats, and you better believe it!" They believed it. There were many sheepish expressions, and those cheat papers started to disappear as fast as they had appeared. He set a standard for the class which eventually graduated the largest group in the school's history.[18]

Living consistent with your values may be uncomfortable and require great courage, but living that way helps you build trust. And trust with yourself and others is essential to your long-term education and career success. More will be said about trust in chapter 4.

6. Develop your decision criteria.

You will likely face several different employment options throughout your life. In fact, while your grandparents may have spent thirty to forty years in the same profession—even working for the same company—today's professionals will change jobs an average of seven times or more. When faced with key decisions about your job, how will you make the right choice? In preparation for answering this question, take some time to develop your decision criteria for determining your best options. For example, a president of a successful public company shared his criteria with me. He has identified five factors that influence his options. They are, in order of priority:

- I have to be excited to go to work. Of course there are the occasional days when I wish I could be anywhere else, but overall, I need to look forward to going to work. My job needs to capture what I call my "shower time," meaning it is what I think about when I wake up, when I get ready for my day, and as I drive to work.
- It has to be developmental for my future. I've got to feel like I am adding to my inventory of skills and experiences.
- I have got to be able to deal with my boss. I may not like him, but I have to respect him.

- I have to be comfortable about the perks (salary and benefits). While this is very important, it is not my #1 criterion. If the preceding criteria are not satisfactory, the money generally won't compensate.
- I have to be comfortable where I live. Geography is important to me. When my wife and I first married, we felt more mobile. Now that we have children in school, we are less willing to uproot our family.[19]

Another executive shared a similar set of decision criteria, again, in order of priority.

- I have to enjoy being around the people with whom I work. I am able to make almost anything fun, as long as I work with good people. And almost anything can be drudgery if I don't enjoy my coworkers.
- I have to have passion around my company's mission. That doesn't mean that I will only work for companies that cure cancer or are involved in other noble pursuits. Sometimes it means the "how" of my work is as important as the "what" of my work. For example, if my job provides opportunities where I can flex my creative muscles and innovate, I find I am more engaged.
- I need to feel stretched or challenged in my work. I want to feel like I have to bring my "A-game" each day in order to succeed. I get a rush from the pressure of staying sharp.
- I want the opportunity for influence. I don't necessarily have to have tons of people reporting to me, but I need to feel like my opinion is sought after and valued.
- I need to feel I am fairly compensated for my contributions.[20]

These are just examples. Your own unique situation and priorities will vary, but developing your own criteria will help you sort through the opportunities you consider.

7. Develop your personal network.

There is a popular party game involving the actor Kevin Bacon called "Six degrees of Kevin Bacon." In this game, one player names a random movie star. The other player then has to make a connection within six movies between a movie that movie star was in and a movie that Kevin Bacon was in. For example, say the first player said, "Dick Van Dyke." The second player might say, "Dick Van Dyke starred in *Mary Poppins* with Julie Andrews. Julie Andrews was in *Princess Diaries* with Anne Hathaway. Anne Hathaway was in *The Devil Wears Prada* with Meryl Streep, and Meryl Streep was in *The River Wild* with Kevin Bacon." (It only took four movies in this example.)

Try this with a group of friends, but instead of using Kevin Bacon and his movies, pick another prominent person—perhaps a Church leader or business leader. You will be surprised at how closely connected you are to these people, even if you don't know them personally. This is a simple example of networking. Networking is a necessary and important skill for your career management. Begin now to create a network of people that you can draw upon for advice, connections, and experience. This does not necessarily mean a list of people you call to ask for work. Rather, it means developing a list of influencers—people who can provide insight about you and can connect you with opportunities as they come.

Do you know of any married couples that met as a result of a blind date or "set-up"? This is a great example of the benefits of networking. These couples would never have met if they hadn't accessed the power of their network. Finding a job is no different. The reality is that most jobs are gained through relationships. You will be surprised at how large your list of influencers becomes. You are likely far more connected than you know. It can be extremely helpful when you are searching for a job to talk with as many people as you can. Few people do this. Instead of taking the time and effort to build a network, many send resumes out to potential employers en masse and then take the first job that presents itself. Networking can help you gain tremendous insight into what jobs might work, and what jobs might not be an appropriate fit. After a few years, some people find themselves stuck in a field of work where they have experience and earning potential, but they don't like what they do. Networking can help provide a clearer picture of your aptitudes, inclination, and options before you officially begin your career.

There are two types of networking: formal and informal. Formal networking is what you do when you look for a job. In fact, until you find official employment, it is your job. Everyone has three networks—the people you know directly, the people these people know, and, you guessed it, the people those people know. The process of building these networks is fairly simple. To begin, start with the particular field or industry where you have an interest and write down the names of every person you know in that industry. Give these people a call and ask for twenty minutes of their time. Ask them what they like and don't like about their jobs, and how they would advise you in your career. During this discussion, ask yourself: "Can I do this job? Will I do this job? Does this fit me personally?" At the conclusion of the interview, let them know how valuable the interview has been for you. Thank them, and then ask, "Do you know anyone else that might be willing to talk with me about this subject?" Add these names to your network and repeat the process.

After your call, send the person a hand-written thank-you card. This is an important step—don't forget it! Once you land a job, send each person you interviewed a hand-written thank-you letter, and mention in that letter your willingness to return the favor with other people in their network. Be sure to keep a journal of your networking activities and take copious notes. You never know when you might need to reference the conversation. Have a place where you can keep track of thank-you notes sent, phone numbers, record of conversations, and so forth.

After you are employed, you need to continue your networking efforts. Informal networking is staying connected and involved with the people who have helped you and who are important to you. This can be in the form of a periodic phone call or email. As an example, say you have left a job, but you know your former boss loves golf. If you run across a fun article on golf, send it him in a short email. Send Christmas cards, write a blog, or build your network on Facebook or other social-networking sites. We live in a time where technology greatly enables networking, and these resources can be a tremendous advantage to you. Don't just reach out to your network when you are in need of something. Stay connected, add value to others in simple ways, and continually seek to build your network.

8. Develop a personal mission statement.

Stephanie, 24, and a new elementary school teacher, shared with me an insight she gained about what she wanted her life's contributions to include. She said, "I want to leave a legacy. As a new teacher, I had a parent tell me that her son was a better person for having known me. Those words had a significant impact on me. I realized that I don't have to be well-known to make a difference—I just have to leave places and people better than I found them. A contribution of this sort cannot be measured in the way the world measures success, but the effects are never-ending."

Each of us has unique abilities and talents that will make a difference in the world. Often, however, our challenge is in discovering these abilities and talents. Creating a personal mission statement—or personal manifesto—will help bring your contributions into focus. Just as the United States Constitution has directed the very structure of our government and is the basis for day-to-day life, your mission statement will serve as an important guide for what you do and for what you will become. The development of your mission statement can be a difficult but illuminating experience. It will help you narrow your focus and tighten your commitment for your ultimate profession. W. H. Murray, organizer of the 1951 Scottish Himalayan expedition, writes:

> Until one is committed, there is hesitancy, the chance to draw back, always ineffectiveness concerning all acts of initiative and creation. There is one elementary truth, the ignorance of which kills countless ideas and splendid plans; that the moment one definitely commits oneself, then Providence moves too.
>
> All sorts of things occur to help one that would never otherwise have occurred. A whole stream of events issues from the decision raising in one's favor all manner of unforeseen events, meetings and material assistance which no one could have dreamed would have come their way.
>
> I have learned a deep respect for one of Goethe's couplets: "Whatever you can do or dream you can, begin it. Boldness has genius, power and magic in it. Begin it now!"[21]

It is amazing what happens when you make a commitment to your mission. When combined with determined action, you create a sense of momentum that is hard to stop. This is what it means to live by design rather than by default. Imagine meeting yourself ten years from now. Who are you? What are you doing? Where are you living? What contributions are you making? Describe your family. How do you make this vision of the future a reality in your life?

The following line represents your life. The beginning marks your birth, and the end represents your death. Place an X on where you currently are on this line. Now, look at the time you have left. What will you do with this wonderful gift of time?

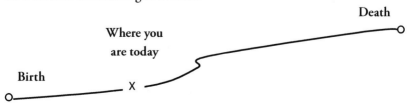

Death

Where you
are today

Birth

X

Influential Leaders

I was never passionate about scouting as a young man. I don't confess it proudly, but honesty demands it. With all the wit, wisdom, and judgment of my thirteen years, I had resisted scouting, and at times I even fought to avoid participation. I had a long-suffering scoutmaster and deacon's quorum advisor who demonstrated tremendous patience with me and who always went the second mile to ensure that I was doing what I needed to do, pulling my weight, and contributing my part. I know I gave him grief and caused him to raise his voice a few times in exasperation, but I also knew he loved me. He had a certain exuberance for the Lord's work that was hard to resist. I remember him taking a week off work to take us to scout camp. His singing "Oh what a beautiful morning" at the top of his lungs very, very early each morning still echoes in my head. I also remember the testimony he shared over campfires and his excitement for the progress we made in our lives. As I got just a bit older, this scoutmaster became my bishop. He saw me through my high school years, guided our family and others through trials and tragedy, prepared me for my mission, and was there to preside over my homecoming.

I remember distinctly the advice and counsel he gave me as I was dating my wife, and his encouragement and support as Michele and I prepared to marry. My wedding reception is mostly a blur—there was so much going on that I actually remember very little. But I do remember that just as it ended, Bishop Harding and his wife joined Michele and me for a few quiet moments to express their congratulations. Given my experience with this man over the years, it was one of the highlights of the entire evening. Just a few weeks later, I received word that this good man, who had served for over seven years as bishop, was killed in a tragic accident in Spanish Fork Canyon, leaving behind his wife and ten children, a struggling business, and a deeply affected ward.

From the world's perspective, this man did not achieve great success. He was not rich, he lived in a small house, and he did not receive any national acclaim. All he did was change lives, and his impact will be felt for generations and, I believe, throughout eternity.

Think about your own contributions to and your mission in life. What do you want to be remembered for? What will be your lasting legacy?

Consider the process of building a house. What would happen if the construction commenced without a detailed blueprint? It is almost ludicrous to imagine, yet many live their lives in exactly that fashion. Indeed, some spend more time planning a two-week vacation than in planning the rest of their lives. A choice movie, *Dead Poet's Society*, features a private school for boys in the northeastern United States. During their initial day at school, the wide-eyed and anxious boys proceed from one class to another, receiving the standard initiation speech from each of their teachers. You watch their progression from class to class—first chemistry, then Latin, then trigonometry. Finally, they meet their new English teacher, Mr. Keating, played by Robin Williams. They discover that he is quite different from the other teachers. With a more unique and creative teaching style, he pushes the boys to reach beyond their comfort zones to attain unexpected levels of understanding and appreciation.

During their second day of class when they receive their textbook, Mr. Keating has one young man read the introductory essay to the literature text, which discusses a scientific and formulaic way of rating and understanding poetry. As the boy begins to read, it becomes clear to the class that Mr. Keating doesn't like the essay. He then stops the young reader and asks the boys to rip the introductory essay completely out of the textbook. It takes a minute for the boys to follow this advice, but soon pages are being torn from the book with enthusiasm. It is as if the essay's very presence alongside the works of Keats, Blake, Wordsworth, and Shakespeare threaten the enjoyment and meaning and value the literature represents. As Mr. Keating says to his students, "In my class, you will learn to think for yourselves. . . . You will learn to savor words and language. No matter what anybody tells you, words and ideas can change the world." Mr. Keating then gathers his class together, and in a hushed, dramatic tone, declares, "We don't read and write poetry because it is cute. We read and write poetry because we are members of the human race. And the human race is filled with passion. Medicine, law, business, engineering . . . these are noble pursuits, and necessary to sustain human life. But poetry, beauty, romance, love . . . these are what we stay alive for!" His final admonition is this: "The powerful play goes on and you may contribute a verse. What will your verse be?"[22]

What a wonderful and appropriate question for each of us to consider! What will your individual "verses" be? How will you make your contributions to the world?

Creating—or better said, discovering—your personal mission statement is a difficult but very powerful process. It will help bring clarity to the things you value, and will help define how you spend your time and the contributions you make. It will bring a greater sense of meaning to your work. I once read a statement that shocked me: "95 percent of Americans have never taken the time to think about goals or mission."[23] Is this true for you? My guess is it is not. I hope you have spent a great deal of time thinking about goals and your ultimate contributions to the world. In either case, however, it is worth an investment of your time to consider the following process for writing your personal mission statement. To begin, take a moment and think about the following questions and see what recollections they bring to you.

- Name the five wealthiest people in the world.
- Name the last five Heisman trophy winners.
- Name the last five winners of the Miss America Pageant.
- Name ten people who have won the Nobel or Pulitzer Prize.
- Name the last half dozen Academy Award winners for best actor and actress.
- Name the last decade's list of World Series winners.[24]

How did you do? The point is, none of us remember yesterday's headlines. These are no second-rate achievers; they are the best in their fields. But the applause dies, awards tarnish, achievements are forgotten, and accolades and certificates are buried with their owners.

Here's another quiz—see how you do on this one:

- List a few teachers who aided your journey through school.
- Name three friends who have helped you through a difficult time.
- Name five people who have taught you something worthwhile.
- Think of a few people who have made you feel appreciated and special.
- Think of five people you enjoy spending time with.

Easier? Here's the lesson: The people who make a difference in your life are not the ones with the most credentials, the most money, or the most awards. They are the ones that *care*.

Think about those who have made a difference to you. Was there a leader that helped change the trajectory of your life or the lives of others? Perhaps it was an influential teacher—someone who caused you to stretch your skills and think beyond your current mind-set to future possibilities. Perhaps it was a friend, a coach, or a Church leader. It may have been a boss or colleague at work; maybe a parent, grandparent, aunt, or uncle. Think about their leadership. What was it that was most meaningful? What did they do that caused you to want to follow them or take their advice?

Rob, 24, shared this experience with me:

> There have been so many people who have helped me become who and what I am, but one person who helped me so very much during a very difficult time in my life comes to mind. He was a sincere friend, and a man who wanted nothing more than for me to understand my potential and my place in the plan of my Heavenly Father, despite the difficulties that I encountered in my life. He took time that I know he had very little of, and used that time to help carry me through a doubt and fear-filled time in my life.

Make a list of the influential leaders in your life and note the traits that you would like to incorporate into your own leadership style.

Influential Leaders	Traits You Want to Emulate
_____	_____
_____	_____
_____	_____
_____	_____
_____	_____

Your influential leaders serve as terrific models to follow. Through your associations with them, you have firsthand knowledge about what is effective and what is not. As you create this list, you will discover that those who have had the greatest impact on you convey an almost tangible sense of love and concern, and demonstrate an ability to paint a vision for you above what you can see yourself. Albert Schweitzer describes these people this way, "In everyone's life, at some point, our inner fire goes out. It is then burst into flame by an encounter with another human being. We should all be thankful for those people who rekindle the inner spirit."[25]

Consider the following questions and jot down your ideas regarding each question in the space below:

- What do I want to have in this life (physical possessions)?
- What do I want to do (accomplishments, travel, and so forth)?
- What do I want to be (attributes of character)?

Have	Do	Be

What roles do you play in your life? Student? Daughter? Son? Husband? Wife? Employer? Employee? Friend? Certainly you are a child of God. Take a minute to identify the different roles you play and write them in the space below. Once you have identified your roles, write a statement that you would like others to say about you in this role. This is an aspirational activity—write what you would like them to say. For instance, if you identified "Daughter" as one of your roles, what would you like your mother or father to say about you as it relates to this role?

Role   Statement

_____   _____

                                       _____

                                       _____

                                       _____

                                       _____

                                       _____

_____   _____

                                       _____

                                       _____

                                       _____

                                       _____

Finally, take a few moments to explore the following questions:

Assuming you had sixty seconds to live, what would you leave as your last words to your family? _____

_____

And what advice on life would you give to children two generations out? _____

_____

48

Assume you just inherited a large sum of money. What would you do differently with your life? _____

_____

What are you thankful for? _____

_____

What brings you the greatest happiness? _____

_____

The purpose of these exercises is to give you a look at your values from a few different angles and to help bring clarity to what is truly important. Creating a personal mission statement is a process that deserves your best focus, and if done thoughtfully, it will serve as a compass in your decision-making throughout your life and will stand as a guide to help you determine how you will contribute. A mission statement can take many forms. It might be a couple of paragraphs. It might be represented by a picture or a poem. For me, it is only ten words. Though someone else might look at my mission statement and wonder why these words are so significant for me, each word is filled with meaning because of the process I engaged in to craft them. This is a very personal activity, and the end product is unique to each individual. Here is an example of a personal mission statement from Ralph Waldo Emerson:

> To laugh often and love much; to win the respect of intelligent persons and the affection of children; to earn the approbation of honest citizens and endure the betrayal of false friends; to appreciate beauty; to find the best in others; to give of one's self; to leave the world a bit better, whether by a healthy child, a garden patch or a redeemed social condition; to have played and laughed with enthusiasm and sung with exultation; to know even one life has breathed easier because you have lived—this is to have succeeded.[26]

With this example and the earlier exercises in mind, follow these four steps and take some time to create a draft of your own mission statement.

1. Review your responses to the earlier exercises.
2. Take five minutes to write everything that comes to your mind. Don't bother editing, spelling, or punctuation—just write, and don't let the pencil or keyboard stop.
3. Refine your mission statement. Review your first draft and

rewrite it. Challenge yourself by looking at what you have created through two lenses: first, does it represent the best that is within you? And second, does it inspire you? Edit and rewrite.

4. Continue to refine your mission statement over time. Review it regularly, and make adjustments as you go.

9. Be results-focused.

Authors Ram Charan and G. Colvin examined the reasons why business leaders lose their jobs. They discovered that 70 percent of strategic failures are due to poor execution of leadership. In other words, leaders failed to get the required results. They generally had good plans, but somehow those plans never translated into actual performance. They also found that the leader's failure was "rarely for a lack of smarts or vision."[27]

As you pursue your work, develop a reputation for producing results. Don't confuse activity with actual performance. Too often we get sucked into the "whirlwind" of daily minutiae—reports that have to be done, phones that need to be answered, endless email, and pointless meetings to attend. Frequently, however, these activities have little to do with what really needs to be done.

Think about your own life. Do you ever feel consumed by the daily grind? Do you ever wonder if you are really accomplishing anything of value? I often ask business people, "If you had no strategic goals or organizational priorities, would you still be busy?" Their answer: "Yes!" There are always tasks to perform. All too often, however, the work we actually do has very little to do with the work that really needs to be done. Developing a results mind-set will help differentiate you from the masses.

A recent research project polled over 225 thousand workers across more than two thousand teams and identified six barriers to effective and consistent execution:

- *Lack of clarity.* Only one in six workers feel their organization sets clear goals.
- *Lack of commitment.* Only one in ten workers feel they fully embrace the goals of an organization.
- *No translation to action.* Only one in five has clearly defined work goals. Most don't know how their specific job connects to the larger organization's strategic objectives and priorities.
- *No enabling.* Fewer than half (46 percent) feel they have adequate resources and freedom to do their jobs.

- *No synergy.* Fewer than a third feel they can express themselves candidly at work. Inter- and intra-departmental conflicts routinely get in the way of the goals.
- *Lack of accountability.* About half of all workers report that they feel they are accountable for their performance, and only one in ten has at least a monthly meeting with his boss to discuss his job.

You will find these barriers in almost any workplace. Be aware of these barriers and decide now to be part of the solution rather than part of the problem. Find ways to look beyond the obstacles and focus on getting the right results. Remember the timeless wisdom of my wife's grandmother, Grandma Winder: "The world is not interested in excuses . . . only results!"

10. Don't give up—stay the course.

Like it or not, your work will be a significant contributor to your self-worth, and you will have difficult days. You may find yourself in a situation that doesn't fit your best talents. Perhaps you have an employer who you feel doesn't value your contributions or doesn't allow you freedom to utilize your full range of talents. Or you may find yourself, for whatever reason, suddenly out of a job, as was one man who expressed the resulting frustration as something equal to a woman's devastation when she receives word that she is barren. Exaggerated as this may seem, the man could find nothing more fitting to describe his anguish.

Part of the earthly plan includes our eating bread by the "sweat of [our faces]" (Moses 4:25). This means that our work experience will sometimes be difficult. There will be challenging and disappointing days, days when you wonder if there is a light at the end of the tunnel. Rest assured there is. Another man who found himself back in the job market after twenty years with one company described his feelings about his job search like this: "Though the whole process is a roller-coaster ride, when I was through I always seemed to have unseen support that buoyed me up. Maybe it was a beautiful fall day where I could take a bike ride, or an encouraging word from someone. I just felt the watchful eye of my Heavenly Father through the process."

Don't be afraid of failure. If you don't fail miserably at some point in life, you are not trying hard enough. Sometimes these experiences are necessary because they teach you things you need to learn. And they are often the catalyst to move you toward what the Lord really wants you to do. The United States Corps of Engineers says it succinctly, "The difficult we do immediately, the impossible takes a little longer."[28]

John Wooden is largely regarded as college basketball's most successful coach. Over a twelve-year span, his UCLA teams won ten NCAA championships, and at one point had a sixty-one-game winning streak. What most fail to remember, however, is that his teams toiled in relative obscurity for fifteen years before they won their first championship, achieving a won-loss record of only 43–63. Year after year, coach Wooden developed the underlying foundations, philosophies, and systems that ultimately led to his success. But it took time.

Similarly, Sam Walton, founder of Walmart, struggled for years to gain a foothold with a single dime store. It took him seven years to obtain his second store, and twenty-five years to go to thirty-eight stores. Eventually, after a lot of slogging through trial and error, and an abundance of blood, sweat, and tears, his work began to pay off. Between 1970 and 2000, Walmart built over three thousand stores and achieved more than 150 billion dollars in revenues. "People have the impression that Walmart was just this great idea that turned into an overnight success," Walton observed. "But, it was an outgrowth of everything we did from 1945 . . . and like most overnight successes, it was about twenty years in the making."[29]

Ultimately, you need to have faith that the Lord knows you and knows what is best for you. He expects all of us to do our best and to make an honest effort in all we do. There is no substitute for hard work, and we should pray as we work. In fact, Amulek reminds us that it is not only appropriate, it is imperative that we "Cry unto him: Cry unto him when ye are in your fields, yea, over all your flocks . . . over the crops of your fields, that ye may prosper in them. Cry over the flocks of your fields, that they may increase" (Alma 34:20, 24–25).

Elder Holland provides this encouragement:

> "Wherefore, be not weary in well-doing, for ye are laying the foundation of a great work. And out of small things proceedeth that which is great.
>
> "Behold, the Lord requireth the heart and a willing mind; and the willing and obedient shall eat the good of the land of Zion in these last days" (D&C 64: 33–34).

I am asking you not to give up "for ye are laying the foundation of a great work." That "great work" is you—your life, your future, the very fulfillment of your dreams. That "great work" is what, with effort and patience and God's help, you can become. When days are difficult or problems seem unending, I plead with you to stay in the harness and keep pulling. You are entitled to "eat the good of the land of Zion in these last days," but it will require your heart and a willing mind. It will require that you stay at your post and keep trying.[30]

As you explore your opportunities, be sure to make a thorough assessment of your aptitudes, talents, and passions. Broaden your perspective about the world and your options, and stay true to your mission and values. Be diligent in your efforts and go the extra mile. Strive to be results-oriented. Develop a passion for your work, and build your personal network and leverage it appropriately. Ultimately, if you do these things with diligence, persistence, and faith, while maintaining clear and appropriate priorities, you will experience a sense of fulfillment and success.

Notes

1. Harvey Mackay, *Beware the Naked Man Who Offers You His Shirt: Do What You Love, Love What You Do, and Deliver More Than You Promise* (New York: Ballantine, 1996), 83.

2. In Conference Report, May 1982.

3. M. Russell Ballard, "Let Us Think Straight," BYU Devotional, 1983.

4. "Beyond the Call," *Pursuit of Happyness,* DVD, Directed by Gabrielle Muccino, 2006, Columbia Pictures, Inc., released 2007.

5. Samuel L Parker, *Mac Anderson, 212* (Illinois: Simple Truths, 2006), 8–10.

6. Ibid., 26.

7. Ibid., 34.

8. Jim Collins, *Good to Great* (New York: Harper Collins Publishers Inc., 2001), 127–8.

9. Ibid., 128.

10. In Conference Report, Apr. 1982.

11. Jack Welch, HSM Conference, Radio City Music Hall, New York, 2007.

12. Jim Collins, *Good to Great* (New York: Harper Collins Publishers Inc., 2001), 109.

13. Ibid., 110.

14. Ibid.

15. Robert Frost, *The Poetry of Robert Frost* (New York: Henry Holt and Company Inc., 1969), 275.

16. Janet Scharman, "The Lord Thy God Shall Lead Thee by the Hand," BYU Devotional, 1 December 1998.

17. Muhammad Yunus, "The Grameen Bank." *Scientific American*, 16 June 1999, 114–19.

18. Stephen M. R. Covey, *The Speed of Trust* (New York: Free Press, 2006), 65.

19. Personal interview, name withheld, 14 May 2007.

20. Ibid., 16 May 2007.

21. David Bornstein, *How to Change the World: Social Entrepreneurs and the Power of New Ideas* (New York: Oxford University Press US, 2004), 291.

22. "On Poetry," *Dead Poets Society,* DVD, Directed by Peter Weir, 1989, Touchstone Home Video, Inc.

23. Author unknown, "Are Sabotaging Your Goals," http://www.self-growth.com/articles/AreYouSabotagingYourGoals.html.

24. Author unknown

25. David Ross, *1001 Pearls of Wisdom* (New York: Chronicle Books, 2006), 238.

26. Karlin Sloan, Smarter, *Faster, Better: Strategies for Effective, Enduring, and Fulfilled Leadership* (New York: Wiley and Sons, 2006), 185–86.

27. Ram Charan and Geoffrey Colvin, "Why CEOs Fail,*" Fortune*, 21 June 1999, 69–70.

28. David Vaskevitch, *Client/Server Strategies: A Survival Guide for Corporate Reengineers* (New York: IDG Books, 1993), 153.

29. Jim Collins, *Good to Great* (New York: Harper Collins Publishers Inc., 2001), 191.

30. Jeffrey R. Holland, "However Long and Hard the Road," 18 January 1983.

3
Financial Management 101

The Financial Choice

> I commend to all the virtues of industry and thrift, which I believe
> go hand in hand. The labor and thrift of the people make a nation, a
> community, or a family strong.[1]
>
> —Gordon B. Hinckley

You might ask, "Why should I care about financial management? I'm
a poor college student who barely survives financially month to month. Is
saving money even realistic for someone in my situation?" Below are some
of the responses I received from young adults on the topic of financial
management:

> Life is dynamic, and not a lot of expenses are as foreseen as they
> were earlier in life.
>
> —Jacob, 23

> The biggest question I have regarding finances is how to invest.
> In college I never took any financial management classes. Being a
> single working female, I know it is important to invest for my future,
> but I don't even know where to begin. I save my money, but how do
> I know where and how to invest it. That is a very scary concept for
> me.
>
> —Lynne, 24

> I only recently got my first credit card. I was too nervous to take
> that seemingly risky financial move. I should have started building
> credit a long time ago.
>
> —Marie, 24

I am just barely making it every month!

—Tracy, 24

Financial limitations are no excuse for financial irresponsibility. Every choice you make has cause and effect, meaning you will ultimately have to pay the piper. As with everything else at this time of your life, the habits you establish now set the foundation for all that follows. It is not uncommon for successful wage-earners to find themselves in deep financial peril because they failed to plan or use proper judgment. Similarly, there are many professionals who, despite relatively lower incomes, enjoy wonderful financial security and lifestyles because of good, sound financial decision-making.

An important part of being an adult is effective management of finances. I have a good friend who is one of the most intelligent, capable, and talented people I know. His talents have yielded wonderful professional and financial success, but upon his return from his mission he revealed his financial naïveté when he asked his father, "What is income tax, and do I have to pay it?" My guess is that while most of you have a pretty good idea about income tax, some of the basic blocking and tackling of financial management may not be your second nature. If this describes you, read on!

As you embark on the next several years, you will face increasing financial pressures, but before you get to your future, you must meet the demands of now. You have rent and utilities to pay and groceries to buy. Perhaps you have tuition to pay, books to buy, as well as clothing, gifts, phone bills, dates, gas, cars, car repairs, and movies and other entertainment to pay for. And the list goes on. At some point, there will be rings to purchase and mini-vans to buy. The day will come sooner than you think when you want to purchase a home. All of this requires cash. And when children arrive, the expenses mount. Diapers alone can cost as much as $50 to $75 per month for one child.

So much could be said about financial management, and this chapter is not intended to be a definitive document, nor will it provide investment strategies. There are many excellent books on this topic, and broad reading will enrich your perspective and provide you with a well-rounded understanding of your opportunities. Further, you might consider carefully selecting a financial advisor who can provide professional assistance. My intention in this chapter is more basic, that is, to overview some of the fundamentals of managing money and debt so you can establish a healthy financial footing.

Socrates is reputed to have said, "The beginning of wisdom is the definition of terms."[2] So let's first define a few financial terms and look at some essential questions. We will then review selected tools and training to help you on your financial journey. Finally, we will look at the realities of debt, and introduce some strategies for getting out of trouble.

KEY TERMS, DEFINITIONS AND ESSENTIAL QUESTIONS

My intention here is to provide a brief tutorial for those who might be struggling with their financial vocabulary, and to present an overview and review for those with more fiscal experience.

Principal. The face value of an obligation. For example, if you have a car loan of $5,000, the principal amount is $5,000.

Interest. The cost of using money. Interest is generally referred to over a year's period. For example, 10 percent interest on a loan usually means 10 percent paid over a year. If you borrow money, you pay interest. If others borrow from you and you charge interest, you earn it.

Simple Interest. The interest calculation based on the original principal. For example, a $100 deposit with 8 percent simple interest would pay a return of $8 per year (100 x .08).

Compound Interest. The interest calculation based on the principal plus the accumulated interest amount. For example, a $100 deposit with 8 percent compound interest would become $108 the first year (100 x .08); $116.64 the second year (108 x .08); and $125.97 the third year (116.64 x .08). The difference between the same $100 invested at 8 percent with simple interest and compound interest over that three-year period is $26.21 ($124 with simple interest versus $150.61 with compound interest). Obviously, as the invested balance gets higher, compound interest grows your money in a materially different and accelerated way.

What is the difference between a credit card and a debit card? Credit cards are issued by banks and other financial institutions. Credit cards are accepted by nearly every store to provide a purchasing vehicle. When you use a credit card, you are actually borrowing money. Credit card companies provide fraud protection, limiting your liability to only $50 if your card is stolen and subsequently used, and the credit card company is obligated to investigate if you submit a written request.

When you use a debit card, the money for your purchase is taken directly from your bank account. Debit cards limit your liability to $50 for the first two days, and then the liability goes to $500. Because your debit card is linked to your personal bank account, fraud is more common and can devastate your financial situation. Report lost or stolen cards *immediately*!

Are all credit cards the same? No, cards vary greatly. Interest rates can range anywhere from 7 percent to 30 percent. Some cards charge annual fees, and interest rates differ from card to card. As you explore your options for a credit card, carefully look at the interest rate. Be cautious of low "introductory" rates that may change to substantially higher rates after just a few months.

Annual Percentage Rate (APR). This is the interest rate charged on unpaid balances.

What is a credit report? A credit report is a record of your debt-payment history. It will track payments for all types of loans, including bank loans, car loans, credit cards, charge cards, gas cards, student loans, foreclosures, and alimony.

Why does a positive credit rating matter? A positive credit rating is important for major purchases like a car or a home. Without this history, lending institutions are reluctant to provide loans.

How do I establish a positive credit rating? Positive credit can be established in several ways. You can apply for a credit card or debit card from your local bank or credit union. You can apply for a small loan, or establish a payment history with a gasoline card or department store card. Much will be said about debt in this chapter. While it is important to have a positive credit history, be cautious about getting several cards. If you obtain a credit card or small loan for the purpose of establishing credit, use it only for that purpose. Be sure to pay all obligations on time, as late payments will damage credit and defeat the very purpose of establishing a positive credit rating.

Asset. Anything that has exchange value (money or other items). For example, $1,000 in the bank represents $1,000 in assets, as that money could be exchanged for something else. If an individual paid for a car with a value of $6,000, that individual would have $6,000 of assets.

Liability. A claim on assets. A liability is the opposite of an asset. A liability is something that detracts or takes away from your net financial worth. For example, if you have taken out a loan for $6,000 to purchase a car, you would have the liability of $6,000.

Risk. The measurable possibility of not achieving value. When you invest your money, time or other assets, you have to determine the appropriate level of risk you are comfortable with. Generally, the more you risk, the greater the return. However, as you consider where to invest your time and resources, use caution when you hear claims of instant riches. Usually, if it sounds too good to be true, it is.

Creditor. A person or institution who lends money.

Bankruptcy. Bankruptcy is a legal term stating one's inability to pay a debt. Bankruptcy is an extreme measure that can cause the liquidation of personal assets to repay creditors and can severely impact an individual's ability to obtain future credit. A bankruptcy will remain on one's credit record for several years.

PREPARATION

Let's take a look at four financial assessment and planning tools to help you create a budget and plan for improving your financial situation. The first worksheet is a questionnaire designed to help you understand your current record-keeping, spending, and saving habits. It will help you identify specific areas for improvement and will serve as a guide as you develop your budget. The second worksheet provides a snapshot of your current financial position. It will help expose gaps in your financial discipline and provide additional clarity on your monthly expenditures and savings patterns. The third worksheet will assist you in developing your monthly budget. The final worksheet will help you gain control of your debt and work toward eliminating it.

The United States Navy provides training to its sailors on sound financial management principles and practices. Like some of you, new sailors are required to manage their finances and many are ill-equipped to do so. The Navy developed tools and training for its sailors, and the following questionnaire has been adapted from this training. Take a minute to review the questions below and assess your current spending habits. This questionnaire is divided into four sections:

1. Do I keep accurate records?
2. How well do I plan?
3. Do I have a problem with debt?
4. Am I honest in my tithes and offerings?

WORKSHEET #1: RECORDS AND SPENDING

1. **Do I keep accurate records?** Indicate how well you keep

accurate records by marking either (T) True, (F) False, or (S) Sometimes in the blank next to the question.

_____ I make a record of all checks I write in my check register.

_____ I make a record of ATM withdrawals in my check register.

_____ I keep all credit card receipts and check them against my monthly bill.

_____ I reconcile my monthly bank statement with my check register.

_____ I have a system for keeping and organizing bills when they come in so I can pay them on time.

2. How well do I plan? Indicate how well you plan for your financial future by marking either (T) True, (F) False, or (S) Sometimes in the blank next to the question, or otherwise answer the question.

_____ I pay myself first by saving a portion of my income each month.

_____ I have a monthly budget for larger bills so that when they come due I am not faced with an unexpected burden.

_____ I have financial goals for 1 year: _____; 3–5 years: _____; and 7–10 years: _____ .

_____ I keep a file with copies of receipts for income tax purposes.

3. Do I have a problem with debt? Indicate how well you avoid or manage debt by marking either (T) True, (F) False, or (S) Sometimes in the blank next to the question, or otherwise answer the question.

_____ I have more than one credit card of any type and use them frequently.

_____ I write checks without sufficient funds in the bank and hope they don't clear until my next payday.

_____ I pay for group activities with my credit card, collect the cash from the people who owe, and spend the cash instead of paying off my card.

_____ It takes three months or more to pay my credit card off in full.

_____ I pay only the minimum amount due on my credit cards each month.

_____ I have incurred late charges on my bills _____ times in the last three months; _____ times in the last six months.

_____ I have bounced _____ checks in the last three months; _____

checks in the last six months.

_____ I use cash advances from one credit card to pay off others.

_____ I am $_____ and _____ months behind in car, and other consumer debt payments.

_____ I am $_____ and _____ months behind in rent or mortgage payments.

_____ Concerns over money affect my health and/or my relationships.

4. Am I honest in my tithes and offerings? Indicate your level of participation with the law of tithing and other offerings by marking either (T) True, (F) False, or (S) Sometimes in the blank next to each question.

_____ I pay an honest tithe on each paycheck I receive.

_____ I pay tithing on gross, not net.

_____ I contribute to fast offerings each month.

_____ I contribute to the general Church missionary, perpetual education fund, and/or other offerings.

Use this questionnaire to help guide you as you determine where you need to focus your efforts. Establishing proper record-keeping habits will help you avoid unpleasant surprises. Developing the habit of paying yourself first by saving some money each paycheck will generate a sense of security and self-reliance, and give you the flexibility to invest as the years progress. If you answered "false" or "sometimes" to any of the questions regarding records or planning, you have identified a specific area for improvement. Similarly, if you answered "true" or "sometimes" to any of the questions regarding debt, see that as a yellow caution flag and carefully evaluate your approach to debt and credit. Avoiding unnecessary debt will free you from the bondage that accompanies buying on credit.

As you carefully examine your financial position and habits, take a few seconds and establish a snapshot of your current financial situation by providing the information requested on the worksheet on the following page.

Worksheet # 2: Income and Expenses

Income and Expenses	Amount	Don't Know
Current net (take home) earnings per month		
Current average expenses per month		
Amount I usually have left over after all expenses each month		
Amount I spend each month on rent		
Amount I spend each month on utilities and insurance each month		
Amount I spend on groceries each month		
Amount I spend eating out each month, fast food, vending machines, convenience stores		
Amount I spend on entertainment, movies, sports each month		
Amount I spend on clothing each month		
Amount I spend on car payments, gas, maintenance each month		

Income and Expenses	Amount	Don't Know
Amount I spend on cell phone, Internet connections, and related services each month		
Amount spent on CD's, DVD's video games, books, maga-zines, and so forth each month		
Currently, I have how much debt?		
Currently, I have how much in savings?		
Currently, I have how much in investments (IRAs, stocks, bonds, mutual funds, and so forth)		
Amount I contribute in tithes and other offerings		

This snapshot, combined with Worksheet #1, can help you evaluate your current situation and help you plan as you work to establish a budget. As you complete this exercise, if you are unable to accurately answer any of the questions, you know you have gaps in your budgeting process. The first step to effective budgeting is knowing how much you currently spend.

BUDGETING

What is a budget? A budget is a plan that helps you manage and control spending. Consider the following "Ten Principles to Budgeting and Prioritization" as you prepare to draft your initial budget. Review these principles within the context of your own life. Every situation is different, but remember, principles are natural laws. Principles govern, whether we acknowledge them or not.

10 Principles to Budgeting and Prioritization

1. Spend less than you earn. This is what I refer to as the "Uncle Dan Rule," after my wife's uncle. As I discussed this chapter with him and other financial experts, this first principle is always mentioned in the strongest terms. It is far too tempting to exceed your income when expanded purchasing power is so readily available. Resist that urge and simply live within your means. A recent study showed that 43 percent of families in the United States spend more than they earn.[3]

2. Be content to be frugal. This is closely related to the first principle. I heard the saying once that if you can live for ten years the way 90 percent of the population won't, you will live like 90 percent of the population can't for the rest of your life. Remember, it took your parents many years to accumulate all their possessions. It didn't happen overnight, and you should not expect it to happen overnight for you. Remember Elder Holland's council:

> Smile at an old pair of shoes. . . . Cherish a used book. Though some of you may be living in almost desperate financial straits, I promise you there is a way. Such times may be burdensome. Such sacrifice may be hard. But it does not have to lead—for you it must not lead—to despair and destruction and defeat. In the words of Henry David Thoreau:
>
> "Most of the luxuries, and many of the so-called comforts of life are not only dispensable, but positive hindrances to the elevation of mankind. [Walden (1854), 1, "Economy"] Love your life, poor as it is. . . . The setting sun is reflected from the windows of the almshouse as brightly as from the rich man's abode." [Walden (1854), 18, "Conclusion"]
>
> Now no one here need be so dramatic as to peer out of an almshouse, but you may be going without some things, you may even consider yourself poor. Well, "Love your life, poor as it is." "If God so clothe the grass of the field, which today is, and tomorrow is cast into the oven, shall he not much more clothe you, O ye of little faith?" (Matthew 6:30).[4]

Much more will be said about avoiding debt in principle #6 below.

3. Pay yourself first. Establish the habit of putting away some savings and/or investments each month. A good rule of thumb is to pay the Lord His 10 percent, and then pay yourself 10 percent before anything else. If you are not in a position right now to save 10 percent each month, save *something*. Create an emergency fund and develop the discipline to make more deposits than withdrawals. Jana, 23, shared her experience with me:

> I have learned the value of saving. With the convenience of direct deposit, I have set up savings accounts, and I never miss saving because the money gets deposited automatically. I have two different savings accounts. One gets a smaller percentage from my paycheck and is used for extra expenses, like a vacation or when I want to buy something I haven't budgeted for. I deposit a larger percentage of my paycheck in the other account. I don't touch this money. It is used for the so-called "rainy day."

4. Embrace the power of compounding. When Benjamin Franklin was seventy-seven years old, he adjusted his will to include a payment of five thousand dollars to both Philadelphia and Boston. This fund was intended to help young needy people in each city. Each city's fund was to remain intact for two hundred years, though the cities were permitted to withdraw half a million to pay for public works needs after the first one hundred years. Even with the five hundred thousand dollar withdrawal, each city's fund was worth in excess of twenty million after two hundred years!

You don't have 200 years to wait, you say? Fair enough. Consider this: if a generous uncle invests two thousand dollars for his niece on her first birthday at 9 percent interest (and does nothing else with this money— ever), it will be worth a half a million dollars by the time she is sixty-five, yielding an annual income of about forty-six thousand dollars for the rest of her life. Through the magic of compounding, your money will double every eight years (assuming 9 percent interest). To figure how this works, take the rate of return (interest) and divide it into seventy-two. That will tell you how long it will take to double your money. For example, if you invest $1,000 at 10 percent interest, your $1,000 will become $2,000 in 7.2 years and $4,000 in another 7.2 years.

5. Establish and stick to a budget. Worksheet #3 on page 74 will help you create your initial budget if you haven't created one already. Budgeting is the practice of keeping track of expenditures and will bring discipline to your spending habits. Budgeting does not mean you can't spend your hard-earned cash, or that you have to deny yourself of all luxuries. It does mean that you save and spend according to a plan based on priorities.

6. Avoid debt like the plague. This is the big one. You may be tempted to apply for credit cards because of how it expands your purchasing power. It can relieve immediate financial pressure, but be cautious—it can be a trap. You may know people who have applied for and received multiple credit cards. When the balance on one reaches its limit, they make payment on it with a second card, run up the balance on the second card, and then begin on a third. This is a game that will end badly. Good Morning America reported that many Americans spend 25 percent or more of their net monthly income on credit card payments.[5] ABC News reported that Americans owe an average of nearly nine thousand dollars in credit card debt and use cards for average, everyday expenses like utilities, groceries, medical bills.[6] Consider the following statistics on consumer debt:

- 75 percent of all Americans are 3 paychecks away from bankruptcy.
- In 2008, more people filed for bankruptcy than graduated from college.
- 70 percent of Americans live paycheck to paycheck.[7]
- Consumer debt has increased an average of 8 percent annually over the last 20 years, with the average family now carrying $58,500 in debt.[8]
- The Fastest growing group of bankruptcy filers are those people who are 25 years of age or younger.[9]
- Unites States credit card debt: $790 billion.[10]

I once worked with a family whose annual income was approximately $40,000, and they used several credit cards to leverage their financial situation. This lead them to a false sense of security. Without giving it much thought, the family quickly accumulated hefty credit card balances. Daily necessities like groceries, doctor visits, and medications were charged on credit cards. But so were toys for the kids, exercise equipment, home improvements, a new deck for the yard, and purchases from TV infomercials. It was never their intention to become financially strapped, but one purchase led to another, and before they knew it, their aggregate monthly credit card payment was nearly half of their entire gross monthly income; credit card debt was in excess of $45,000 (remember, their annual income was only $40,000). In addition to their mortgage payment and multiple car payments, their monthly service on their credit cards was approximately $1,575. Since their gross monthly income was $3,750 (with a net monthly income of approximately $2,500), they were in way over their heads. Their only course of action, they supposed, was to apply for yet more credit to supplement their cash requirements. Do the math—if they only paid the minimum balance each month with no additional spending—*ever* (a highly unlikely scenario)—they would be required to pay monthly for more than 24 years for a total payment of $78,625. Yikes! So just to get by, they continued to apply for and receive additional cards.

To make matters worse, because they lived off credit, they were targeted more specifically by credit card companies and received additional credit card offers. But because of their unfavorable credit rating, the banks and credit card companies required a higher interest rate on the new cards and the dance with disaster continued. It became a downward spiral they couldn't escape. Eventually they reached the painful point of accountability, which strained their marriage. Dramatic measures and tremendous sacrifice were all that could save them. Don't let this happen to you! If you find yourself in a financial trap, make a plan now to address it and then stick to that plan. Heed the council by Elder J. Reuben Clark:

> Interest never sleeps nor sickens nor dies; it never goes to the hospital; it works on Sundays and holidays; it never takes a vacation . . . once in debt, interest is your companion every minute of the day and night; you cannot shun it or slip away from it; you cannot dismiss it; it yields neither to entreaties, demands, or orders; and whenever you get in its way or cross its course or fail to meet its demands, it crushes you.[11]

Is all debt bad? Not necessarily. Simply put, there are two kinds of debt: good debt and bad debt. While it is preferable to avoid debt entirely, there are times when it is necessary to assume some debt. The difference between good debt and bad debt is straightforward: good debt provides a return, bad debt doesn't. Examples of good debt include education and the purchase of a home (within your means). Bad debt includes all consumer debt (TVs, furniture, clothing, and so forth).

What happens when you have $5,000 in credit card debt? How long will it take to pay it off if you pay just the minimum payment each month? And how much will you end up paying? $5,000 at 14 percent interest (some credit cards are lower, many are higher) will require a minimum monthly payment of $175 and will take more than 13 years to pay off. Here's the scary thing: that initial $5,000 will eventually cost you $7,421.09 in total payments. And this total does not include the opportunity cost of that $5,000. If you were to have invested the same $5,000 at 6 percent interest for the same period, you would have earned $18,307, for a total difference of $10,886!

I conducted a survey of young single adults, ages 18–30 living in apartments near a university. Most involved in the survey were students, but some had recently completed their education and had begun their careers, and all shared a similar economic status. These apartments received between ten and twenty credit card applications *per week*!

While obtaining a credit card is easy, misuse of these cards can cost a lot, even if you are not over-extended. One USA Today study explained:

> In recent years, banks have become more aggressive in imposing fees and raising interest rates, says Robert McKinley of CardWeb.com. Many banks now hit you with fees of up to $39 per incident if you pay your bill one minute late or spend $1 past your credit limit. On top of this, some banks impose record-high penalty interest rates up to 32 percent on those who pay late or spend past their limit just once. Some card issuers also jack up rates on consumers who pay late on some other bill, such as a mortgage or utility bill.[12]

Journalist Kathy Chu writes:

> Credit card marketers today are as aggressive as ever—just more creative—about reaching students. Some solicit students by phone or e-mail, and flood their mailboxes with credit card applications. Other marketers set up tables around heavily trafficked campus areas, hawking free sandwiches or pizzas to hungry students to get them to sign up for a credit card.
>
> At universities that restrict credit card solicitation, marketers legally bypass the rules by moving across the street from campus. It takes about five minutes to fill out a credit card application. In a few months, students can fall deep in debt, charging [groceries] and designer jeans, as well as school supplies, to these cards, according to consumer advocates. "These credit card issuers circle the campus like sharks circling a fish," says Elizabeth Warren, a Harvard Law School professor. "Companies are turning over every possible rock to find a live human being to take one of their credit cards and use it. The college-age student is a prime target."

This year, Citigroup has more than doubled the number of college campuses, to more than 200, where it's marketing its bank accounts and credit cards.[13]

This article continues, as it relates the sad news that one student took her own life, due in part to her depression with her seemingly hopeless financial situation:

Consumer groups and parents say that banks make it too easy for college students to get credit and to become mired in debt. [One parent asked,] "How could a college student who works 12 hours a week get a credit card and get another one before she makes a payment on the first?" In 2004, the latest year for which figures are available, three out of four college students had credit cards, and more than 40 percent had at least four, according to student lender Nellie Mae. As students advance through school, their card debt tends to swell. Seniors carry an average debt load of $2,864, nearly double a freshmen's average of $1,585.[14]

You might ask, "Is it okay to have one credit card?" Yes . . . for emergencies or to establish a positive credit rating. Credit cards are not inherently bad. They are a useful financial resource. But it is easy to abuse them if you are not careful. If necessary, put a post-it note on it to help remind you to use it judiciously. It sounds a bit silly, but in reality it is far less silly than racking up thousands of dollars in debt.

7. **Create a financial plan.** Begin with the end in mind. Think about where you want to be financially in five, ten, and twenty-five years. What do you need to do today in order to accomplish these goals? If you are in school, stay in school. If you are out of school and beginning your career, take some time to set your goals and plan your future. Consider your future financial plans in three categories: (1) protection, (2) savings, and (3) growth.

Protection includes ensuring that you are adequately insured, including having appropriate medical, car, disability, and life insurance. If you are married, you should establish a will and trust.

Savings include regular bank savings, money market, and other savings accounts, 401Ks (which most employers offer), pension benefits, and tax-deferred savings.

Growth includes such things as real estate, stocks, and bonds.

Again, this chapter is not intended for the creation of investment strategies, so consider consulting a financial professional who can help you create a plan that has the right risk and balance for you and your situation.

8. Know your priorities. Make sure you are spending your money on those things that are truly important to you. Having a huge DVD collection is nice, but will it help you achieve your financial goals ten years from now? Be careful about how much you spend on fast food. Don't get more car than you need or can afford. We learned this lesson early in our marriage. I became enamored with the idea of driving around in the hot red car with a killer sound system. I manufactured lots of reasons to buy it. First and foremost, we would look really good driving it. It would make a statement. We could afford it. Also, because it was new, it was reliable and wouldn't give us trouble. We would have lots of room to drive others around. And it was European, so it would appreciate in value. In other words, it was a good investment.

Wrong! Despite my initial rationalization to the contrary, cars are not an investment, they are only a cost. And after getting saddled with a high monthly payment, we learned that we didn't really look that good in the hot red car. We actually looked rather foolish. The door soon got scratched, the sound system gave us trouble, the trunk inexplicably filled with water (could have had something to do with my two-year-old) and smelled musty. We suffered though several months of unnecessary financial bother until we finally unloaded the beast at a loss. If we were looking to make a statement, we succeeded. We just didn't like the particular statement.

Remember, it is okay to spend money, as long as it is according to your priorities. I have heard a lot of young men say they wish they could date, if only they had the money. Make dating a priority. If you are married, budget some money each week to go out with your spouse. Align your savings and spending with the things that really matter. Consider the following advice:

> As we reflect on our lives, maybe we should also reflect over the trends of our society and how we measure up. We spend too recklessly, laugh too little, drive too fast, get too angry too quickly, stay up too late, get too tired, read too seldom, watch TV too much, and pray too seldom. We have multiplied our possessions but reduced our values. We talk too much, love too seldom, and lie too much. We've learned how to make a living, but not a life; we've added years to life; not life to years.

We have bigger houses and smaller families; more conveniences, but less time; we have more degrees, but less common sense; more knowledge, but less judgment; more experts, but more problems; more medicine but less wellness. We've been all the way to the moon and back but we have trouble crossing the street to meet the new neighbor.[15]

9.   Get as much education as you can. Be willing to sacrifice to do it. Each of you possesses unique gifts, but these gifts must be carefully cultivated through dedicated study. As you face the deadlines, pressures, papers, finals, and other delights of school, I fully appreciate that there are times in your studies when the best you feel you can do is "get through." Like a weary traveler, walking through a blinding snowstorm and struggling just to endure, you put your head down and hope you will somehow make it. Believe me, I've been there.

But consider the privilege you have to obtain an education. Find fulfillment in the process of your schooling. Do your best to develop a passion about a particular subject and find real joy in the learning process. For me, it came when I discovered the literary treasures of Shakespeare, Yeats, Tennyson, Mark Twain, Ernest Hemmingway, Zora Neal Hurston, and many others. Even if your goals are to stay at home and raise a family, you should work to gain an education. It will help in your efforts with your children and enrich your life in many other ways. President Gordon B. Hinckley said: "The Lord wants you to educate your minds and hands, whatever your chosen field."[16]

10. Pay tithes and be generous with your offerings. What about tithes and offerings? Is it realistic, given the financial straits many of you face, to be expected to contribute in this way? Elder Robert D. Hales taught:

> The temporal and spiritual blessings of tithing are specifically tailored to us and our families, according to the Lord's will. But to receive them, we must obey the law upon which they are predicated. In the case of tithing, the Lord has said, "Bring ye all the tithes into the storehouse, that there may be meat in mine house, and prove me now herewith, saith the Lord of hosts, if I will not open you the windows of heaven, and pour you out a blessing, that there shall not be room enough to receive it." (Malachi 3:10)
> Would any of us intentionally reject an outpouring of blessings from the Lord? Sadly, this is what we do when we fail to pay our tithing. We say no to the very blessings we are seeking and praying to receive. If

you are one who has doubted the blessings of tithing, I encourage you to accept the Lord's invitation to "prove [Him] now herewith." Pay your tithing. Unlock the windows of heaven. You will be abundantly blessed for your obedience and faithfulness to the Lord's laws and commandments. Be assured that these blessings are poured out equally upon rich and poor alike. As the hymn says, it is "sacrifice [that] brings forth the blessings of heaven," not the sum of our contributions. Members who freely give a full 10 percent of their annual income receive all of the promised blessings of tithing, whether the amount is a widow's mite or a king's ransom.[17]

Brandon, 21, wrote of the blessings he receives through tithing: "Paying my tithes has always helped me in my life. I feel that tithing has always opened the windows of heaven not only in spiritual ways, but also with ideas for investments and business ideas. Many people expect blessings from tithing to come in the form of a new job, or a raise, or finding $20 in their pocket. I believe that blessings from tithing can come in many ways, including business or investment ideas, inspiration to perform better at work, as well as direct monetary blessings."

As for fast and other offerings, you are not expected to "run faster than [you have] strength" (Mosiah 4:27). That said, even your seemingly insignificant donations will be consecrated to your benefit and will reinforce important habits that will bless your life and that of others.

Kaylee, 21, said, "I want to be someone who spends more time being generous and less time selfishly spending my money. Generosity is born from charity and helps create Zion in our communities."

Jon M. Huntsman, founder of Huntsman Chemicals, has achieved substantial wealth over the years. And as his wealth has grown, so has his ability for philanthropy; however, his younger years were anything but opulent. Michael Pineager writes:

> In the early days of their marriage, Brother and Sister Huntsman had a meager income. Sister Huntsman was in charge of their books and could account for all their expenditures except $50 each month. When she approached her husband about it, he told her not to worry. She remained unaware of how the money was being spent until several months later when she heard a needy mother stand in fast and testimony meeting and thank an anonymous donor who had given her $50 each month. After Sister Huntsman told this story, Jon Huntsman acknowledged that it was true and said: "If you cannot give when you have little, you will not be likely to give when you have everything."

> Not everyone who gives generously becomes wealthy. . . . I am
> convinced the Lord gratefully accepts gifts of whatever size so long as
> we give them with the right attitude.[18]

Everything we have comes as a blessing from a loving Heavenly
Father. It is not too much for the Lord to ask of us, after giving all He has,
to return 10 percent for the administration and activities of the Church.
Develop the habit of paying a generous fast offering, and contribute to
the Perpetual Education Fund and other general funds. These activities
don't require your last dollar. Of course, we pay our tithes and offerings
because it is a commandment, and because we love the Lord. We don't
necessarily pay them in exchange for blessings, but the blessings do come.
The Lord has provided powerful promises to all who are faithful with this
commandment, and these promises have been verified and validated by
millions since they were given. Add your name to that list.

Just prior to his appointment as President of Brigham Young University, Jeffrey R. Holland addressed the issue of finances to an audience of
young adults. He said:

> If as a student you are the way I was, you may be discouraged over
> money matters—and almost everyone is, at least some of the time. A
> recent study indicated that financially related problems outranked all
> other factors in marital difficulty by a margin of three to one. And the
> pressure can be about that great on single students as well. If shared
> misery provides any consolation for you, take heart—you have friends.
> From the day I walked into my first college class until I staggered out
> the exit of my last—a period of time stretching over twelve years and
> four degrees—I was responsible for every cent of my education. I know
> that many in this audience are getting through school exactly the same
> way—part-time jobs, loans, working spouses, an almost desperate plea
> for scholarships, postponed personal comforts, and all the rest. These
> things can be troublesome, but you have an obligation—to yourself if
> no one else—to see that they are not destructive. Prepare. "The arrow
> seen before cometh less rudely." Take advantage at this tender age to
> learn to use a budget, to sit down at a table spread out with your debts
> and come to grips with the economic facts of life. It's none too soon
> if you've made it to college and still have not had to establish personal
> fiscal priorities to decide what you will have at the expense of some
> things you will not have. Get it down on paper and deal with it there.
> That is the counsel given to husbands and wives, and the same solution
> works for others. The alternative is to leave it churning in your stomach

and head and heart, all of which are susceptible to their own forms of ulcer.[19]

With the Ten Principles to Budgeting and Prioritization in mind, use Worksheet # 3: Prepare Your Budget to first track your actual expenditures, then make the necessary adjustments and revise your budget.

Worksheet # 3: Prepare Your Budget

Income	Total
Monthly Income	$
Other Income	$
Gross Monthly Pay	$
Monthly Take Home (Net)	$

Budget Item	Monthly Budget	Actual Monthly Expenditure
Tithing	$	$
Savings and Investments (self)	$	$
Rent or Mortgage	$	$
Car	$	$
Insurance	$	$
Gas and Car Maintenance	$	$
Tuition	$	$
Books	$	$
Cell Phone	$	$
Home Phone	$	$
Utilities (Gas, Electric)	$	$
Television	$	$
Groceries	$	$
Fast Food and Restaurants	$	$
Credit Card Debt	$	$

Laundry and Dry Cleaning	$	$
Personal Items (soap, deodorant)	$	$
Entertainment	$	$
Clothing	$	$
Emergencies	$	$
Other Donations	$	$
Other	$	$
Other	$	$
Other	$	$
Total	$	$

Debt elimination

So much is said about avoiding debt. But what do you do if you heed the council too late? How can we address and even eradicate the debt we have acquired? Please know there is hope, but it will require a plan, some discipline, and work. Mellody Hobson, president of Ariel Capital Management, teaches the "Three C's" of credit card debt elimination, which can help as you build your plan.

Call: Credit card companies will often renegotiate the interest rate if you are having trouble making the payment. The average annual interest rate (APR) on credit cards is 13 percent, while some credit cards charge as much as 20 percent or higher. Examine your card's interest rate carefully. If you are paying higher than 10 percent, call the credit card company and discuss your options. Credit card companies would rather charge a lower rate and receive some payment than receive nothing because the consumer (you) is in too deep and can't pay the bill. Consultations of this sort are not unusual—in fact, it happens all the time.

Cancel: Once you have eliminated a balance on one card, cancel the card so it no longer serves as a temptation.

Cut: Cut or otherwise destroy the card so you can no longer use it. This is a drastic measure, but may be a necessary one. This will not only prevent you from using it, but it will also eliminate others from using it.[20]

If you have multiple credit or charge cards, use Worksheet #4: Debt

Elimination to assist as you create your debt reduction plan. In his conference address, "Guide to Family Finance," Elder Marvin J. Ashton introduced a "Debt Elimination Calendar"; this worksheet is adapted from that process.

First, identify all sources of debt, with an accurate payoff balance, interest rate, and minimum monthly payment. Once that is identified, take the debt with the highest interest rate and apply all extra payments to that debt's principal—as much as you can. Doing this, as opposed to spreading extra payment across all cards, will accelerate the ultimate debt pay-off. Once the first debt is paid in full, apply the entire amount you had been paying for that debt to the next debt in line. Once that debt is paid in full, apply the entire amount you paid for the first two to the third debt in line. Continue doing this until all balances are paid in full.

In the example below, Casey has a total outstanding debt of $585, with a minimum monthly payment of $75. This debt is the combination of two credit cards and two retail store cards. While none of the individual balances are huge, the cumulative payment is significant, given his monthly income. However, Casey is current with his payments, and has even budgeted an extra $25 per month toward paying off his debts. He begins with the highest interest rate—in this case the Mastercard—and applies $40 (minimum payment of $15 plus the extra payment of $25).

> *Note: this example assumes that the minimum monthly payment for each debt goes exclusively toward interest and every dollar above the minimum payment directly impacts principal. In actuality, a very small percentage of the minimum payment goes to principal. However, this example is directionally accurate, if not precise to the last percentage.

Worksheet #4: Debt Elimination, Casey's Plan

Creditor	Balance	Interest Rate	Minimum Payment
Visa #1	$225	14 percent	$25
Mastercard	$75	18 percent	$15
Retail Charge Card #1	$120	18 percent	$15
Retail Charge Card #2	$165	14 percent	$20
Totals	**$585**		**$75**

	Master-card Monthly Payment	Retail #1 Monthly Payment	Retail #2 Monthly Payment	Visa Monthly Payment	Total Monthly Payment
Month 1	$40 ($15+$25)	15	20	25	$100 (min+$25)
Month 2	40	15	20	25	$100
Month 3	40	15	20	25	$100
Month 4		55 ($15+$40)	20	25	$100
Month 5		$55	20	25	$100
Month 6		$55	20	25	$100
Month 7			$75 ($20+$55)	25	$100
Month 8			$75	25	$100
Month 9			$75	25	$100
Month 10				$100 ($25+$75)	$100
Month 11				$100	$100
Month 12				$100	$100

Notice how the payment accelerates once the first debt is retired. Using this process, it will take Casey twelve months to completely eliminate his debt with only $25 extra per month.

This process will take a little time, but you will be surprised at the difference a plan and a little discipline can make in just a few months. Now use the blank worksheet below to track your own progress as you become debt-free.

Worksheet #4: Debt Elimination

Creditor	Balance	Interest Rate	Minimum Payment
Totals			

	Debt 1	Debt 2	Debt 3	Debt 4	Debt 5
Month 1					
Month 2					
Month 3					
Month 4					
Month 5					
Month 6					
Month 7					
Month 8					
Month 9					
Month 10					
Month 11					
Month 12					

As you consider your financial goals, work to make money your servant and not your master. Elder Joseph B. Wirthlin admonished:

> We have earthly debts and heavenly debts. Let us be wise in dealing with each of them and ever keep in mind the words of the Savior. The scriptures tell us, "Lay not up for yourselves treasures upon earth, where moth and rust doth corrupt, and where thieves break through and steal; But lay up for yourselves treasures in heaven." (Matthew 6:19–20) The riches of this world are as dust compared to the riches that await the faithful in the mansions of our Heavenly Father. How

foolish is he who spends his days in the pursuit of things that rust and fade away. How wise is he who spends his days in the pursuit of eternal life.[21]

There will be pressures and obligations, but do your best, have faith, and follow the principles of effective financial management; review your priorities and remember: "Before ye seek for riches, seek ye first the kingdom of God. And after ye have obtained a hope in Christ ye shall obtain riches, if ye seek them; and ye will seek them for the intent to do good—to clothe the naked, and to feed the hungry, and to liberate the captive, and administer relief to the sick and the afflicted" (Jacob 2:18–19). If you "seek first the Kingdom of God and His righteousness" (3 Nephi 13:13) you will be blessed with what you need, and the very windows of heaven will be opened unto you and pour you out blessings so great that you do not have room enough to receive them (see Malachi 3:10).

Notes

1. Gordon B. Hinckley, *Standing for Something* (New York: Times Books, 2000), 79.

2. Icon Group International, *Wisdom: Webster's Quotations, Facts and Phrases* (New York: ICON Group International, Inc., 2008), 6.

3. Gwendolyn Audry Foster, *Class-Passing: Social Mobility in Film and Popular Culture* (Southern Illinois University Press, 2005), 62.

4. Jeffrey R. Holland, "For Times of Trouble," BYU Devotional, 18 March 1980.

5. Good Morning America, May 21, 2007 Report

6. ABC News Report, see also http://debtsolutionsource.org/eliminate-credit-debt/eliminate-high-interest-credit-card-debt.

7. https://www.amazines.com/article_detail.cfm?articleid=655056

8. http://www.bankruptcylawinformation.com/index.cfm?event=dspStats.

9. Committee on Banking, Housing and Urban Affairs, 2002.

10. Tim Westrich and Christian Weller, "House of Cards," Feb. 2008, 3.

11. In Conference Report, Apr. 1938, 103.

12. Kathy Chu, *USA Today*, 10 October 2006.

13. Ibid.

14. Ibid.

15. Author unknown, published in *Shortcut to Spirituality: Mastering the*

Art of Inner Peace by Bob Gottfried (North York, Ontario: Deeper Dimension Publishing, 2004), 29.

16. Gordon B. Hinckley, "A Prophet's Counsel and Prayer for Youth," *Ensign*, Jan. 2001, 2.

17. In Conference Report, Oct. 2002.

18. J. Michael Pineager, "The Lord's Goods," BYU Devotional, 16 November 2004.

19. Holland, "For Times of Trouble."

20. Mellody Hobson, "Three C's," *Good Morning America*, 21 May 2007.

21. In Conference Report, Apr. 2004.

4

WHY WOULD ANYONE FOLLOW ME?

The Leadership Choice

Yours is a great responsibility in this day when the need for courageous leadership is so urgent. You can become those leaders![1]

–Ezra Taft Benson

Here are a few questions to consider regarding leadership:
- What does it really mean to be a leader?
- Are some people born with leadership skills and therefore destined for greatness?
- Is leadership manifest only through specific positions or callings?
- Can leadership skills be developed?
- Where does one start?
- How do you have lasting influence with others?
- Leaders have followers, right? So how do you help others catch the appropriate vision of your initiatives in such a way that they are not only willing to get things done for you and sometimes even willing to make sacrifices to help you accomplish your goals?
- In order to lead others, what groundwork do you need?

Leadership is essential for one who occupies a supervisory role. But leadership skills are also critical for those in the middle, and just as impor-
tant for the anyone in an entry-level position of an organization or team. Ask yourself: "Why would anyone follow me; of all the choices one could make, why would someone choose me to lead?" Compare and contrast different leaders in your life: What is it that makes you want to follow some

and not others? What is it about George Washington, Mother Teresa, Gandhi, or Martin Luther King Jr. that inspires you? What about Church leaders? Do you trust your bishop, stake president, or the prophet because they are in positions of authority, or is it something else? Would you trust them even if they didn't hold these positions? Do others trust you? I was intrigued and touched the day following the passing of President Gordon B. Hinckley. Many of the youth of the Church wore their Sunday best to school in his honor that day. The Washington Post noted this gesture:

> On Monday morning this week, 12 hours after the passing of the 97-year-old leader of the Church of Jesus Christ of Latter-day Saints, President Gordon B. Hinckley, an extraordinary and spontaneous thing happened. Young teenagers in Salt Lake City began showing up for school that day, dressed not in their usual jeans and winter clothing, but in their "Sunday best." Young men sat in classes in white shirts and ties, suits and coats. Thousands of them did this, with no prompting from parents or other adults and to the surprise of teachers. The idea, it seems, started with a few and then spread at unbelievable speed through text messaging, child to child. This was their way of showing respect to a man seven times their age and several generations their senior. Such was the power of this one extraordinary leader of the Church of Jesus Christ of Latter-day Saints to touch the lives of ordinary people.[2]

What was it that connected this ninety-seven-year-old man to teenagers across the world? Why did they feel so attached?

This chapter explores different aspects of leadership. We will discuss some definitions of leadership, why it is crucial to develop these skills, and then review some fundamental elements of effective leadership.

I recently had the opportunity to speak to a fifth-grade class about the subject of "Leadership." These students considered three statements related to the topic: (1) "A leader is someone who . . . ," (2) "A leader in my life is . . . ," and (3) "I can be a leader by . . . ." They shared some wonderful insights that are both simple and profound:

A leader is someone who . . .
- is kind and nice
- is trustworthy
- shows courage
- doesn't have to be rich or poor
- you can rely on

- you can respect
- leads people down the right track
- never gives up
- wants teamwork
- tells the truth
- is friendly
- takes charge when something goes wrong
- has gratitude
- does the right thing
- is loyal
- takes responsibility
- doesn't have to have a special job like the president, a teacher, or a principal
- takes a stand
- does what he believes in
- has courage to do scary things

A leader in my life is . . .

- me
- my parents
- my dad
- my teacher
- my mom
- my brother
- my uncle

I can be a leader by . . .

- being loving
- helping other people
- not bullying others
- being a friend to those who need a friend
- being good to my little brother
- breaking up fights
- being courageous
- being trustworthy
- being daring and taking risks for others
- being nice to my siblings. Sometimes I'm a little bit cranky.
- stepping up at any moment of the day.

- being kinder and more confident in people
- never giving up
- facing my fears

What remarkable insights from a group of youngsters! Let's pursue some more mature views and see if we can add to this, starting with a definition.

Leadership is about influencing others, and in order to do this, you must first lead your own life. In other words, leadership of and influence on others begins with leadership of self. It is what the United States Army calls "the great force multiplier." For them, great leadership can lift ten men or women to do what otherwise might require one hundred. Effective leadership brings out the best in yourself and others, allowing you to maximize your time, efforts, and resources.

The great Archimedes (287–212 BC), one of the world's finest mathematicians, was a man before his time. Not only did he invent integral calculus and the field of hydrostatics, but his numerous contributions include a unique numbering system, the most accurate approximation of π (Pi) to date, a new way of approximating square roots, and an examination of the properties of levers and pulleys. On one occasion, his friend King Hiero had a ship mired in the harbor, and despite the efforts of many men, the ship would not budge. Archimedes declared to the king "Give me a place to stand on and I will move the earth." The king asked Archimedes to prove his statement by freeing the stuck ship. Using his knowledge of leverage, Archimedes built a machine that allowed him to single-handedly move the ship. By using levers and the appropriate positioning of the fulcrum, one man's efforts did what many men combined could not do.[3]

So it is with our efforts. Our contributions may seem small and insignificant at first, but the ultimate impact can have far-reaching effects. Like Archimedes's fulcrum and lever, leadership allows one to accomplish great things, even when faced with challenges that seem beyond normal abilities.

Leadership is the ability to influence yourself and others in achieving sustained results. In the process of achieving results, leaders convey vision, develop trust, establish confidence, remove barriers, and inspire the best efforts and talents of others.

According to the November 11, 2000 *US News and World Report* cover story, the population of the Church is predicted to grow to approximately 265 million members worldwide by 2080. This would put the Church "second only to Roman Catholics among Christian bodies. 'Mormonism,' says Rodney Stark, professor of sociology and religion at the University of Washington, 'stands on the threshold of becoming the first major faith to appear on Earth since the prophet Mohammed rode out of the desert.' "4

That is an incredibly bold estimate, and other studies show the number substantially lower. Assuming it is *only 10 percent accurate*, and Church membership grows to between twenty-five and thirty million members, just think of the substantial need for leaders in the Church! You will be the ones counted on to lead and will be expected to be ready to contribute. In a July 1996 press conference, President Gordon B. Hinckley was asked, "What do you see as the greatest challenge facing the Church as you enter the twenty-first century?" His answer was simple: "Growth." Regarding the growth of the Church and subsequent need for leadership, President Hinckley added, "All our local leaders are presided over by volunteer workers not compensated financially in any way. As we grow, it becomes necessary to train leaders, and that is a challenge. That is the same challenge Brigham Young faced. We have faced it all through the years and will continue to face it as the Church grows across the world."5

Indeed, the Church and the world need your leadership. And more important, your families need your leadership. As President Wilford Woodruff intimates, "There never was a generation of the inhabitants of the earth in any age of the world who had greater events awaiting them than the present. . . . And an age fraught with greater interest to the children of men than the one in which we live never dawned since the creation of the world."6

It might be helpful to think about leadership in two ways: formal authority (influence as a result of a specific role, title, or position), and moral authority (leadership associated with a way of being, and the ability to persuade and influence even if no official role or title exists). In fact, as you think about your leaders, you may discover some of them have had or currently have formal leadership positions, and you may have realized that some had tremendous influence without an official title. Sometimes it is the informal leaders that inspire the most and that make the greatest impact because of their moral authority. Leadership is not just the domain of those in certain positions. It is everyone's responsibility. And everyone—those in positions of authority and those not in such positions—can benefit from a discussion about developing leadership skills.

Most of this section deals with the development of the leadership skills necessary for any individual, regardless of role or calling or position. However, it is worth taking time to talk about serving in a specific calling, as there may be times in your life when you are asked to accept a responsibility for which you don't feel particularly prepared. Take comfort in President Monson's inspired statement: "Whom God calls, God qualifies."[7]

My grandmother used to tell a story about her days as an elementary school teacher. One snowy winter afternoon, as one of her young students was leaving school for home, Grandma stopped to help him put on his galoshes. They were clearly too small for his shoes, but after several minutes of tugging, twisting, and struggling, she finally succeeded in pulling them on. The boy then replied, "These are not my galoshes." Exasperated, my grandmother then spent the next several minutes going through the process of removing them, after which the boy replied, "These are not my galoshes. They're my sister's. But I couldn't find mine this morning, and my mother made me wear hers." So once again, my grandmother had to go through the process of putting the galoshes on.

Over the years—and perhaps sooner than you think—you will have opportunities to provide leadership that don't exactly "fit" your talents. Keep "tugging, twisting, and struggling" anyway. Make the conscious decision to be an active and willing participant in building the Lord's kingdom. I have heard so many former full-time missionaries declare with boldness how much they loved serving. Unfortunately, I have seen some of these same missionaries, when a few years or even just a few months pass after their return home, lose their passion for the Lord's work.

Instead of viewing leadership and service as a privilege, some view it as a burden. Home teaching or visiting teaching becomes routine, just something that has to be done, if indeed it is done at all. Preparing a Sunday School lesson for a bunch of thirteen-year-olds who don't want to be there is hard, even more so when *you* don't want to be there. Service projects, family home evening, scout camp, and youth conference can either be a blessing or a curse, depending on your paradigm or your attitude.

Look for and pray for opportunities to serve in the kingdom, without respect to the so-called "importance" or visibility of the calling. Be willing to serve with diligence and enthusiasm in whatever capacity you are called to serve. "Every great and commanding movement in the annals of the world is the triumph of enthusiasm. Nothing great was ever achieved without it," observed Ralph Waldo Emerson.[8]

Prepare now for any opportunity that may come your way. I recently met a young man, 26, who, after receiving his degree at Brigham Young University, moved with his new wife to a large inner-city environment. He found himself in a large ward with many first-generation members. Just a few months after moving into this complex ward with its many and unusual needs, he was called to serve as the bishop. Now that particular calling may not be given to many twenty-six-year-olds, but others will come, and we must prepare to serve where we are called.

In the October 2007 priesthood session of General Conference, President Henry B. Eyring offered this important counsel, suggesting three keys to service and leadership: (1) remember the Lord and how He has sustained you in the past. Be assured He will do so in your current and future assignments. (2) Pray for those you serve. Said President Eyring, "When you forget yourself to pray for the circle of others, your service will be extended in your heart. It will change not only your service but your heart. That is because the Father and His Beloved Son, whom you are called to serve, know and love so many people your service will touch, however limited to a few it may seem to be to you."[9] (3) Go to work. President Eyring reminds us that our job as leaders is to bless others:

> And that always takes moving out and doing something, usually something hard to do. So you can expect, in addition to assurance of God's help and the command to forget yourself, the clear prompting by the Holy Ghost to go and do something which will bless someone's life. That may be as obvious as going prayerfully to visit a person or a family or a quorum member to whom you are assigned to serve. For a father it may be to correct one of his children.
>
> Whether what you do is to correct or to teach the gospel of Jesus Christ, you will do it better if you remember what success will be. You are to help Heavenly Father and His Son, Jesus Christ, make eternal life possible for those you serve. To do that, the Spirit must take a testimony down into their hearts. And that testimony has to lead them to choose to keep the commandments of God, whatever storms and temptations may come.[10]

Remember that while leading and influencing others is an important role, just about everyone will need to fill at some point in their lives through formal responsibilities at home, at work, in the community, or at church. Everyone has the responsibility to lend their influence toward the accomplishment of good things, even if no formal role is involved.

Ryan, 26, provides this perspective:

> Leaders make others better just by being around them. They don't have to say anything, or sell them on their leadership abilities, or be particularly charismatic. They simply exude confidence. Thus, people feel more confident in themselves simply by being around a true leader. It is genuine confidence that cannot be taught by a self-help book. It comes from actually knowing—not just believing—who you are and your divine potential as a son or daughter of God.

Much of my perspective on leadership comes from my association with Stephen R. Covey and Hyrum W. Smith, men who have devoted their lives to the study of this subject. I strongly encourage readers to thoroughly study *The 7 Habits of Highly Effective People* and *What Matters Most*, as well as *The 8th Habit*. The content of these books has become fundamental for the leadership development efforts of individuals across the globe, as well as organizations in both the public and private sectors. I also suggest a careful reading of two other excellent books: *7 Habits of Highly Effective Teens* (even if you are way past your teenage years) by Sean Covey, and *The Speed of Trust*, written by Stephen M. R. Covey. I acknowledge the work of other colleagues in developing additional leadership content, processes, and tools that have literally benefited millions, and influenced my thinking and philosophy.

LEADERS UNDERSTAND THAT PRINCIPLES GOVERN

In the physical world, natural laws prevail. For example, gravity is defined by the *American Heritage Dictionary* as, "The natural force of attraction exerted by a celestial body, such as Earth, upon objects at or near its surface, tending to draw them toward the center of the body."[11] The law of gravity is operational whether I acknowledge it or not. If I choose not believe in it as a principle that applies to me, it does not invalidate its effect on my life. I will still fall if I step off a tall building. Natural laws are impartial; they don't favor one person over another. As Sean Covey writes, "Principles aren't mine or yours. They aren't up for discussion. They apply equally to everyone, rich or poor, king or peasant, male or female. They can't be bought or sold. If you live by them, you will excel. If you break them, you will fail. It's that simple."[12]

Knowing how principles operate can empower you to great things. For example, a large aircraft weighs over 750 thousand pounds. Yet an understanding of the law of gravity and other principles of flight, such as lift, thrust, and drag, allows us to get these large chunks of metal to fly safely through the air at amazing speeds.

Society's natural laws are as timeless and universal as the physical laws, and bring predictable results. If we ignore or violate them, we will fail. As noted filmmaker Cecil B. de Mille said, "It is impossible to break the law. We can only break ourselves against the law."[13] These are among the social laws we must follow if we are to prosper:

- Honesty
- Integrity
- Respect
- Personal Accountability
- Vision
- Prioritization
- Abundance
- Empathy
- Inclusion
- Balance

I'm sure you have met people who have obtained great success (as the world defines success). They may have gathered riches, or achieved a degree of notoriety or fame by stepping on others, and seeking their own objective at the expense of everything else. Is it possible to get results by violating the so-called principles of human effectiveness? Well, the answer is both yes and no. It is certainly possible to achieve a short-term objective at the expense of others. I once determined to win a game of Monopoly by bending the rules to meet my own selfish needs. As the banker, it was easy to slip a few extra bills under my section of the board with each transaction. Ultimately, I won the game. In fact, it wasn't even close, and I celebrated in front of my family with great enthusiasm. But when my children learned the truth of how I won, they refused to play with me for a long time.

Think of your school experience. Have you ever crammed for a test or put off a project until the last minute? Cramming is a learned behavior with many. I, for instance, developed quite an ability to get an acceptable grade in my classes by cramming. But what are the consequences? Can you get the right grade or test score? The answer is yes. I did. Do you remember, long-term, what you studied? Not usually. So if the purpose of your college experience is to "get the grade," cramming may work in a shoddy way. But if the purpose of your college experience is to learn, to gather lasting knowledge, and to gain a true education, there are better ways to study.

Both my parents and much of my wife's family grew up on farms. Does cramming work on the farm? In other words, can you put off planting all spring and summer, work real hard in September—plant quickly and water intensely—and expect a rich and robust harvest in October? Of course not. The principle of "you reap what you sow" (see D&C 6:33) is in effect here. The same is true in your relationships. You cannot ignore them and expect them to flourish. You cannot demonstrate a pattern of dishonesty and expect people to continue to trust you. Short-term gains might be possible, but long-term success will elude you.

I like the concept of secondary greatness versus primary greatness. Secondary greatness is greatness or success as it is defined by the world, and includes wealth, notoriety and prestige. Primary greatness has little to do with worldly wealth or notoriety. It has everything to do with your contributions, your relationships with others, and with how you bless others' lives. This greatness comes only by obedience to principles. You can't fake it.

I have had the privilege of traveling through many different nations and love the richness of different cultures and people. In fact, I have been able to visit six of the world's seven continents. (I'm still waiting for a reason to go to Antarctica.) I love to sample the various foods and study the different traditions each region presents, and while I love the diversity I have experienced across the globe, I have learned that members of the human family have a lot more in common than most people would think. One of the things we share is principles. They exist for and apply to all peoples and cultures.

LEADERS UNDERSTAND THE POWER OF PARADIGM-SHIFTING

Joel Barker, author of *Future Edge*, tells a story of a man driving along a mountain road at night. As he was rounding a curve, a man on the side of the road shouted, "Pig!" "Well," thought the man, "that was about the rudest thing I have ever heard! I can't believe the gall of some people! I do not know that man and have done nothing to offend him. Why would he choose to call me a pig?" Just then, as the man turned the corner on the road, he saw a pig in the middle of the road, slammed on his brakes, and narrowly missed driving off the steep edge. The man hadn't been trying to insult the driver; he had known there were pigs in the road and he was trying to warn him.[14]

This little illustration highlights one of the foundational elements to effective leadership: the ability to examine and challenge your viewpoints. Our view of the world (our paradigms) has a tremendous influence on what we, individually, are able to accomplish. Our paradigms drive our attitudes, affect our confidence, and influence our relationships. Each of us possesses unique mind-sets that shape what we do every day. These mind-sets represent how we view ourselves, how we see others, and our perspective of the world. It's like viewing the world through colored lenses. One of the key skills for effective leadership is the ability to examine and challenge our own viewpoints and perspectives.

Consider your own views: What role do your paradigms play in the results you achieve? The view we hold of ourselves and others can either limit or liberate us. Sometimes our perspectives are simply wrong, and yet we still behave according to those perspectives. Frequently, we base our perspective of who we are, our abilities, and our talents on what we think others think of us. For example, if I believe others will think that I am not capable of doing something, I could let that negatively impact what I do. Do you ever limit yourself based on faulty paradigms or perceptions that are only partially correct? Bear in mind, if you want to make incremental improvement, change your behavior. If you want to make geometric improvement, change your paradigm. Let's look at some examples:

When my wife and I were newly married, we shared a car. It took a high level of communication and coordination to make our competing schedules work. For example, I had early classes at the university several miles from home. My wife's work also started early and was quite a few miles in the opposite direction. Following my morning classes, I would go to work, which, in turn, was also some distance from school. Our daily routine was something like this: Michele would drop me off at school early enough for her to make it to her office by 8:00 AM. She would return to pick me up at noon and we would have lunch together. She would then deliver me to my job and return to work. Finally, at around 5:30 PM, when we had completed our work for the day, she would meet me again and we would return home together. We put many miles on our car that semester.

On one particular day, I had several assignments and tests at school, and needed to be in class a bit early. Furthermore, I had some pressing projects at work, which required more time and attention than I seemed to have. Before we left our apartment that morning we discussed the schedule, and she agreed to be prompt in picking me up. Therefore, I walked confidently to meet her in the parking lot at noon, and met only disappointment, when I didn't see our car anywhere in sight. Forced to wait, my impatience grew exponentially as the minutes mounted. This was before the days of cell phones, and I had no way of calling her. I suppose I could have gone to a classroom or some professor's office and found a phone, but I was convinced that if I left, she would pull up, find me missing, and assume I had found another way to work. So I just waited . . . and waited. Finally, after about forty-five minutes, she pulled into the parking lot. By then, I suppose I bellowed out my frustrations boldly. However, Michele calmly explained that she had had a crisis at work and had no way of reaching me, and while she had empathy for my feelings, my only recourse was to deal with it. I reluctantly admitted that unforeseen things can happen to even well-planned schedules, and I was left to swallow my frustration and adjust my day.

As a result of time lost that day, the following day's schedule was especially tight, with several additional assignments due at school, and more awaiting me at the office. I now had no margin for error. Again, we discussed the situation and coordinated our schedules, so when I stepped out of my class at noon, I fully expected to see her in the parking lot waiting for me. She wasn't . . . and my temperature began to rise. I waited and waited and waited. Fifteen minutes turned to an hour. I started to worry that something had happened to her. After another hour, I determined that if nothing had happened to her, something would happen once she finally showed up! Of course things occur to our schedules from time to time that are beyond control and the routine can occasionally require alteration. But this was absurd!

Suddenly, in the midst of my pacing, fretting, and fuming—and after more than two hours—I had stunning insight: I had driven the car that day! Michele was waiting for me! I gulped hard as I struggled to discover what I might say to her, who surely would not be waiting for me with serene resignation.

We chuckle now as we look back on that experience. But at the time, I felt thoroughly embarrassed. I perceived the situation a certain way and as a result of an inaccurate view of reality, I developed very negative feelings that evolved into less-than-exemplary behavior.

Don't underestimate the power of a paradigm. One of the traits of a great leader is the ability to remain open and realize that no one has all the information all the time. Be careful about judgments you make of others. Remember that your perspective is based on your experience and is by nature incomplete. A friend of mine coined this profound statement: "Nobody knows everything about anything." Our perspectives are always limited and sometimes, like my car experience, they are dead wrong. Honestly evaluate your heart: Do you ever judge others unfairly based on poor or limited information? Do you ever judge yourself the same way? Recognize and remember that you are capable of many things.

Sometimes we do things simply out of habit. Hyrum W. Smith tells the following story about a newly married couple.

> While preparing Sunday dinner, the new bride took a ham, cut off both ends, placed the ham in a roasting pan, and put it in the oven. The husband was perplexed, and asked, "Why did you cut the ends off the ham?"
>
> His wife said, "It makes it taste better."
>
> "How do you know?" the husband relied.
>
> His wife responded, "My mother told me."
>
> The next Sunday, while visiting his in-laws, the husband pulled this mother-in-law aside and asked her the same question, "Why did you cut the ends off the ham?"
>
> Her response was the same as her daughter's: "It makes it taste better."
>
> Again, the husband's response, "How do you know?"
>
> His mother-in-law said, "That is what my mother always did."
>
> He then called the 93 year-old grandmother: "Why did you always cut the ends off the ham before you baked it?"
>
> The grandmother replied, "Because my roasting pan was too small. That was the only way I could get it to fit."[15]

Be open to viewing problems and situations in new ways. Don't get stuck in the rut of old thinking. Remember, how you see the world (your paradigms) influences what you do (your behaviors), which determines the results of what you do. If you don't like the results you are getting, examine your paradigms and adjust them as you see fit.

Your influence with others grows as you help them broaden their perspectives of their own capabilities. Early in my career, a colleague and I were asked to open our company's first field office, about two thousand miles away, and I was expected to represent my organization to the highest levels of government officials and corporate leaders. Grateful for the appointment and enthusiastic about the opportunity, I still could not quell all my youthful trepidations. A conversation with one of my leaders the day I left did much to reassure me. I told him of my excitement and assured him that I would generate significant sales opportunities for the senior members of our firm. He stopped me mid-sentence and very directly reminded me that I was a now senior member of the firm and didn't need to rely on anyone else. As simple as it was, that short conversation completely changed the way I viewed myself and my capabilities. I elevated the expectation I had of myself to match the expectations and trust this leader held for me. His view of me helped me shift my own thinking and became a catalyst for new and enhanced behaviors. It caused me to stretch and work in different and better ways.

Being a leader, regardless of circumstance or position, is a paradigm. As we have discussed, effective leadership is a requirement for any formal position, but it is also a requirement for life in general. Think about what it would mean if you saw yourself as a leader in your calling as a Primary teacher, versus simply putting in your time. How would you approach your weekly assignment? Would you prepare your lesson for the day's class during sacrament meeting, or would you be prayerful and thoughtful throughout the week and consider the needs of each of the children in your class? Would you know their concerns? Would they feel your love for them individually? Legrand, 29, shared this insight with me: "The greatest leaders I have ever known have the ability to see people for what they can be. What's more, they actually believe those individuals have the ability to achieve that potential. They possess true charity—the ability to see others how Heavenly Father sees them. These leaders then do all in their power to help them attain this potential."

Can you remember a teacher from your own life who demonstrated this kind of leadership? I remember Sister Carpenter, my primary teacher when I was six. I don't remember a specific thing she taught me from the manual, but I remember that she cared about me. To this day, I feel her love and concern. I wanted to be better because of her influence. Are you having this kind of impact on those you serve, even if you are in a position other than Elders Quorum president or Relief Society president? How are you bringing leadership to your individual growth and development? Are you, as Elder Neal A. Maxwell taught, taking the sacrament without letting it take you back to Gethsemane or back to the temple? How about leadership in your personal prayers?[16]

LEADERS DEVELOP TRUST

Trust is another important part of effective leadership. Think of different relationships where trust is either evident or not. How do you feel about those relationships where trust is high? How effective is your communication with these people? In my experience, communication is easy, simple, and fast in relationships with a high level of trust. Even if I am dealing with a difficult issue, I find that I am able to resolve it and come to consensus with the other person quickly. In high-trust relationships, I can misspeak, and not feel like I am constantly walking on egg shells, worrying that I will offend someone by something I said. Conversely, when trust is low, it seems that no matter what I say, my words are taken out of context. Communication seems nearly impossible, even on the most trivial matters.

During a somewhat casual conversation, a colleague made what seemed to be an unrealistic commitment. Over time, conditions at my organization had changed to such a degree that it looked like this commitment could not be met—not because the individual was incapable, but simply as a matter of circumstance. I was surprised one day when he called me into his office to let me know he had met his commitment. His effort had come at great personal sacrifice, but he made sure he followed through because he had made the commitment. I had always trusted him, but that day I gained an even deeper and more profound appreciation for his integrity and knew that he could be trusted in any circumstance. Over the course of several years, I participated in many difficult discussions with him where we faced important strategic issues, and even when the stakes were high and pressure was intense, our communication was clear and easy.

In contrast, I recall another individual whose relationship with his coworkers always seemed clouded by ulterior motives. Even simple conversations with him were difficult, as nearly every word aroused suspicion and offense. Trust is the great accelerator. When trust is high, everything is faster and less complicated. When trust is low, everything is encumbered.

In his book, *Speed of Trust*, Stephen M. R. Covey discusses the power of trust in our personal, interpersonal, work, family, and societal lives. He explains that trust is a function of two key things: our character (who we are, our values, and integrity), and our competence (our skills and capabilities). If you and I were engaged in a business relationship and you knew that I had all the right professional qualifications and talent, but that I didn't keep my word on important issues, you would not trust me. My lack of character would prevent you from doing business with me. Often it is our competence that gets us in the door to certain opportunities, but it is lack of character that gets us excused. Think of examples of high-profile athletes and executives with world-class competence who no longer hold the public's trust because of some very high-profile lapses in character.[17]

On the other hand, Covey shares the example of tennis champion Andy Roddick. During the third round of the Italia Masters tournament in Rome, Roddick was battling Fernando Verdasco from Spain. On match point, in favor of Roddick, Verdasco hit a shot that was called out by the line judge. The crowd cheered for Roddick, who had apparently just won the match, and his opponent came to the net to shake hands. Covey writes:

> Andy Roddick didn't accept the point. Instead, he said that the ball was "in" and called the umpire's attention to a slight indentation on the clay court which showed the ball had landed on—not beyond— the line. Surprised, the umpire allowed Roddick to overrule him, and the point was awarded to Verdasco.
>
> Everyone was amazed. In a game not typically played on the honor system—but on the umpire's calls—Roddick had made a call against himself and went on to lose the match.
>
> Though Andy Roddick lost the match that day, he gained something far greater. He gained credibility. He gained trust. How did this display of integrity give him credibility? Look at it this way: How are the umpires going to respond the next time Andy Roddick challenges a call? Most likely, they will treat his challenge with the utmost respect. His reputation is known; his credibility will precede him.
>
> Also, how do you think Andy Roddick felt about himself? How might he have felt if he chose to accept the win, knowing all along that the ball really wasn't out?[18]

Remember the words of the great educator Karl G. Maeser: "I have been asked what I mean by word of honor. I will tell you. Place me behind prison walls—walls of stone ever so high, ever so thick, reaching ever so far into the ground—there is a possibility that in some way or another I may escape. But stand me on the floor and draw a chalk line around me and have me give my word of honor never to cross it. Can I get out of the circle? No. Never! I'd die first."[19] Our character *does* matter!

Think about trust and your relationships in terms of a bank account—making deposits and taking withdrawals. Deposits include keeping commitments, kindness, keeping promises, apologizing and forgiving, being honest, showing respect, listening to understand, and so forth. Withdrawals include opposite behaviors: violating commitments, arrogance, pride, breaking promises, holding grudges, being dishonest, showing disrespect, failure to listen, and so forth. Now think of your relationships. What do you do that builds trust? What do you do that destroys trust? Relationships are fragile things, and need constant care and attention. Take a moment and consider a key relationship in your life. Could the trust be better? What are you doing that is potentially eroding trust? And what can you do to improve the level of trust? Create an action plan for improving trust.

Key relationship: _____

Trust level: Low   1—2—3—4—5—6—7—8—9—10   High

Withdrawals   Deposits

_____   _____

_____   _____

_____   _____

_____   _____

_____   _____

One of my heroes, Mohandas K. Gandhi, was among the most significant personalities and leaders of the twentieth century. His impact on the world was colossal, yet he held no political office. He was about five feet six inches tall, and was scrawny, frail, and dressed funny (at least according to modern conventions). He struggled with school, lived in abject poverty for most of his life, and had few possessions beyond his glasses, a piece of cloth to cover himself, and a tin cup. And all he ever did was liberate 600 million people. His passive-resistance movement literally brought what was the most powerful empire on the planet at the time (Great Britain) to its knees. He changed, on a massive scale, the course of human events for much of the world.

One day a woman from a small village brought her fifteen-year-old son to Gandhi. The boy was a diabetic, and his mother was concerned about his eating habits, as he was eating an unhealthy amount of sugar. The mother knew if she could get Gandhi to ask her son to stop eating sugar, he would, because her young son held so much respect for Gandhi. She explained this to Gandhi, who replied simply, "Come back in three weeks." Puzzled and frustrated, the woman left with her son. Three weeks later she returned, and again asked if Gandhi would speak with her son. This time Gandhi gently asked the boy to stop eating so much sugar. The boy respectfully replied that he would. Grateful but perplexed, the mother inquired why he had to complicate the process by insisting on a return visit. Why did he oblige her to make a second trip? Gandhi replied, "Because three weeks ago, I was eating sugar."[20]

Gandhi's tremendous influence had nothing to do with formal leadership roles. It had everything to do with his honor and integrity. He would never ask someone to do something he wasn't willing to do himself.

Undoubtedly, you have heard or read Shakespeare's oft-quoted words from *Hamlet*, as Polonius, the king's senior aid, wisely advises his son Laertes before a long journey: "This above all: to thine own self be true, and it must follow, as the night the day, thou canst not then be false to any man."[21] Powerful words! What we often forget when quoting this passage, however, is the shallow character behind those profound words. Readers of *Hamlet* will remember Shakespeare's brutal irony as Polonius fails to heed his own advice, eventually meeting his own death because of lack of character. Never forget that "what you are communicates far more eloquently than anything you say or do."[22]

Imagine you are called by an associate who requests an early meeting with you at a location an hour away. While the meeting's time and location are inconvenient, the agenda is important to you, so you accept the appointment. You plan and prepare your day so you can arrive early, attend the meeting, and return to accomplish the myriad other things you need to get done that day. However, your associate never shows. You wait an hour, and then return home, frustrated. Suppose later that afternoon, the associate calls back, apologizes and gives some excuse, then asks for the same meeting the following morning. Recognizing again the importance of the agenda, you somewhat grudgingly accept, though it will once again come at a price; you will have to sacrifice other things you need to accomplish. You make the long drive early in the morning, arrive on time, and again, your associate doesn't show. You drive back, frustrated, and resolve not to do business with that individual again. If you felt frustrated after the first incident, this time you feel it twice as strong. The behavior demonstrated by the delinquent individual shows a lack of respect for others and skewed priorities.

I use this little illustration to make this point: It is important that when you make a commitment to another person you keep it. Each of us should do all in our power to fulfill our promises to others. But how often do we make commitments to ourselves, and do that same thing the delinquent associate did in the illustration? Are the commitments we make to ourselves any less important than those we make to others?

YOU ARE RESPONSIBLE

Ultimately, each of us has the freedom to choose our own response to the circumstances we face. This can be very tough, and requires the development of our "proactive muscles." One of the great lessons of life is the notion that you are responsible for your choices. That is not to say that any of us determines the conditions we face, but we are responsible for how we respond to these conditions.

Remember back to your high school psychology class when you studied Pavlov and his dogs. You will recall that Pavlov, the 1904 Nobel Prize in Physiology and Medicine, was researching the theory of "conditional reflexes." Each time Pavlov fed his dogs, he would first ring a bell. He did this over and over, so that whenever the dogs heard a bell, they would salivate in anticipation of eating. Eventually, Pavlov could ring a bell and the dogs would salivate, even if he didn't feed them. Where there was a stimulus (the bell), there was an immediate response (the salivating). Unlike Pavlov's dogs, we are not determined by the stimuli in our lives. We might be highly influenced by these stimuli, but ultimately we have the ability to choose our response in any circumstance—to live our life and not have our life live us.

Each of us is predisposed to certain individual tendencies. Our background, upbringing, experience, and DNA have a lot of influence on who we are. For example, you may have endured an abusive relationship or struggled with financial difficulty. Perhaps you have the natural tendency to be short-tempered or impatient. Or maybe you find it difficult to feel motivated to do anything productive on rainy days. Yet despite these significant influences, you inherently have the freedom to choose your response. Sometimes we face conditions we can't change, yet we must adjust to and choose how we respond to various circumstances.

Dr. Viktor Frankl offers a case in point. Frankl was a Jew living in Nazi Germany during Hitler's tyrannical rule. Like millions of other Jews, Frankl was imprisoned in concentration camps, spending time in both Auschwitz and Dachau, two of the most heinous of these camps. While there, he experienced the worst of what any man can impose on another. The prisoners were deprived of adequate food, separated from loved ones, and forced to watch the senseless murders of countless innocent people. I cannot imagine a more daunting and inhumane scenario for any human to face. "The devil laugheth and his angels rejoice," Nephi tells us, suggesting the horror that only devils could applaud (3 Nephi 9:2). Yet despite the atrocities he faced, Frankl came to a startling conclusion: his Nazi captors could impose their physical will upon him, but they could never determine who he was as a person. At the conclusion of this experience, Frankl observed that while his liberty had been virtually eliminated, his freedom to choose was greater even than his captors'. He learned that what could not be changed could be faced and addressed in the best personal way. He wrote: "We who lived in concentration camps can remember the men who walked through the huts comforting others, giving away their last piece of bread. They may have been few in number, but they offer sufficient proof that everything can be taken away from a man but one thing: the last of the human freedoms—to chose one's attitude in any given set of circumstances, to choose one's own way."[23]

One of the most powerful concepts I have learned in my life is this: when you focus your energy on things over which you have no control, your personal influence shrinks. You may be concerned about the weather or what other people say, or perhaps you worry that so-and-so is doing such-and-such. This is debilitative thinking, and will only serve to diminish your ability to accomplish. On the other hand, if you choose to focus your time and energy on the things you can control, your influence increases dramatically. You recognize you cannot control others; you can only hope to influence others. You understand the concept of "eating an elephant one bite at a time" and don't get entombed by what you can't do.

In 1984, the nation of Ethiopia was still suffering from a prolonged famine. News reports focused on relief efforts, highlighting children with haunted gaze and swollen bellies. The relief workers were forced to make the horrifying choice of how to administer limited supplies, sending the relatively strong to the area where they could receive food and medical attention while the hopelessly weak were left to die.

Bob Geldof, a musician and a member of the Boomtown Rats, an Irish punk-rock group, watching one of these news reports with a friend, became deeply affected. "How is it," he said to his friend, "that we can just sit by, doing nothing, while others are struggling and dying in these conditions?" His friend expressed empathy and remarked at how terrible it was. "But what can you do about world hunger?"[24]

I find myself in the friend's situation. I see myself watching the same program and my heart goes out to those who suffer. "Too bad the situation is on the other side of the world," I think. "I would like to do something about it." Then I wonder what is on the other channels, or what time the anticipated ball game is starting.

Thankfully, Bob decoded to do something different. He met with his band, discussed the situation with them, and they decided to hold a series of benefit concerts with the proceeds going to the Ethiopian relief efforts. He coordinated logistics with the theatre and facility owners, and went to work on enlisting the support of other musicians. His goal was to shoot as high as he could—to get the most famous musicians of the day involved. It worked. Soon people like Elton John, Phil Collins, and Michael Jackson signed on.

What started as one man's desire to make a difference grew into one of the largest charity and benefit efforts the world has ever seen: "Band Aid" in Europe and "Live Aid" in the United States. Millions of dollars were raised and thousands of lives were impacted.[25]

Here's another example of a rapidly expanding circle of influence, this time a little closer to home. My friends Karen and Bob Hahne were in their forties, with a house full of young children, when they received a call at home one evening. Karen happened to answer the phone. It was LDS social services. The Hahnes had adopted several children years before, so it wasn't entirely unusual to receive a call from social services. However, because of their ages, their files had been closed and the fact that their social worker had retired made this call unanticipated. Then came the unexpected: the caller told her they had just learned of a baby boy who needed a home and asked, would Karen be interested in adopting another child? Before Karen could answer, the caller added, "This child was born with Down syndrome. He will have many special challenges and will require unique care."

Without hesitation, Karen knew they needed to have this baby as part of their family. They gave social services an emphatic and enthusiastic "Yes!" and they started a new chapter in their lives with their new son, Reed.

Reed, as promised, presented many challenges. The first professional they encountered told them to "love him, but don't expect too much." Others advised them that Reed should never attend the public school system. He would be figuratively crucified, they were told. Another concerned individual asked them, "How can you do this to your other children?" Their response, "How can we not give them this wonderful blessing!"

Over the next few years, the Hahnes worked with Reed. As expected, his development was delayed, but progress began. Gradually, Reed was responding to their care. They exposed him to fine music, the theatre, and other culturally rich and stimulating experiences. I ran into them on several occasions at plays and concerts. Reed learned to talk, exuding enthusiasm for life. The Hahnes continued to explore every possibility to assist in his growth and development. They pursued government and community initiatives, only to learn there were few options. Realizing they couldn't just sit and fret about what was not available to them, Karen and Bob determined to go beyond present resources. They learned there were other parents of special needs children who also struggled for resources and support (financial, physical, spiritual and emotional). So they started a small group called, "Up With Downs Early Pre-School," which met a couple of days a week in a local high school, then later in a donated room of a doctor's office and provided education for both children and parents.

Word began to spread. More and more parents came seeking education and support. Two mothers who knew they needed funding wrote a grant, and much to their surprise, got it. The program, now known as "Kids on the Move" grew beyond those facilities, and it became clear they needed their own building. With little funding and escalating demand, the Hahnes and other parents persevered. They raised money (projects, begging, coercing), got government grants, and enlisted the help of a generous community. Miracle after miracle followed. Today, Kids on the Move is a substantial school for children from birth to age three, and the program's influence extends well beyond the school, and deep into homes and communities. The program currently serves over 1,500 families each year and employees 80 people.

And what about Reed? This young man, whom "experts" considered a hopeless case, has grown into a wonderful contributor to society. Not only did he learn to talk, he learned to excel. He attended Mountain View High School in Orem, Utah, where he had many friends. For their school "Preference" dance, Reed was voted one of the school's "most preferred," and successfully served on student council his senior year. He later served two service missions (during the first one he helped first grade children learn to read and write), and is currently attending college with excellent grades. He is a regular speaker at high school assemblies and firesides. He was won national awards for advocacy and addressed many national and state conventions. Not bad for a young man who wasn't expected to do or accomplish anything.

Bob and Karen Hahne's relentless determination and faith traveled hand in hand with hardship, discouragement, and the occasional dead end. Ultimately, however, their perseverance has blessed thousands of lives and brought hope to many families who had nowhere else to turn.

Bob and Karen Hahne's relentless determination and faith traveled hand-in-hand with hardship, discouragement, and the occasional dead end. Ultimately, however, their perseverance has blessed thousands of lives and brought hope to many families who had nowhere else to turn. Never underestimate the power of choice. Fine-tune your ability to make decisions and take initiative based on your values, not just on prevailing conditions. Remember the words of Margaret Mead: "Never doubt that a small group of thoughtful citizens can change the world. Indeed, it is the only thing that ever has."

THE KEY TO THE MANY IS THE ONE

In Matthew 18:12–13, the Savior teaches an important leadership principle: "How think ye? if a man have an hundred sheep, and one of them be gone astray, doth he not leave the ninety and nine, and goeth into the mountains, and seeketh that which is gone astray?

"And if so be that he find it, verily I say unto you, he rejoiceth more of that sheep, than of the ninety and nine which went not astray."

One of the important traits for a leader to possess is the ability to recognize, amid all the noise and tumult of life, the needs of the one. How we treat the individual will determine our ultimate effectiveness as a leader with the larger groups.

My brother-in-law has made a habit of sending weekly letter to the extended family. This letter serves as his personal and family journal, and he graciously shares it with all of us. In this letter he recounts the happenings of each week and adds his insight, feelings, and musings. He writes in a wonderful conversational style, and I look forward to receiving his letter every week. He recently sent a note that particularly touched me, which, I believe, is relevant to this leadership principle. He writes of one of his son's missionary experiences when, on preparation day, he and his companion were visiting a family in a rural part of their area, and he and his companion decided to ride their bikes to visit another family, some ten miles away. My brother-in-law writes:

> One of the older boys of the member family wanted to go with the Elders on this bike excursion and so the household was searched for a bike that he could use. All he could find was a little pink bicycle that his little sister sometimes rode that really didn't fit him well and didn't have all the nifty gears to help accommodate the ups and downs of the journey. The tires were low, the chain was rusty, but the young man was excited to ride with the Elders. Both Elders had nice ten-speed bikes with good bearings, fully inflated tires, lubed chains, and stylish paint.
>
> For the first few miles they all biked the rural roads together, but it became clear after four or five miles that the young man on the little pink bike was at a serious disadvantage and had fallen behind. At a point about midway through the ride the trio stopped for a rest. The young man on the little pink bike was obviously winded and struggling. It occurred to my son that he might be able to help things along by letting the young man ride his bike while he took a turn on the smaller bike. As they proceeded down the rolling country road my son began to realize what a challenge it was to ride this bike. When the "up" side of the hill came, there was only one gear to use. When the "down" side of the hill came, the under-inflated tires and poor bearings didn't allow for much coasting. It was a constant struggle. My son's legs grew very weary as they neared their destination.

After arriving and taking care of business, the young man faced the grim prospect of riding the little pink bike back to his home. My son, feeling the need to ease the burden, traded time on the little pink bike on the return trip.

As my son related this story he drew an analogy of those who come into this world saddled with "little pink bikes." Their self-esteem might be low, their social skills are rusty, and it's a struggle for them to handle the ups and downs of life. These are not the "beautiful people" of the world with whom we like to associate. These are they that have many needs and are very often overlooked.

Yesterday afternoon I was the only one home when a phone call came in. I looked at the caller ID and saw it was from an out-of-state psychiatric hospital. I picked up the phone and heard a young woman's voice on the other end. She identified herself and asked for my son. I recognized this young woman's name and remembered that she was one of those in high school whom my son had gone out of his way to befriend. I remembered she was short, plump, had thinning hair, heavy acne.

I found myself—all of a sudden—becoming protective of my son's time. After talking for a minute, I became more and more agitated at her persistence that I get her number to my son. Ultimately, however, I agreed to do it.

As I called my son to talk with him, I hatched a way that he could call her but be able to end the call in short order. She had told me she couldn't talk after 9:00 PM, so I suggested to my son that he call her after 8:30, thus assuring a shorter call. My son listened, then told me that he knew how to let the young woman know when he had to leave and that he would be okay. "Not to worry, dad," he said. "She is one that has been given a little pink bike to ride through life." He told me that he loved me and then we hung up. I sat and pondered his words.

I have been listening to audiotapes of a fictional account of a family living at the time of Christ and of their interactions with the Savior. As I was listening this morning, the narrator told of one of the story's characters that happened to be near the Savior as he recited the following parable:

But he, willing to justify himself, said unto Jesus, And who is my neighbour?

And Jesus answering said, A certain man went down from Jerusalem to Jericho, and fell among thieves, which stripped him of his raiment, and wounded him, and departed, leaving him half dead.

And by chance there came down a certain priest that way: and when he saw him, he passed by on the other side.

And likewise a Levite, when he was at the place, came and looked on him, and passed by on the other side.

But a certain Samaritan, as he journeyed, came where he was: and when he saw him, he had compassion on him,

And went to him, and bound up his wounds, pouring in oil and wine, and set him on his own beast, and brought him to an inn, and took care of him.

And on the morrow when he departed, he took out two pence, and gave them to the host, and said unto him, Take care of him; and whatsoever thou spendest more, when I come again, I will repay thee.

Which now of these three, thinkest thou, was neighbour unto him that fell among the thieves?

And he said, He that shewed mercy on him. Then said Jesus unto him, Go, and do thou likewise. (Luke 10:29–37)

The narrator then analyzed this parable through the fictional character. This character realized that the priest and the Levite, both holders of the priesthood, had crossed over to the other side of the road, not wanting to be burdened with the "messy" situation. However, the Samaritan not only crossed over to the man who was beaten, but also bound his wounds, administered antiseptic, and helped him on his donkey. None of this was convenient. The Samaritan then took the man to an innkeeper, paid for the expenses, and expressed his willingness to incur additional debt on behalf of the injured man.

Like a bolt of lightning, the characters became real to me. The man on the side of the road became the young woman who had called asking for my help. Her "little pink bike" was broken and she needed someone to help inflate the tires, lube the chain, and oil the bearings. I was the high priest who felt I was being imposed upon by the inconvenience of a call from the hospital. I had been very willing to stay on my own side of the street and not get my hands dirty, not wanting to let anyone else in my family suffer the same inconvenience. I recalled the long-term help my son had provided to this young woman, and the parallel between him and the Samaritan hit me forcefully.

Hot pangs of guilt flooded over me as the Holy Ghost taught me of a better way. I felt selfish and in need of repentance. I may not be the most "manly" response, but tears poured down my face as the Spirit placed new characters into the setting of that ancient parable.

Each of us will, at some point in our lives, encounter difficulty and discouragement, where we feel we are riding our own little pink bike.

Some will have life-long struggles with particular issues. A leader's ability to recognize these individual needs and attend to them builds trust and confidence in the leader's ability to serve everyone.

Shaun, 29, wrote me:

"To understand leadership—to know a true leader—we only need look to the example of Christ. He served His fellow man. He taught, yes, but He also served. He healed the sick. He comforted the sad, the lonely, the mourning. He was an example. I was told once that the fundamentals of leadership were given by the Savior in His Sermon on the Mount, and I have found that the greatest leaders I have known are those who obtain these attributes of the Savior."

Elder Joseph B. Wirthlin reminded us, "This instruction [to seek after the one] applies to all who follow Him. We are commanded to seek out those who are lost. We are to be our brother's keeper. We cannot neglect this commission given by our Savior. We must be concerned for the one."[26] Dag Hammarskjold, the former U.N. Secretary-General said, "It is more noble to give yourself completely to one individual than to labor diligently for the masses."[27]

Mother Theresa sums it up thus:

> I never look at the masses as my responsibility. I look at the individual. I can love only one person at a time. I can feed only one person at a time. Just one, one, one. . . . So you begin—I begin. I picked up one person—maybe if I didn't pick up that one person I wouldn't have picked up 42,000. The whole work is only a drop in the ocean. But if I didn't put the drop in, the ocean would be one drop less. Same thing for you, same thing in your family, same thing in the church where you go. Just begin . . . one, one, one.[28]

LEADERS PROVIDE VISION AND DIRECTION

Throughout your life, you will have opportunities to be in formal leadership roles, where you are responsible for organizing others and helping them understand their duties and responsibilities. Remember the principle of "no involvement, no commitment." When a leader merely dictates the team's purpose without involving others in the process, that leader will find a low level of commitment and a high level of burnout from others.

At the same time, you can't just rely on the input of others as the sole basis of your direction. A leader is more than a census-taker. In fact, you will learn if you haven't already that it is difficult to please everyone all the time. So don't even try. Involve people in key decision-making processes, let them help you clarify the direction of the team or the initiative, but be prepared to take a stand once you have gathered data and input. Think for a moment about the great leaders in your life. My guess is that they had a unique ability to provide a sense of direction and purpose, a sense of clarity about who you are, and a vision for what you may become. In my own experience, I have found this to be one of the most inspiring traits of a leader—the ability to inspire others to achieve well beyond what they think they can do.

A vision describes a future state of being, and effective leaders convey this sense of vision. As I have studied visionary leaders, I have come to the conclusion that there are few things more powerful than a bold and compelling vision. In 1831, when the restored Church was still in its infancy, with just a few hundred members in New York, Pennsylvania, and Ohio, and with persecution and resistance building from all corners, the twenty-six-year-old Prophet Joseph declared to the world, "And this gospel shall be preached unto every nation, and kindred, and tongue, and people" (D&C 133:37). Though at the time this vision may have been viewed as outrageous, it was inspired, and has come to pass.

Think about President Gordon B. Hinckley's vision for temples. From 1830 to 1998, the Church had built and dedicated some thirty-four temples. In 1998, President Hinckley announced his intention to have dedicated at least 100 temples by the year 2000. A few years earlier, we might have thought having 100 temples would be impossible. Yet at the time of his passing, President Hinckley's vision had been realized, with 124 operating temples and more announced or under construction.

Leaders Execute with Excellence

Vince Lombardi once said, "When all is said and done, more is said than done."[29] Ultimately, leaders are responsible for getting results. It is not sufficient for an individual or team to simply have a good strategy—that strategy must translate into performance. Here are four steps to executing with excellence:

1. Clarify goals. Studies have shown that individuals and teams who have one to three goals will, with focus and attention, achieve them all. However, teams that have five to six goals generally accomplish only one or two. And teams that have 10 or more goals generally accomplish none of them. There is tremendous power in focus. As you prioritize your goals, think about those things that *must* be done, and move lower priorities to the back burner.

. When you work with teams, either in the Church or otherwise, follow this same process. Be sure to establish a clear and shared understanding of the goal. Leaders often assume the objective is understood by everyone, when in reality there is wide and divergent understanding. On one occasion, I was meeting with a group of senior government leaders who were all part of the executive team for a newly-formed agency and had a mandate to build their organization. Prior to my meeting with them, this team had met for several days in a strategic planning session. With some anticipation, I asked the executive team to share their key goals and top organizational priorities. I was fascinated to hear their response—they were all over the map! One person believed their top priority was to be one thing while others felt it should be something completely different. And yet, because of their extensive meetings, they all assumed they were on the same page.

It is best to think of goals with specific time frames, in other words, "x to y by z." For example, if I have a goal to lose weight, my goal would be stated thus: go from 195 pounds to 180 pounds by June 1. I have a starting point, my ultimate objective, and a specific target date. For example, in 1958, the United States Space Program was significantly behind the Soviet Union's program. President Dwight D. Eisenhower stated that as a country, we mush "maximize our effectiveness in space." Nothing specific, nothing measurable, something of a yawn. On May 5, 1961, in a speech before a joint session of Congress, and as the American space program had slipped further behind the Soviet Union's, President John F. Kennedy declared with specificity that the United States would send a man to the moon and return him safely to the earth by the end of the decade. This vision, when coupled with specific time lines, galvanized and energized the entire country, and you all know the result.

2. Establish lead measures. Once you have established clarity around the goal, help to make sure individuals on the team understand how their own roles contribute to that objective. Create a scorecard to track progress. There are two types of measures: lag and lead. *Lag* measures account for what has been done. Using the example again of my weight-loss goal, my lag measure is my weight. *Lead* measures are those things that track progress toward the lag measure. For me, my lead measures are diet and exercise. When I stand on the scale, I can't do anything about what I weigh at that moment (lag measure). But I can influence what I will weigh in three weeks by focusing on and measuring my diet and exercise (lead measures).

3. Inspect what you expect. President Thomas S. Monson has taught: "When we deal in generalities we shall never succeed; when we deal in specifics we shall rarely have a failure; when performance is measured performance improves, when performance is measured and reported, the rate of performance accelerates."[30] While I was serving as a missionary in Philadelphia, my companion and I used to enjoy playing playground basketball in the inner city on our preparation days. It was fun to try to match our skills with the locals. As we approached the basketball courts, I could always tell which groups were keeping score and which groups weren't. There was just a different level of intensity with those who were keeping score. Consider creating actual scoreboards that very simply reflect the goal and lead measures.

4. Establish a system for weekly reporting and accountability. Include a review of the commitments each person made from the prior week and discuss the activities that need to occur in the coming week. The question for each individual should be: what is the one thing that will make the biggest difference toward reaching our goal this week? That becomes the new commitment.

This simple, four-step process will help you and the teams you lead cut through the clutter and chaos of daily life and drive toward the execution of your team's important initiatives.

Just as I began this discussion on leadership, I ask you again to consider this question: "Why would anyone choose to follow me?" Why does anyone choose to follow anybody? What is compelling about great leaders? As you study their lives you will learn that each brought different strengths and competencies. Some had formal leadership roles or titles, others didn't. But each possessed a clear sense of who they were, with a focus on doing better and being better and making a difference for others.

You don't have to be old to be a leader. Joan of Arc was an obscure farm girl of thirteen when she began hearing voices telling her that she would liberate France from England's clutches. The two countries had been embroiled in what is referred to as the "100 Years War." Committed to follow her conscience, young, inexperienced, uneducated, and unknown Joan approached the Dauphin, France's crown prince, and declared to him she was to lead her country to victory. The Dauphin was annoyed at first, but Joan was so bold, confident, and persuasive that he eventually gave her command of all his armies. At one point she gave an order that none of her men believed in. She told her generals that she, personally, would lead the attack. They responded, "Not a man will follow you." Her response was simple: "I will not look back to see if anyone is following me." You all know the result. Joan, through force of will, focus, determination, and providence, was successful in defeating the British and liberating France. Not long after, however, she was betrayed and taken captive. Her captors gave Joan two choices: deny her convictions and live, or maintain her beliefs and be burned at the stake. Listen carefully to the remarkable response that she gives in Maxwell Anderson's play, Joan of Lorraine:

"Every man gives his life for what he believes. Every woman gives her life for what she believes. Sometimes people believe in little or nothing. Nevertheless, they give up their life to that little or nothing. One life is all we have and we live it as we believe in living it and then it's gone. But to surrender what your are—and live without belief—that's more terrible than dying—more terrible than dying young."[31]

I personally feel great encouragement as I consider the following short biographical sketch of one of our country's greatest leaders. This man failed in business in 1831, was defeated for Legislature in 1832, had a second failure in business in 1833, suffered a nervous breakdown in 1836, was defeated for Speaker in 1838, was defeated for Elector in 1840, was defeated for Congress in 1843, was defeated for Congress in 1848, was defeated for the Senate in 1855, was defeated for Vice President in 1856, was defeated for the Senate in 1858. And in 1860, Abraham Lincoln was elected President of the United States.[32]

As you consider the contributions you will make in life, be patient, but be persistent. Don't allow yourself to become discouraged by setbacks or failure. Battling discouragement is a topic germane to both leadership and life in general. Researchers conducted a study involving the walleye pike, a very aggressive fish. The researchers placed the walleye in a large tank filled with water and added several minnows, the walleye's natural food source, and watched as the fish immediately devoured the minnows. The researchers then placed a transparent glass divider in the tank and placed new minnows on one side with the walleye on the opposite side. Again the larger fish went after the minnows, this time hitting its head against the glass with each attempt. Eventually, the walleye stopped attempting to eat the minnows, having learned that the effort would only bring a sore head. Finally, the researchers removed the glass barrier. Now there was nothing separating the predator fish from its prey. But even though the minnows were now swimming all around the walleye, the walleye made no attempt whatsoever to eat them. The researchers learned that at this point, the walleye would starve to death before attempting to eat what was its favorite meal. Such is the power that discouragement can have on us. We may have tried and failed in the past, and because we learned that trying can occasionally bring failure and pain, we assume it will always be so. Don't believe it.

Elder Jeffrey R. Holland tells the story of Thomas Edison:

> [Thomas Edison] devoted ten years and all of his money to developing the nickel alkaline storage battery at a time when he was almost penniless. Through that period of time, his record and film-production company was supporting the storage battery effort. Then one night the terrifying cry of "Fire!" echoed through the film plant. Spontaneous combustion had ignited some chemicals. Within moments all of the packaging compounds, celluloids for records, film, and other flammable goods had gone up in flames. Fire companies from eight towns arrived, but the heat was so intense and the water pressure so low that the fire hoses had no effect. Edison was sixty-seven years old—no age to begin anew. His daughter was frantic, wondering if he was safe, if his spirit was broken, how he would handle a crisis such as this at his age. She saw him running toward her. He spoke first. He said, "Where's your mother? Go get her. Tell her to get her friends. They'll never see another fire like this as long as they live." At five-thirty the next morning, with the fire barely under control, he called his employees together and announced, "We're rebuilding." One man was told to lease all the machine shops in the area, another to obtain a wrecking crane from the Erie Railroad Company. Then, almost as an afterthought, Edison added, "Oh, by the way. Anybody know where we can get some money?" Virtually everything we now recognize as a Thomas Edison contribution to our lives came after that disaster.[33]

You may feel your efforts never produce any lasting consequence.

President Gordon B. Hinckley addressed this issue in a stake conference address, where he related the experience of Elder Charles A. Callis, a member of the Quorum of the Twelve from 1933–1947. Prior to his service in the Twelve, Elder Callis served as the mission president of the Southern States Mission for twenty-five years. Elder Callis shared his experience of a missionary who, at the conclusion of his service admitted he felt he was a failure as a missionary. He had only baptized one person, a twelve-year-old boy, "a poor little kid who lived in the back hollows of Tennessee."

Elder Callis followed up on the boy throughout the years. As the boy grew older, he served as the secretary of the branch Sunday School. Later, he was called into the branch presidency, and ultimately as both branch president and district president. Eventually he moved with his family from Tennessee to Idaho, and had sons and grandsons that served missions. Elder Callis reported that as result of that one baptism "of that little 12-year-old boy, more than 1,100 people have come into the Church."

"Now that," President Hinckley said, "is the power of the gospel, and it works."[34]

I urge you to believe in the future. Believe in yourself. Reach out to others, prepare now to lead, and, most important, act now.

Winston Churchill exemplified the grit and determination necessary for each of us when, in 1940, at age sixty-nine, as the new Prime Minister of Great Britain, he faced the seemingly insurmountable task of defeating Nazi Germany in Europe. In one of his first speeches, he boldly declared, "We shall not flag or fail. We shall go on to the end, we shall fight in France, we shall fight on the seas and on the oceans, we shall fight with growing confidence and growing strength in the air, we shall defend our island, whatever the cost may be, we shall fight on the beaches, we shall fight on the landing grounds, we shall fight in the fields and in the streets, we shall fight in the hills; we shall never surrender."[35]

Leadership is a choice. And it's a choice you must make, for the Lord is counting on you to carry His kingdom to your families, to the Church, and to all of His children.

Notes

1. Quoted by Rodger Dean Duncan and Ed J. Pinegar, "Leadership for Saints, Part 1: Why a Book on Leadership? Why Now?" *Meridian Magazine*, 2002.

2. Michael Otterson, "On Faith: Guest Voices: Gordon B. Hinckley: 1910–2008," *Washington Post*, 29 January 2008.

3. Quoted by Pappus of Alexandria in *Synagoge, Book VIII.*

4. Jeffery L. Sheler, "The Mormon Moment," *US News and World Report*, Nov. 2000, Cover story.

5. Sheri L. Dew, *Go Forward with Faith: The Biography of Gordon B. Hinckley* (Salt Lake City: Deseret Book, 1996), 592–93.

6. Wilford Woodruff, *Journal of Discourses,* Volume 18. 12 September 1875, 110.

7. Thomas S. Monson, "All That the Father Has," *Ensign*, Jul. 1989, 68.

8. Quoted by Orison Swett Marden, *Everybody ahead, or Getting the Most out of Life* (New York: F. E. Morrison, 1916), 299.

9. Henry B. Eyring, "God Helps the Faithful Priesthood Holder," *Ensign*, Nov. 2007, 55–58

10. Ibid.

11. Joseph P. Pickett, *The American Heritage Dictionary of the English Language,* 4th ed. (Boston: Houghton Mifflin, 2000).

12. Sean Covey, *The 7 Habits of Highly Effective Teens* (New York: Simon and Schuster, 1998), 24.

13. Stephen R. Covey, *Principle-Centered Leadership* (New York: Simon and Schuster, 1992), 94.

14. Joel Barker, *Future Edge* (New York: W. Morrow, 1992).

15. Hyrum Smith, story shared with the author through personal correspondence.

16. Neal A. Maxwell, *Men and Women of Christ* (Salt Lake City: Bookcraft, 1992).

17. Stephen M. R. Covey and Rebecca R. Merrill, *Speed of Trust* (New York: Simon and Schuster, 2008), 30.

18. Covey and Merrill, *Speed of Trust* (New York: Simon and Schuster, 2008), 59–60.

19. Ernest L. Wilkinson, *BYU Speeches,* 5 October 1960, 15–16.

20. Ian Clarke, *A Useful Guide to Managing Teams,* (England: Pansophix, 2008), 40.

21. William Shakespeare, *Hamlet*, Act I, Scene iii.

22. Covey. *Principle-Centered Leadership*, 58.

23. Victor Frankl, *Man's Search for Meaning* (Boston: Beacon Press, 1959), 75.

24. BBC: Band Aid and Live Aid, 13 December 2000, retrieved 15 July 2006, http://www.bbc.co.uk/dna/h2g2/A447266.

25. Ibid.

26. Joseph B. Wirthlin, "Concern for the One," *Ensign,* May 2008, 17–20.

27. Stephen R. Covey, *The 7 Habits of Highly Effective People* (New York: Simon and Schuster, 1990), 201.

28. Susan Conroy, *Mother Teresa's Lessons of Love and Secrets of Sanctity* (New York: Our Sunday Visitor Publishing, 2003), 205.

29. David Ulrich, John H. Zenger, Jack Zenger, and W. Norman Smallwood, *Results-Based Leadership* (Massachusetts: Harvard Business Press, 1999), vii.

30. Thomas S. Monson, "The Aaronic Priesthood Pathway," *Ensign,* Nov. 1984, 41.

31. Maxwell Anderson and Andrew Solt, *Joan of Arc* (New York: William Sloane, 1948).

32. Alan R. Schonberg, Robert L. Shook, and Donna Estreicher, *169 Ways to Score Points with your Boss* (New York: McGraw-Hill Professional, 1998), 179.

33. Jeffrey R. Holland, *However Long and Hard the Road* (Salt Lake City: Deseret Book, 1985), 3–4.

34. Gerry Avant, "Christmas gift," *LDS Church News,* Dec 2006.

35. Winston Churchill, *The Life Triumphant* (New York: American Heritage, 1965), 991.

5

GREAT BATTLES ARE WON WITH SMALL SKIRMISHES

The Morality Choice

In the Church we are not neutral. We are one-sided. There is a war going on, and we are engaged in it. It is the war between good and evil and we are belligerents defending the good. We are therefore obliged to give preference to and defend all that is represented in the Gospel of Jesus Christ, and we have made covenants to do it.[1]

—President Boyd K. Packer

Two incredible stories, one from the monumental struggle between the federal states and the confederate states, and another from the equally monumental struggle of the Saints to reach safety in the West, will provide a fitting frame for our discussion of the choice to remain pure.

On July 1–3, 1863, the United States Army was in a very precarious position. During the previous two years, the Army of the Confederate States of America, under the leadership of Robert E. Lee and despite being outnumbered and out-resourced, had won nearly every battle of the Civil War to that point. Support for the war effort was waning in the Northern states, while the Southern states had developed a powerful sense of confidence and momentum. In an effort to accelerate the conclusion of the war, General Lee brought his army into Northern territory, thinking that a decisive victory there would end the war and solidify the confederate's independence as a sovereign nation. General Lee had even penned a letter to President Abraham Lincoln dictating the terms of the North's surrender, which he intended to personally deliver to the White House after defeating Lincoln's army on its own ground.

The Northern army, under the command of General George Meade, collided with their southern brothers during a hot and steamy week at Gettysburg, a small farming community in rural Pennsylvania. On July 2, Colonel Joshua Lawrence Chamberlain, a professor of rhetoric from Bowdain College in Maine, who had just inherited a group of one hundred deserters to go along with his small regiment of approximately three hundred men and who had marched for approximately twenty hours, had been instructed to hold a position atop a small hill called "Little Round Top." Chamberlain was given a position at the end of the Union line and, he was told, his little group would see no action that day. The report was that the Confederate army would attack the center of the Union line. The small regiment settled in for some much needed rest.

Lee, however, had a different strategy. His generals knew if their army could sweep around the back of the Union forces and hit them both from the front and the back, they could cut the Union army in half. It was a brilliant strategy, and nearly caught the Northern army unprepared. But if it were not for Colonel Chamberlain and the efforts of his incredibly brave men, the battle would likely have been lost; the war, for all intents and purposes, would have ended with the country permanently divided, and the institution of slavery would have been firmly established in the Southern states for years to come.

When Colonel Chamberlain saw Colonel William Oates' 15th Alabama regiment charging up the hill toward his men, he knew the consequences of his position. He could not afford to lose, no matter the cost. Though outnumbered more than two to one, the men from the 20th Maine bravely repelled the first assault, but a second charge soon followed. His men took a barrage of bullets and expended most of their ammunition to force the charge back. A third time the Alabama regiment came at them. This time, Chamberlain's small band held, but just barely. As he was preparing for the next assault, he was informed that the battle had taken a terrible toll on his regiment, with nearly 30 percent casualties, and his remaining men were out of ammunition.

Do you ever feel like Colonel Chamberlain and the 20th Maine, when you are faced with insurmountable odds where there seems no way out? For Chamberlain, the very survival of his country depended on his success, and he was nearly out of men and completely out of bullets. As the final charge approached, Chamberlain did the only thing he could think of . . . he shouted to his remaining men to "fix bayonets!" and they charged down the hill at their attackers. This charge so surprised the

Southern army that many of the confederate men dropped their weapons and ran. Others surrendered, not knowing their captors had no bullets!

Chamberlain and his army won the day by being firm and decisive in a moment of intense challenge. Had he not been determined to hold the line at any cost, this small skirmish would have resulted in a terrible defeat for the Union Army. As it was, the 20th Maine Regiment held the day, which allowed the Northern Army, ultimately, to gain victory at Gettysburg. While the war lingered for another two years, the North's victory in this battle devastated the Southern Army and ultimately led to the conclusion of the Civil War. Chamberlain went on to achieve the rank of brigadier general and though wounded seven times, survived well into his eighties. General Ulysses S. Grant honored Chamberlain as the officer selected to receive the surrender of the southern armies at the Appomattox Courthouse, and as a show of respect to his former foe, Chamberlain refused the traditional transfer of swords. As Lee and his men exited the courthouse that morning, Chamberlain ordered his men to stand in salute to their southern countrymen.[2]

There are many admirable elements to Chamberlain's heroics, including his fierce commitment to a cause, his relentless courage in the face of devastating pressure, his willingness to give every ounce of his effort, and his ability to inspire his men to do the same. What a lesson in leadership! As I consider the impact of this battle and the consequences associated with a wrong decision or a willingness to give in, one lesson stands paramount: that great battles are won with small skirmishes. This particular skirmish was just one of hundreds that occurred during the Civil War. The men who stood strong then were no braver or greater than the men who fought in other battles, their sacrifices no less valued. But the significance of Colonel Chamberlain's small battle in this particular moment proved to be a turning point in the history of our nation.

And so it is in our lives. Daily we face small decisions that on their own seem insignificant, in which we have opportunities to compromise our values in little ways that might seem inconsequential—give in on a particular point or surrender here or there. And yet the cumulative effect of either winning the small battles or giving in will help determine our ultimate destination.

I had a profound experience recently that left an indelible mark as I participated in a youth conference for my stake. Five hundred youth, ages fourteen to eighteen, loaded onto non-air-conditioned school buses and traveled seven hours northeast of our homes to the desolate high plains of Wyoming. Our objective was to retrace the pioneer trail, experience first-hand some of what it must have been like in those days of cross-country migration. To establish some authenticity, each youth was limited to just ten pounds of personal gear. We wore authentic pioneer clothing: long pants, long sleeve shirts for the young men, dresses and bonnets for the young women. Bathroom facilities were limited, while sand and rattlesnakes were abundant. We loaded our gear onto handcarts and our journey began.

For four days we traveled along the same trails as our early forebears, adding our blood and sweat and tears to theirs. We slept on the ground and endured rainstorms, lightening storms, fierce winds, hail, 100-degree weather, chafing, blisters, square dancing, and fainting. It was remarkable to see the ruts carved in the rocks along the trail, remnants of the faith and stubbornness of committed Saints of so many years ago, a monument to the literally thousands of wagons and handcarts that made the journey from Nauvoo to the Salt Lake Valley. We had the sacred privilege of visiting Martin's Cove, where members of the Martin and Willie handcart company suffered such hardship so many years ago. We splashed and played in the Sweetwater River. We climbed Rocky Ridge, pulling and pushing handcarts loaded to the brim with gear and equipment for a family of ten. We took the opportunity as we walked and walked and walked to learn a little more of our pioneer history. One story stands out as particularly poignant:

James Kirkwood immigrated to America from Scotland with his family when he was just a boy. Shortly after their arrival in the new world, his father died. Determined to take her four boys to the Salt Lake Valley, James's mother joined the Willie Handcart Company when James was 11 years old. One of his older brothers, Thomas, 19, was crippled, so he had to ride in the handcart. This required James' mother and older brother Robert to pull the cart, so responsibility for James's four-year-old brother, Joseph, fell to James.

On October 20, 1856, the company camped near the base of Rocky Ridge. The company had had very little to eat for several days, and everyone was weak. The day required the steep ascent of Rocky Ridge, and camp lay 13 miles beyond that. It was snowing, and a bitter cold wind was blowing. After a time, little Joseph became too weary to walk, so James carried him. The two moved slowly, and Joseph seemed to grow heavier with each step. James shifted him from his shoulder to his arms, then to his shoulder again. They eventually fell behind the main group, but continued to push ahead. Sometimes Joseph would slip as James's fingers became too frozen. So James would set his brother down, rest a minute, pick him up again, and move on.

After *more than 27 hours*, James and Joseph finally saw the campfires burning ahead of them. They had made it to camp! When they finally arrived at the fireside, James dutifully set his little brother down for the last time. "Having so faithfully carried out his task, James collapsed and died from exposure and over-exertion."[3]

I was truly humbled the next morning, after our group walked that same trail for seemingly endless hours, to see little James Kirkwood's grave marked in a special cemetery near the campsite. Our testimony meeting that morning seemed all the more meaningful to me. The hardships these great people endured were stunning, their example remarkable, and my admiration for them goes beyond my ability to express.

And yet as I examine the trials and hardships of these great people, I am impressed that your generation has its own set of life-threatening or life-altering challenges; challenges that no other generation has faced to such a degree. While our contemporary lives may not require the same physical demands as the early saints faced, we live in an environment where Satan's hold on the hearts of men has become so tight that we see the fulfillment of Isaiah's prophecy, where evil is called good, darkness is called light, and bitter is confused with sweet (see Isaiah 5:20).

Preserving Personal Morality

There is little subtly in the messages the world sends regarding moral purity. The notion that one should avoid sexual relationships outside of marriage is viewed by many as naïve or old-fashioned. The very institution of marriage is being challenged and redefined. More than 50 percent of today's marriages begin with the couple living together, and so much of our society reinforces what seems to have become a social norm: "What I do is my business. Sex is part of the human experience, and marriage has no bearing on it."

Many confuse romance and affection with physical intimacy. In order to be loved, you have to sleep with someone. This behavior is portrayed in nearly every situational comedy on television—not just on the obscure cable channels, but in prime-time programming. Movies and music also play prominent roles in communicating this social value. LDS filmmaker Keith Merrill stated, "Today's movie producers have no more hesitation about showing sexual acts on screen than they do about showing people eating dinner."[4]

I received a letter from Megan, 24, who wrote of the pressures faced by so many young adults:

"I think that everyone wants to feel love. The world tells us that we 'need' to be loved to have any kind of self-worth. This kind of worldly influence tells you that if you are not having physical contact with someone then you don't have value. I think seeing that image daily in our lives can make it difficult to stay morally clean."

Indeed, the pressures to compromise our values, particularly as related to personal purity, are intense. Regarding sex and the standards of the Church, Elder Jeffrey R. Holland pointed out to an audience of young adults, "Some may feel this is a topic we hear discussed too frequently, but given the world in which we live, we may not be hearing it enough."[5]

We have been incredibly blessed to become a partner with God in creating life. This is a sacred privilege, intended for use within the protection of marriage. The proper use of this power creates families, and helps keep them together and strong. Its misuse is the cause of great pain and sorrow, and tears at the very heart of our society. The unintended consequences of this include shattered relationships, devastated families, desensitized morality, and the objectification of others. A 2008 Center for Disease Control study revealed a shocking statistic, that "at least one in four teenage American girls has a sexually transmitted disease." The report makes this stunningly obvious declaration: "To talk about abstinence is not a bad thing . . . Teens tell us that they can't make decisions in the dark and that adults aren't properly preparing them to make responsible decisions."[6]

Today's generation is bombarded from every angle by Satan and his minions. As I mentioned earlier, movies, television, music, and all types of media suggest—even demand—that happiness comes by catering to our most base desires. The Internet makes hidden and destructive evils all too convenient and accessible. And society, as a whole, seems to be sliding closer and closer to the adversary's side. We are seeing the embodiment of Alexander Pope's insight:

Vice is a monster of so frightful mien,
As to be hated needs but to be seen;

Yet seen too oft, familiar with her face,

We first endure, then pity, then embrace.

Imagine holding a balloon in your hand. Imagine it full of air, the sides translucent and nearly ready to burst with the pressure. What would happen if you let it go? It would fly around the room at great speed, dipping in and out, up and down, without direction or coherence, free of rules or rudders or constraints of any kind.

However, like we discussed in chapter 4, the principles of gravity, lift, thrust, drag, airspeed, and so forth ultimately prevail, and the balloon falls to the ground, its power spent. Now compare that to an aircraft, which, on a relative scale, has similar power of movement. To maximize effectiveness and provide the highest form of protection, certain constraints are in place. Wings provide lift, and the tail and rudder provide direction and stability. A pilot skillfully knows when and how to engage the various controls. He also knows that a violation of the natural laws of flight will lead only to sorrow and death.

Like the principles of flight, our Heavenly Father has provided principles of happiness. Regarding morality, one of these principles of happiness, our leaders have declared, "Physical intimacy between husband and wife is beautiful and sacred. It is ordained of God for the creation of children and for the expression of love between husband and wife. God has commanded that sexual intimacy be reserved for marriage."[7]

Note the message: physical intimacy is good and is part of God's plan. It is an expression of love and will help unify a couple and allow them to participate in bringing spirit children into the world. What an incredible blessing! But it is also crystal clear that physical intimacy is to be reserved for the marriage relationship.

We are taught further: "Do not have any sexual relations before marriage, and be completely faithful to your spouse after marriage. Satan may tempt you to rationalize that sexual intimacy before marriage is acceptable when two people are in love. That is not true. In God's sight, sexual sins are extremely serious because they defile the power God has given us to create life. . . . Alma taught that sexual sins are more serious than any other sins except murder or denying the Holy Ghost."[8]

The world sees these constraints as ridiculous, confining, old-fashioned, and unnecessary. You and I know better. Elder Jeffrey R. Holland provides three important reasons why sexual transgression is so significant.

First, when we transgress in this way, we treat lightly how life is created. LDS doctrine teaches that "the spirit and body are the soul of man." (D&C 88:15) When one casually "toys" with the "God-given—and satanically coveted—body of another" he "toys with the very soul of that individual, toys with the central purpose and product of life. . . . In trivializing the soul of another we trivialize the Atonement which saved that soul and guaranteed its continued existence."

Elder Holland writes:

"So in answer to the question, 'Why does God care so much about sexual transgression?' it is partly because of the precious gift offered by and through his Only Begotten Son to redeem the souls—bodies and spirits—we too often share and abuse in such cheap and tawdry ways. Christ restored the very seeds of eternal lives (D&C 132:19,24), and we desecrate them at our peril."[9]

Second, human intimacy is a sacred symbol of the union between a man and a woman. We have received the commandment to become "one flesh" (see Genesis 2:24), and, as Elder Holland writes:

> That commandment cannot be fulfilled, and that symbolism of "one flesh" cannot be preserved, if we hastily and guiltily and surreptitiously share intimacy in a darkened corner of a darkened hour, then just as hastily and guiltily and surreptitiously retreat to our separate worlds—not to eat or live or cry or laugh together, not to do the laundry and the dishes and the homework, not to manage a budget and pay the bills and tend the children and plan together for the future. No, we cannot do that until we are truly one—united, bound, linked, tied, welded, sealed, married.[10]

Finally, and closely related to the other two reasons, sexual intimacy is not only a symbol of unity between two people, it is a sacrament between those people and God, "between otherwise ordinary and fallible humans uniting for a rare and special moment with God himself and all the powers by which he gives life in this wide world of ours." Said Elder Holland:

> Indeed, if our definition of sacrament is that act of claiming and sharing and exercising God's own inestimable power, then I know of virtually no other divine privilege so routinely given to us all—women or men, ordained or unordained, Latter-day Saint or non-Latter-day saint—than the miraculous and majestic power of transmitting life, the unspeakable, unfathomable, unbroken power of procreation.[11]

Many of us take the blessings of the gospel for granted. It is, as Elder Glen L. Pace wrote, as if we are passengers on a train. The train represents the Church, and as we are traveling, we occasionally look out the window and view the world as it passes by. We may be tempted to resent the confines of the train, to think it might be more fun outside where people are laughing and enjoying themselves. So we jump off to join them, only to find that it is not as much fun as Lucifer would have us believe, or we become injured, so we work our way back to the tracks and the train ahead.

> With a determined spirit we catch up to it, breathlessly wipe the perspiration from our foreheads, and thank the Lord for repentance.
>
> While on the train we can see the world and some of our own members outside laughing and having a great time. They taunt us and coax us to get off. Some throw logs and rocks on the tracks to try and derail it. Other members run alongside the tracks, and while they may never go and play in the woods, they just can't seem to get in the train. Others try to run ahead and too often take the wrong turn.
>
> I would propose that the luxury of getting on and off the train as we please is fading. The speed of the train is increasing. The woods are getting much too dangerous, and the fog and darkness are moving in.
>
> Although our detractors might as well "stretch forth [their] puny arm[s] to stop the Missouri River in its decreed course, or to turn it up stream" (D&C 121:33) as try to derail this train, they are occasionally successful in coaxing individuals off. With all the prophecies we have seen fulfilled, what great event are we awaiting prior to saying, "Count me in?" What more do we need to see or experience before we get on the train and stay on it until we reach our destination? It is time for a spiritual revival. It is time to dig down deep within ourselves and rekindle our own light.[12]

So as it relates to a physical relationship while dating, what is the line we shouldn't cross? At what point have we gone too far and need to talk with a bishop or other priesthood authority? My answer is found in the following paragraph from the Strength of Youth pamphlet:

"Before marriage, do not do anything to arouse the powerful emotions that must be expressed only in marriage. Do not participate in passionate kissing, lie on top of each other, or touch the private sacred parts of another person's body, with or without clothing. Do not allow anyone to do that with you. Do not arouse those emotions in your own body."[13]

This is wise council. But my concern about detailing the "Bishop's

Line" is that people tend to race as close to the line as possible without crossing over. As long as they do not get *too* physical, they might think, they are okay. This is a perilous path, one that quickly leads to activities far more serious and hurtful. I believe most of the young people who get into trouble with moral purity do not do so intentionally. Rather, they get too close to the line, and then passions take over and judgment and restraint are lost.

Let me suggest another way to think about this. Consider the following matrix:

	Affection	Arousal
Dating	Develop good habits.	The real line.
Marriage	Continue to court—always!	Important part of a healthy marriage.

DATING AND AFFECTION

When dating, you should be affectionate. So much is said in the Church about not being involved in steady dating before you are of age and are ready to marry. This is sound advice. However, once you reach the right age, it is very appropriate to date with a purpose. You should pair off. You should specifically pursue those activities that will lead you to marriage. Not only is the pursuit of marriage a good idea, it is a commandment. And you will find it very difficult to develop a relationship to the point of marriage if you don't pair off, hold hands, or even kiss. Showing appropriate affection while dating is an imperative as you progress in your relationship toward marriage. Men, this means you should be considerate of your date's feelings. Don't say or do things that could be considered disrespectful or degrading. Women, be thoughtful of your date. Don't belittle or unnecessarily pick at his faults. Don't make jokes at each other's expense. Remember Elder Holland's council:

> In a dating and courtship relationship, I would not have you spend five minutes with someone who belittles you, who is constantly critical of you, who is cruel at your expense and may even call it humor. Life is tough enough without having the person who is supposed to love you leading the assault on your self-esteem, your sense of dignity, your confidence, and your joy. In this person's care you deserve to feel physically safe and emotionally secure.[14]

Remember, sarcasm in relationships is destructive. Both parties should give careful thought to the needs and interests of the other. Cultivating the habit of seeking the welfare, comfort, and happiness of the other will reap great rewards throughout your life. Be deliberate in your affection, and actively seek to bless the lives of others. This common sense is not always common practice.

MARRIAGE AND AFFECTION

You have all seen marriages where the couple, despite having been together for many years, maintains wonderful affection for one another. They continue to hold hands and open doors for one another. They are respectful toward each another, and seem genuinely interested in the needs and wants of the other. These relationships do not happen by accident. They are created every day through consistent acts of service. A recent BYU study of the elements of a successful marriage analyzed the effects of communication and kindness. Conducted over several years, with deep analysis of various relationships, this study revealed the importance of both communication and kindness (see chart below).

CHARACTERISTICS OF SUCCESSFUL MARRIAGES

85 percent High Kindness Low Communication	93 percent High Kindness High Communication
29 percent Low Kindness Low Communication	19 percent Low Kindness High Communication

Not surprisingly, marriages that exhibited effective communication and consistent kindness had a 93 percent chance of success. Conversely, marriages that had consistently poor communication and low levels of kindness had only 29 percent chance of success. In other words, if you communicate well and are kind to one another, you stand a very good chance of remaining happy and staying together. And if you don't, your chances for success are a lot less.

On the other side, marriages that had good communication but demonstrated low kindness had only a 19 percent chance of success. This percentage is lower than those marriages that had poor communication.

Why? Because these couples were well-trained to be better fighters. This study showed that communication without kindness doesn't work. And perhaps most interesting, marriages that had poor communication, but consistently demonstrated high kindness succeeded 85 percent of the time! What does this mean? At the end of the day, kindness and affection rule the day.[15]

A close friend of mine recounts that while dating his wife, they went to see her grandparents. Her grandfather was eighty-five and her grandmother was eighty-three. Age had slowed their movements, but their mental acuity was still intact. It was late spring, and the couple had a small cherry orchard. While my friend was visiting, the grandfather brought the first ripe cherry of the season into the house to show his wife, and then proceeded to cut it into two pieces so they could enjoy it together. For him, the experience of eating the fruit was not complete unless he could share it with his wife. My friend was touched by his future grandfather's tenderness toward his wife of over sixty years. Follow this example as you plan your marriage. Continue to court your spouse after you marry and have a set date night. Pray together and hold family home evening—even when it is just the two of you. Go to church together and attend the temple often. Discuss spiritual matters with each other. Don't let the pressures of life get in the way of what is truly important.

Connie, 24, offers this insight:

> Have you ever been able to just feel the love a happily married couple feels for one another? I work as a nurse and one of my favorite things is to walk into a room where the patient is in the bed and the spouse is in the chair next to them. They do not even have to be look-ing at one another. Something about the presence of their spouse shows the immense concern and care they have for one another. Nothing else matters except the well-being of the other.

Consider the wonderful celebration you will have on your fiftieth wedding anniversary. Think about who will be there: you will have your children and grandchildren; possibly even a great-grandchild or two. You will invite close friends to celebrate the occasion with you. Each of your guests will take a minute and pay tribute to the two of you, and share how your examples have blessed their lives. Then the two of you will take a minute and pay tribute to each other. What do you want others to say that day? What will you say about your spouse? What will your spouse say about you? How will you express your feelings? Think now about what you want in your relationship, and make a plan to create this reality through your daily kindness and affection.

Marriage and Arousal

As stated earlier, physical intimacy between a husband and wife is an important part of a healthy marriage. This intimacy is for the purpose of bringing children into the world, but it is also an expression of love and is intended to bring a couple close together. Authors Stephen Lamb and Douglas Brinley wrote regarding this subject:

> Much to their credit, [young adults] pursue personal purity in spite of their natural curiosity, considerable pressure from peers, and a well-orchestrated effort "in the hearts of conspiring men in the last days," (D&C 89:4) to lead them away from virtue and truth. Simply put, they learn to say "no" to sex because they know it is wrong for them, just as they learn to say "no" to drugs, alcohol, and other dangerous things.
>
> It is not surprising, therefore, that some youth approach marriage with uncertainty and internal conflict about sexual matters. They wonder about saying "yes" to their spouse after saying "no" for so long. Perhaps in our attempts to encourage young people to be chaste, we sometimes send an unbalanced message. Have we failed to convey the peace of mind that comes through self-control before marriage and the exultant joy of proper intimacy afterward? Have we not fully explained that God himself instructed His children to participate in sexual relations as an important aspect of the marriage covenant?
>
> LDS couples, young and old, need to know that sexual relations within marriage are not merely acceptable to the Lord; they are encouraged and ordained by Him.[16]

President Kimball, who spoke and wrote often about many sensitive subjects, taught this principle with clarity. He said:

> The Bible celebrates sex and its proper use, presenting it as God-created, God-ordained, God-blessed. It makes plain that God himself implanted the physical magnetism between the sexes for two reasons: for the propagation of the human race, and for the expression of that kind of love between man and wife that makes for true oneness. His commandment to the first man and woman to be "one flesh" was as important as his command to "be fruitful and multiply."[17]

Some couples may have the mistaken perspective that sexuality has a single purpose, that of bringing children into the world. Again quoting President Kimball, "We know of no directive from the Lord that proper sexual experiences between husbands and wives need be limited totally to the procreation of children."[18] As Brent A. Barlow, professor of Family Science at Brigham Young University writes, "While creating children is an integral and beautiful aspect of marital intimacy, to use it only for that purpose is to deny its great potential as an expression of love, commitment, and unity."[19]

DATING AND AROUSAL

Any activity before marriage that brings feelings of sexual arousal is inappropriate and should indicate that you should stop what you are doing—even if you are nowhere near the "line." Remember, it is very appropriate—even essential—to be affectionate while dating. However, you should be considerate. Always show respect for one another. But prolonged kissing or making out, french-kissing, lying on top of one another, and other things that move the relationship from affection to passion are inappropriate, even if you have not "crossed the line." One more make-out session will not provide greater confirmation of true love. In fact, in my experience, relationships based the physical aspect or that get too physical too fast have more conflict and frustration than those relationships that are respectfully affectionate. The decision to marry is colossal, one with eternal consequences, and you will both want and need the guidance of the Spirit in making this most important decision. When a relationship is inappropriately physical, you separate yourself from that Spirit. Further, rational thought and judgment are seriously impaired when passions are aroused. You don't want to find yourselves participating in inappropriate activities that you otherwise would never consider. It is not uncommon for bishops to hear, "I can't believe this happened. It is not what we intended or desired. We just got carried away."

I also want to briefly discuss pornography. Avoid pornography like the plague—don't even start. If you have started, stop immediately. Just a few years ago, one was required to purchase a seedy magazine or rent a so-called "adult-themed" movie in order to access pornography. Today, it is available to all with the click of just a few buttons. It is accessible in every home with access to the Internet. You can't just *try* to avoid it—you must fortify against it. These fortifications include installing Internet filters, unsubscribing to premium movie channels, and refusing to have a live

Internet connection in your bedrooms.

Pornography is big business and big money—make no mistake about it. It is developed and distributed by conspiring men and women who want to take your money (see D&C 89:4). And if they destroy your soul in the process, it is of no consequence to them. In fact, the further into this trap they can lead you, the more money they will collect.

Pornography generates nearly $100 billion in annual revenues, exceeding the combined annual revenues of the world's top technology companies, including Microsoft, Google, Amazon, eBay, Yahoo!, Apple, Netflix, and EarthLink. Every second of every day, $3,075.64 is spent on pornography, with 28,258 individual viewers. In the United States alone, there are 244,661,900 pornographic web pages. This number grows daily, as a new pornographic video is being created every thirty-nine minutes.[20]

This problem is not exclusive to men, and my message applies to both sexes. But it is more pervasive among men than it is among women. President Hinckley provided this clear admonition:

> Brethren, we can do better than this. When the Savior taught the multitude, He said, "Blessed are the pure in heart: for they shall see God" (Matthew 5:8).
>
> Could anyone wish for a greater blessing than this? The high road of decency, of self-discipline, of wholesome living is the road for men, both young and old, who hold the priesthood of God. To the young men I put this question: "Can you imagine John the Baptist, who restored the priesthood which you hold, being engaged in any such practice as this?" To you men: "Can you imagine Peter, James, and John, Apostles of our Lord, engaging in such?"
>
> No, of course not. Now brethren, the time has come for any one of us who is so involved to pull himself out of the mire, to stand above this evil thing, to "look to God and live" (Alma 37:47). We do not have to view salacious magazines. We do not have to read books laden with smut. We do not have to watch television that is beneath wholesome standards. We do not have to rent movies that depict that which is filthy. We do not have to sit at the computer and play with pornographic material found on the Internet.
>
> I repeat, we can do better than this. We must do better than this. We are men of the priesthood. This is a most sacred and marvelous gift, worth more than all the dross of the world. But it will be amen to the effectiveness of that priesthood for anyone who engages in the practice of seeking out pornographic material.[21]

As members of the Church, we are a covenant people. One of the covenants we make is to avoid *any* sexual relationship with anyone other than our spouse, to whom we are legally and lawfully wedded. Participation in pornography is a violation of that covenant, and must be taken seriously. If you have questions, I urge you to talk with your bishop. Follow this injunction in the Strength of Youth pamphlet: "If you have committed sexual transgressions, begin the process of repentance now so you can find inner peace and have the full companionship of the Spirit. Seek the Lord's forgiveness. Talk with your bishop. He will help you obtain the forgiveness available to those who truly repent."[22]

One evening, while I was living on the East Coast of the United States, a friend and I were driving down a lonely country road. We passed a small pond, and being curious young men, decided to go exploring. The air was filled with loud and insistent croaking, which immediately informed us that this pond contained frogs, a fact that was confirmed as we approached the water and heard splashing with nearly every step, as frogs jumped in the water to avoid us.

I somehow got the idea that I needed to see how frog legs tasted, so we set out to catch our dinner. Eventually we succeeded in bagging two rather large victims. You have probably heard of the analogy of boiling a frog—how if you put a frog directly in boiling water, it will jump out. But if you put a frog in cold water and then turn on the heat, it will stay in the water until it is dead. Not sure how else to dispose of our new amphibious friends, we decided this would be a good opportunity to see if this actually worked. When we reach our house, I put a pot of water on the stove. Just as it came to a rolling boil, I dropped both frogs into the water. Sure enough, the frogs immediately jumped out. I then took a new pot, filled it with cool water, placed the frogs in it, and turned on the stove. The frogs sat tranquilly, with no effort to escape, and remained there as the water temperature gradually began to rise. In just a few minutes, it was clear the frogs were dead. Here is the interesting part: as I went to retrieve them, I discovered the water was not even boiling.

Like the frogs in the water, you and I face precarious situations that have serious implications, situations where our moral fortitude is tested. Most of the time when faced with the "big" temptations, we generally have the presence of mind to run away. It is not usually the "big sins" that get us. It is the little compromises we make that cause most of our trouble, and eventually are what lead to the big things. We find ourselves in cool, comfortable water, but with each compromise, the heat goes up. Little by little, degree by degree, the water is warm, then hot, then a rolling boil, and we find ourselves in a situation that is counter to our character, upbringing, and moral values. And we wonder how we could get to such a place.

Remember this final admonition from Elder Holland:

> Of all the titles he has chosen for Himself, Father is the one he declares, and creation is His watchword—especially human creation, creation in His own image. His glory isn't a mountain, as stunning as mountains are. It isn't in sea or sky or snow or sunrise, as beautiful as they all are. It isn't in art or technology, be that a concerto or computer. No, His glory—and His grief—is His children. We—you and I—are His prized possessions, and we are the earthly evidence, however inadequate, of what He truly is. Human life is the greatest of God's powers, the most mysterious and magnificent chemistry of it all, and you and I have been given it, but under most serious and sacred of restrictions. You and I—who can make neither mountain nor moonlight, not one raindrop or a single rose—have this greater gift in an absolutely unlimited way. And the only control placed on us is self-control—self-control born of respect for the divine sacramental power it is.[23]

The experience of kneeling across the altar at the temple with your sweetheart is a transcendent experience, and one of the most extraordinary spiritual experiences you will have in your life if you are prepared. Don't cheat yourselves of this wonderful moment. Don't try to push the line or get as close to trouble without actually doing something that requires a discussion with your priesthood leader. Hold yourselves to a higher standard, and hold your partner in greater respect. Remember, respectful physical intimacy between a husband and wife is part of marriage. You have feelings of attractions and physical desires because that is how Heavenly Father made you. They are appropriate and part of the plan, but they must be manifest in the proper time and way, and *never* before marriage.

Notes

1. "Do Not Spread Disease Germs!" *BYU Studies*, Summer 1981, 271.

2. Thomas Wheeler, *Leadership Lessons from the Civil War* (New York: Currency Doubleday, 2000).

3. Clayton Corey Newell, *Latter Days* (New York: Macmillan, 2001), 191.

4. Bruce C. Hafen, "The Gospel and Romantic Love," BYU-Idaho Devotional, 28 September 1982.

5. Jeffrey R. Holland, "Of Souls, Symbols, and Sacraments," BYU Devotional, 12 January 1988.

6. Center for Disease Control Press Release, 11 March 2008, retrieved 13 October 2008, http://www.cdc.gov/STDConference/2008/media/release-11march2008.htm.

7. *For the Strength of Youth: Fulfilling our Duty to God* (Salt Lake City: Intellectual Reserve, 2001), 26.

8. Ibid.

9. Jeffrey R. Holland, "Of Souls, Symbols, and Sacraments."

10. Ibid.

11. Ibid.

12. Glenn L. Pace, "Spiritual Revival," *Ensign*, November 1992, 11–12.

13. *For the Strength of Youth: Fulfilling our Duty to God*, 27.

14. Jeffrey R. Holland. "How do I Love Thee?" BYU Devotional, 15 February 2000.

15. Notes taken from a presentation at Campus Education Week, Brigham Young University, 1999.

16. Douglas E. Brinley and Stephen E. Lamb, *Between Husband and Wife* (American Fork: Covenant Communications, 2000), 17–18.

17. Spencer W. Kimball, "Thoughts on Marriage Compatibility," *Ensign*, May 1974, 7.

18. Ibid.

19. Brent A. Barlow. "They Twain Shall Be One." *Ensign*, Oct. 1975, 4.

20. Jerry Ropelato, "Internet Pornography Statistics," May 2007, retrieved 29 May 2007, http://www.Internet-filter-review.toptenreviews.com/Internet-pornography-statistics.html.

21. Gordon B. Hinckley. "A Tragic Evil Among Us." *Ensign*, Nov. 2004.

22. *For the Strength of Youth: Fulfilling our Duty to God*, 28.

23. Holland, "Of Souls, Symbols, and Sacraments."

6

Getting Up After the Fall

The Repentance Choice

Anyone who imagines bliss is normal is going to waste a lot of time running around shouting that he's been robbed. The fact is that most putts don't drop, most beef is tough, most children grow up to be just people, most successful marriages require a high degree of mutual toleration, most jobs are more often dull than otherwise. Life is like an old time rail journey . . . delays, sidetracks, smoke, dust, cinders and jolts, interspersed only occasionally by beautiful vistas, and thrilling bursts of speed. The trick is to thank the Lord for letting you have the ride.[1]

—Jenkins Lloyd Jones

There is an urban legend about a bricklayer who had been injured at work. His insurance company asked him to write a letter explaining the circumstances of the accident. He wrote the following:

Dear Sir:

I am writing in response to your request for additional information. In block 3 of your accident report form I put "trying to do the job alone" as the cause of my accident.

You said in your letter I should explain more fully and I trust that the following details will be sufficient. I am a brick layer by trade. On the day of the accident I was working alone on the roof of a new six-story building. When I had completed my work I discovered I had about 500 pounds of bricks left over. Rather than carry the bricks down by hand, I decided to lower them in a barrel by using a pulley that fortunately was attached at the side of the building on the sixth floor.

Securing the ropes at the ground level, I went to the roof, swung the barrel out and loaded the bricks into it. Then I went back to the ground level and untied the rope, holding it tightly to assure a slow decent of the 500 pounds of bricks.

You will note that in block number 2 of the accident report form I weigh 135 pounds. Due to my surprise at being jerked off the ground so suddenly, I lost my presence of mind and forgot to let go of the rope. Needless to say, I proceeded at a rather rapid rate up the side of the building.

In the vicinity of the third floor, I met the barrel coming down. This explains the fractured skull and broken collar bone. Slowed only slightly, I continued my rapid ascent, not stopping until the fingers of my right hand were two knuckles deep into the pulley. Fortunately by this time I had regained my presence of mind and was able to hold tightly to the rope in spite of my pain. At approximately the same time, however, the barrel of bricks hit the ground and the bottom fell out of the barrel.

Devoid of the weight of bricks, the barrel now weighed approximately 50 pounds. I refer you again to my weight in block number 2 as 135 pounds. As you might imagine, I began a rather rapid descent down the side of the building. In the vicinity of the third floor, I again met the barrel coming up. This accounts for the two fractured ankles and lacerations of my legs and lower body.

The encounter with the barrel slowed me enough to lesson my injuries when I fell onto a pile of bricks. Fortunately only three vertebrae were cracked. I am sorry to report, however, as I lay on the bricks in pain, unable to stand and watching the empty barrel six stories above me, I again lost my presence of mind and let go of the rope. The empty barrel weighs more than the rope, so it came back down and broke both my legs. I hope I have furnished the information you required as to how the accident occurred because I was trying to do the job alone.[2]

Benjamin Franklin stated, "In this world nothing is certain but death and taxes."[3] In addition to these two certainties, I would add a few others. Life will bring you moments of sublime happiness juxtaposed against moments of discouragement, moments of faith and moments of fear, and moments of success and moments of failure. There is opposition in all parts of our life. Lehi reminds us that we are intended to experience joy, but in order to gain that experience, we also meet with doubt, sorrow, and even despair (see 2 Nephi 2:11).

This chapter addresses two causes of the sorrow we experience in life: first, the sorrow that comes with sin, and second, the sorrow that comes with life in general. Some of the trouble we encounter is self-imposed and some is not. But regardless of how we encounter it, how we respond to it, ultimately, will define us. Thankfully, and unlike the unfortunate bricklayer, we won't have to face either of these challenges alone. We have the help of the Master available to us at any time. The following story illustrates how the Master can help us reach our true potential.

> Wishing to encourage her young son's progress at the piano, a mother bought tickets to a piano recital given by the famed Paderewski. They arrived in time to claim their seats in the second row. The young boy stared in wide-eyed wonder at the majestic concert grand piano on the stage. The Mom began talking to a nearby friend and failed to notice her son slipping away and heading for the piano on stage. The house lights began to dim . . . the spotlights hit the piano only to find the little boy at the piano bench, innocently picking out Twinkle, Twinkle Little Star. Before the woman could have presence of mind to retrieve her son, the famous Paderewski appeared on stage and quickly moved to the keyboard. "Don't quit! Keep playing," he whispered to the boy. Leaning over, he reached down with his left hand and began filling in a marvelous lower keyboard accompaniment. With his right hand, he reached around the other side, encircling the child, and added a running obligato. Together, the old master and the young novice mesmerized the crowd.[4]

This little vignette represents my core belief about the Master. As we turn to Him, we will feel ourselves encircled about in the arms of His love. Our efforts, insufficient as they may seem, will be enlarged and expanded. Magnified through Him, if we will "keep playing," our works can become masterpieces. President Ezra Taft Benson declared:

> Men and women who turn their lives over to God will find out that he can make a lot more out of their lives than they can. He will deepen their joys, expand their vision, quicken their minds, strengthen their muscles, lift their spirits, multiply their blessings, increase their opportunities, comfort their souls, raise up friends, and pour out peace. Whoever will lose his life to God will find he has eternal life.[5]

Such is the divine power of Jesus Christ to save our souls. I hope you can begin to more fully understand His great love for you and His desire for you to find peace, joy, and happiness in this life as you travel back to him. He stands ready to perform miracles in your life if you will let Him. Like Enos, I question in humble yet profound awe, "Lord, how is it done?" (Enos 1:7).

Consider the story of Moses as a metaphor for life. Certainly Moses encountered huge obstacles as he led the children of Israel out of Egypt and into the desert. In Exodus we read there were "about six hundred thousand on foot that were men, beside children." In addition, "a mixed multitude went up also with them; and flocks, and herds, even very much cattle" (Exodus 12:37–38).

Imagine the logistics of such an endeavor! First, they all had to be fed. According to the United States Army Quartermaster General, Moses had to have some fifteen hundred tons of food each day. This would have required two freight trains, each one mile long. In addition, they would have needed four thousand tons of firewood each day just to cook their food. And remember they were in the desert for forty years!

What about the problem of water? If they only used enough to drink and wash a few dishes, it would have required eleven million gallons each day, enough to fill a freight train with tank cars some eighteen hundred miles long.

And how about crossing the Red Sea with the vast numbers of all the children of Israel? If they had crossed over a narrow path, double-file, the line would have been eight hundred miles long and would require thirty-five days and nights to get through. Since the armies of Pharaoh would not allow thirty-five days and nights, there had to have been a space approximately three miles wide in order to cross, and they would have had to walk five thousand people abreast.

When they stopped for camp each night, a campground two-thirds the size of Rhode Island would have been required, or a total of 750 square miles. This much space just for nightly camping! Do you think Moses had this all figured out before he left Egypt? Of course not. But Moses had faith in God, and knew that in Him, all things were possible. And if God can do that for him for forty years, imagine what he can and will do for us as we turn to Him.[6]

THE PROCESS OF PERFECTION

Regarding sin, Satan would have us believe that we sin because we are fundamentally bad. Nonsense! Remember Paul's statement, *"All* have sinned and come short of the glory of God" (Romans 3:23, emphasis added). This does not excuse sin, but we must understand that our Father knew we would struggle in mortality, and that we would fall and scrape our spiritual knees from time to time.

The Lord said, "I the Lord cannot look upon sin with the least degree of allowance" (D&C 1:31). Alma taught, "No unclean thing can inherit the kingdom of God" (Alma 40:26). And we have twice received this forceful injunction: "Be ye therefore perfect, even as your Father which is in heaven is perfect" (Matthew 5:48; see also 3 Nephi 12:48). These statements, however, were not admonitions given to perfect people. They were given to mortal sinners—imperfect people—who, like us, made mistakes every day. Nevertheless, perfection through Christ is possible; in fact, it is imperative. While we are not commanded to live a sinless life, we are commanded to have faith unto repentance (see Alma 34:17) and to become "perfected in him" (Moroni 10:32), and He has provided a way for us to bring the power of the Atonement into our lives. This process requires all we have, for "it is by grace that we are saved *after all we can do*" (2 Nephi 25:23, emphasis added).

C. S. Lewis discussed the process of perfection in *Mere Christianity*. He suggests we count the costs associated with this process:

> Make no mistake," [the Lord] says, "if you let Me, I will make you perfect. The moment you put yourself in My hands, that is what you are in for. Nothing less, or other, than that. You have free will, and if you choose, you can push Me away. But if you do not push Me away, understand that I am going to see this job through. Whatever suffering it may cost you in your earthly life, whatever inconceivable purification it may cost you after death, whatever it costs Me, I will never rest, nor let you rest, until you are literally perfect—until my Father can say without reservation that He is well pleased with you, as He said He was well pleased with Me. This I can do and will do. But I will not do anything less.[7]

Nephi called this perfection process "[pressing] forward with a steadfastness in Christ" (2 Nephi 31:20). Indeed, that is exactly what we must do—press forward despite the obstacles, insecurities, pain, and discouragement we may encounter. In other words, if we allow Christ to be our beacon, exemplar, and Savior—through thick and thin—we will have eternal life.

Have Hope for Repentance

In his book, *Believing Christ*, author Stephen L. Robinson eloquently makes the distinction between simply believing in Christ and truly believing Him when He says we will be forgiven of our sins if we repent. You may feel you simply don't warrant forgiveness because your transgressions are too serious, or perhaps you simply make too many mistakes no matter how hard you try. The nature of the sins might not be that serious, but mistakes—several every day—keep occurring. It is simply too hard to be perfect. If you feel this way, welcome to the club.

A belief in Jesus Christ as our Savior and Redeemer requires that we believe Him when He says, "though your sins be as scarlet, they shall be as white as snow; though they be red like crimson, they shall be as wool" (Isaiah 1:18). Joseph Smith taught that there are only two sins that cannot be forgiven in this life: denying the Holy Ghost—in other words, coming out in open rebellion against the Lord and the plan of salvation despite having received a perfect knowledge of its truthfulness—and murder.[8] Since it is most unlikely that you have committed either of these sins, you need to have the understanding that there is nothing you have done, serious as it might be, for which you cannot receive a full forgiveness.

Consider the following scriptures. Next to each reference I have provided a synopsis of the message. Each of these should provide a perspective on how the Lord views the sins of those who repent. As you engage in your repentance process, I suggest a thorough study of each of these.

Scripture	Summary
Ezekiel 18:20–28, 31–32	The righteous shall live and transgressions shall not be mentioned.
Jeremiah 31:34	The Lord will not remember our sins when we repent.
D&C 58:42	When we confess, forsake and repent of our sins, the Lord remembers them no more.
Alma 36:3	Trust in God and you will be lifted up at the last day.

My point with these scriptures is this: When we violate the law, we suffer the consequence of our actions and we will fall short of exaltation if we fail to repent. But when we sincerely repent, all the wrongs we have done are washed away. One young woman from Hong Kong wrote:

"When I decided to be active in the Church after two years of inactivity, I knew I had a lot of repenting to do, and I feared Heavenly Father would not forgive me. I was wrong. He let me feel His love and strengthened me by his mercy. I knew I could live a better life if I was willing to change. He let me see miracles and feel His love along the way."

Our immortality and eternal life are the Lord's work and glory. His Atonement is infinite and eternal, but it is also personal. He knows us and loves us. I have experienced His boundless and all-consuming love and forgiveness. And I have experienced the peace that comes when I turn my sins and my sorrows over to Him. I envision his loving arms stretched out in anticipation of my embrace, as he calls to me, "Come unto me all ye that labour and are heavy laden, and I will give you rest" (Matt 11:28), and as he says to me and my family, "You are my friends" (D&C 93:45). Through his suffering, his love, and his sacrifice for us, we find peace, happiness, and expansion. Remember, "he was wounded for our transgressions, he was bruised for our iniquities; the chastisement of our peace was upon him; and with his stripes we are healed" (Isaiah 53:5; see also Mosiah 14:5).

I received a letter from a friend containing a story of his neighbor who was serving two back-to-back, twenty-year sentences for some serious sexual crimes. This man went to prison claiming his innocence, shouting with a loud voice for all who could hear that he had been misjudged. My friend obtained visitation rights, and several years later, in a heavily guarded room with myriad steel doors that clanged shut as he entered the room, the neighbor said to my friend:

"I need to beg for your forgiveness. You need to know that I did those things I was accused of and more. I am tired of lying. I am tired of the weight of my sin. I want to be free of it. No matter what I have to go through, I want to be free of the weight and darkness that comes with my sin. Will you forgive me?"

My friend wrote the following in his letter to me:

> About two weeks ago, I got word that my neighbor was up for his second parole hearing and that he would like me to attend it to support him. I agreed, and I soon found myself sitting in a courtroom at the State Prison with a parole judge sitting in front of us at a very elegant hard-wood podium, my neighbor seated in front of her, maybe twenty feet away, and those that were there to support my friend maybe twenty feet beyond that. My neighbor was dressed in "prison-white," with "Utah State Prison" stamped in large letters across his back.
>
> There were several people from his family, our neighborhood, and our ward there, including the man's wife, our bishop, cousins, uncles, aunts, and his step-father and mother. In all, there were over fifty people in attendance to provide their support.

I looked around the room and knew that each of these people had been contacted in as personal a way as possible, and my neighbor pleaded with each of them for forgiveness.

I saw my friend transform over the years from a wicked man, full of deception and vice, to a man that could look anyone in the eyes and tell them that he had felt the cleansing power of the Savior take his sins away. He said that the fact that his sins had been forgiven did not mean that he was then exempt from serving his debt to society, but you could see the inner peace that was about him. The struggle was over. All that was left was doing the time.

In the end, the parole judge indicated that my neighbor would need to spend a few more years in prison to pay as much as could be paid for his crimes. My friend nodded and understood. The judge did say that she would recommend parole in a few years, and my neighbor seemed pleased with that.

My neighbor learned that salvation is not to be an angel flitting about the clouds with golden wings and walking streets of alabaster on the way to some heavenly mansion. No, salvation is that peace of mind and heart that comes in only one way. It is the loosing of the "ball and chain" of sin through Jesus Christ's sacrifice for our individual mistakes. It is peace of mind and heart in knowing that the only One who counts has paid for and forgotten our sins. That's what salvation from sin is. My friend is still "doing the time" at the State Prison, but he is doing what it takes to have his sins blotted out, to be remembered no more.

Again, repentance is possible for all. Alma the Younger's example reminds us that even the vilest of sinners have hope for lasting change (see Mosiah 28:4). Amulek makes this point crystal clear: "*If* ye will repent and harden not your hearts, *immediately* shall the great plan of redemption be brought about unto you" (Alma 34:31, emphasis added).

In his book, *The Power Principle*, Blaine Lee writes of a woman who didn't have much money to spend on personal indulgences, yet, more than anything else, she dreamed of taking a Caribbean cruise. So she pinched her pennies and sacrificed on indulgences for two years. Finally, she saved sufficient money for her long-anticipated trip. She selected a Caribbean cruise that circled the islands, but didn't go into port, so all her time would be spent at sea. After her extensive preparation, the day finally arrived, and upon embarking, the woman made her way to her cabin and unpacked her belongings. She noticed, however, that many of the passengers were dressed for dinner and making their way to the upper deck.

Embarrassed by her modest wardrobe, she returned to her cabin and made a meal of some crackers and canned meat she had brought along. She repeated this ritual every evening, until the last night on the ship, when she decided she would venture above and treat herself to a gourmet dinner.

Over the course of the night, she thoroughly enjoyed herself. She ordered from the menu, sampled the sumptuous buffet lines, and watched some of the other passengers revel on the dance floor. "So this is what they've been doing up here all week," she mused. "This is what I have been missing . . ."

When she was ready to return to her cabin for the evening, the woman waited for the steward to bring her check. He never came, so she signaled across the room to him. When he arrived, she said, I'm ready for my check." He chuckled uncomfortably. "What are you talking about?" he questioned. "My bill for the meal. I know I have not been up here before, but I'm prepared to pay." The steward couldn't believe what he was hearing. "Of course you are joking, ma'am. All your meals were included with this trip. They're already paid for."[9]

Like this woman, there is so much in our lives for which a price has already been paid. But in order to take advantage of this gift we must turn to Christ. Jacob reminds us that the Atonement satisfies the demands of justice if we sincerely bring its power into our lives. But if we neglect to do this and waste the "days of [our] probation . . . awful is [our] state" (2 Nephi 9:27). We must be willing to make the Church and all it offers a part of our lives. Elder Joseph B. Wirthlin councils:

We have all made mistakes. The question is not whether we will trip and fall but, rather, how will we respond? Some, after making mistakes, stray from the fold. This is unfortunate. Do you not know that the Church is a place for imperfect people to gather together—even with all their mortal frailties—and become better? Every Sunday in every meetinghouse throughout the world, we find mortal, imperfect men, women, and children who meet together in brotherhood and charity, striving to become better people, to learn of the Spirit, and to lend encouragement and support to others. I am not aware of any sign on the door of our meetinghouses that reads "Restricted Entrance—Perfect People Only."

Because of our imperfections, we need the Lord's Church. It is there that His redemptive doctrines are taught and His saving ordinances are administered. The Church encourages and motivates us to be a better and happier people. It is also a place where we can lose ourselves in the service of others.

The Lord knows we will make mistakes. That is why He suffered for our sins. He wants us to get back on our feet and strive to do better. There is joy in the presence of the angels of God over one sinner who repents.[10]

FEEL REMORSE FOR SIN

If you find yourself in the category of those who are experiencing the sorrow brought on through sin, understand that those feelings are part of the healing process. As a bishop, I found it interesting when people would come to me to discuss serious transgressions with a flippant attitude. This was not common, but when it did occur, I knew the person did not fully understand what it meant to bring about the power of the Atonement in their lives.

Remorse for wayward actions is part of the repentance process. We should feel godly sorrow, acknowledging that with every sin we commit, we cause our Savior to suffer. That should bring us significant reflection, and hopefully provide the impetus to never repeat the offense.

But feeling remorse does not mean dwelling on the sin. We must also keep foremost in our mind the Lord's promises that when we repent, He will remember our sins no more (D&C 64:7). It is literally as if they never occurred. Unduly dwelling on past mistakes prevents us from moving forward. As the apostle Paul wrote: "This one thing I do, forgetting those things which are behind, and reaching forth unto those things which are before" (Philippians 3:13). Just as Paul did, we must move forward.

Kenneth L. Higbee writes:

> The Lord does not require us to grovel in remorse as part of repentance. Excessive remorse can lead to a morbid sense of guilt and inferiority and that can lead to a loss of self-respect and can drain a person of the moral energy necessary to complete the remaining steps of repentance.
>
> Repentance involves turning back to living God's commandments as well as feeling remorse for having broken His commandments. Let us not dwell on the latter at the expense of the former. Repentance should actually be a joyful act rather than a mournful one. After calling the people to repentance, Mosiah said, "And behold, I say unto you

that if ye do this ye shall always rejoice, and be filled with the love of God, and always retain a remission of your sins" (Mosiah 4:12). The Lord indicated that there is joy in Heaven every time a sinner repents (Luke 15:7).

After we have repented, the sin should not cause the same remorse it caused before repentance. The Lord said that "every man must repent or suffer" (D&C 19:4). Notice that he did not say repent and suffer.

Unfortunately, although the Lord promised us that He would remember our sins no more after repentance, He did not promise us that we would remember them no more. Many people continue to remember them in remorse, tormenting themselves needlessly, going through the mental anguish they would need to go through if they had not repented. Although the Lord has promised to forgive us when we repent, many people cannot forgive themselves.

As with other failures, once we have repented of a sin, we should not dwell on it. The comparison has been made between a sin and a wound. Suppose that after a wound has been bandaged, we were to repeatedly take off the bandage to examine the wound, each time tearing it open again. Would this not be foolish? Yet this is what we sometimes do with our sins. How much better it would be to put the bandage on the wound and forget it until it heals. Likewise, once we have repented of a sin, let us follow Paul's advice: forget it and look to the future. No matter what our past is like, our future is spotless.[11]

HOW DO I DO IT?

A four-year-old boy was putting together a puzzle of the face of Jesus near Christmastime, when his mother asked, "Do you know who that is?"

He answered, "Yes, it's Jesus." He then asked, "Mom, what happened to Jesus?" His mother told him that some wicked men didn't understand His mission on earth and arranged for Him to be killed. The boy quickly responded, "Does Dad know about this?!" His mother assured him that his dad knew about it and the boy returned to his puzzle.

Several hours later as his father came through the door, the boy ran up to him and said, "Dad, some mean men killed Jesus—what are we going to do about it?!"[12]

I think the boy's question is very appropriate for each of us. Jesus lived, endured, suffered, sacrificed, and died for our eternal happiness. He has provided prophets and leaders to guide and direct us, to give council, and constrain us at times so that we might be eternally happy. The key question for us is: What are we going to do about it? Will we repent?

Megan, 24, wrote to me about the process of repentance:

> I have learned that overcoming sin is not always a quick and easy thing for someone to do. Sometimes overcoming sin is something we have to work hard at, really hard sometimes. It takes a lot of patience both on the part of the people who are trying to help us and with ourselves. We also need people to assist us and be there for us when we are tempted to sin again. It is so important to be accountable to someone. This can really help us as we try to overcome sin.

As you begin this process, consider the following council from the scriptures. As before, I have provided the reference along with a short summary. Take time to read these verses and ponder their meaning in your own situation, including the power of remorse, fasting, abandonment of the sin, obedience to all God's commandments, and obtaining a new heart.

Scripture	Summary
2 Corinthians 7:10	Godly sorrow leads to repentance.
3 Nephi 9:20	God knows all things.
Alma 36:12–22	Sin brings extreme pain, but repentance extreme joy.
Isaiah 58:6	Fasting and service are part the process of relieving burdens.
D&C 58:43	One will confess and forsake his sins when he repents.
D&C 1:32	The Lord will forgive us when we repent.
Alma 5:7, 14	The Atonement will change men's hearts. Has your heart been changed?
1 Samuel 16:7	The Lord sees and knows our heart.

If you are working to overcome a sin that requires the assistance of your priesthood leader, do as President Monson counseled and make a friend of your bishop. President Monson said, "He has been called of God by prophecy and the laying on of hands by those who are in authority. He is entitled to heavenly help in providing you with counsel and guidance."[13]

In the previous chapter, I mentioned one particular challenge that is far too prevalent with young adults, namely the pernicious evil of pornography. Justifiably, we hear a lot about it. This is an area of grave concern, an area where Satan has a well-established foothold. But as serious, destructive, and addictive as it is, it can be overcome. There is tremendous, even transcendent power in the Atonement.

Elder L. Whitney Clayton offers this council:

> If you are already caught in the pornography trap, now is the time to free yourself with the help of the Savior. There is a way out, but you will need His help to escape. Your complete recovery will depend upon your complete repentance. Go to your bishop immediately. Seek his inspired guidance. He will help you put in place a plan of repentance that will restore your self-esteem and bring the Spirit back into your life. The healing power of the Atonement of the Lord Jesus Christ reaches all afflictions, even this one. If you will turn to the Savior with all of your heart and follow the counsel of your bishop, you will find the healing you need. The Savior will help you find the strength to resist temptation and the power to overcome addiction.[14]

For the last several years, I have gone on an annual trip with a group of close friends. The trip generally revolves around an away game of our favorite college football team. We have visited some of college football's most hallowed venues, including Notre Dame, Alabama, Washington, and had adventures in several other locations around the United States, including Phoenix, Seattle, San Diego, San Francisco, Colorado Springs, Las Vegas, Reno, and Albuquerque. While the trip's stated purpose is to attend the football game, we always schedule in as many extreme activities as we can. We call our group, "BEAMS," which stands for "Brotherhood of Excessive Animalistic Marrow-suckers." Sounds disgusting, I know, but it is really an excuse for us to eat without counting calories, watch lots of movies, share key insights for the year, play tons of golf, and participate in other athletic activities that our normal good judgment would prevent. Historically, we have challenged a local elders quorum to a flag football game, but our advancing age and too many injuries have changed that part of our itinerary. Still, our win-loss record in this game is pretty impressive!

Throughout the years we have done some pretty fun things, including repelling, flying light-weight airplanes, riding ridiculous roller coasters, attending ESPN Race School, playing full-contact golf, and massacring each other in paintball.

One year we rented Harley Davidson motorcycles and rode for several hours on California's Highway 1, the Pacific Coast Highway (PCH). This breathtaking, scenic road parallels the coast and is a route everyone should drive in their lifetime.

I admit to some trepidation as I drove out of the parking lot of the bike rental shop. While I have had a motorcycle license since I was sixteen, I had not ridden a motorcycle since I was sixteen, and here I was riding a hog with 1450cc's of raw power. I pulled out of the parking lot, made two turns, and immediately found myself on Highway 101 heading for the Golden Gate Bridge. It was an adrenaline-filled experience, with cars flying past me at seventy and eighty miles per hour. Just across the Golden Gate Bridge, we made our way through a San Francisco neighborhood, and then turned onto the PCH. What a wonderful and relaxing ride!

After a quick food stop at a hamburger shack near Half Moon Bay, I attempted to turn back onto the street and suddenly found myself lying on the road with a smashed up motorcycle on top of me. I am still not sure what happened, except that I wasn't paying attention, did something stupid, and ended up having to pay a large sum of money to fix the problem I had caused. Thankfully I was wearing a helmet and my bike was technically still operable—barely. Not wanting to spoil the trip for my friends, I continued on the ride for several more hours, but my earlier confidence had now turned to overt caution. I was no longer interested in the beautiful scenery, only concerned with avoiding another accident and simply staying alive. Ultimately, my foolish lack of attention sucked the fun out of an otherwise incredible experience.

Finally, our group headed back to the bike shop. At one point on our return ride we were approaching a sharp left-hand bend in the road. On the right-hand side of the road was a sheer rock wall. Because of the angle of the turn, the rock wall loomed straight ahead of us. To the left of the road was a steep cliff with a drop-off of a few of hundred feet. It was dusk, and after my earlier experience, I was worried about any kind of wrong turn. I remember thinking over and over, "Don't hit the rock wall, don't hit the rock wall." I became fixated on the barrier in front of me, and that focus was leading me right for it. Just at the last moment, I allowed my gaze to extend beyond the immediate and very large obstacle in front of me to the road ahead, and as I did that, an interesting thing happened—the bike went exactly where I was looking.

Sometimes our struggles to overcome sin are like that, particularly the battle with pornography. We have made a mistake, and it consumes us. We make the determined decision not to ever do it again, and we tell ourselves, "I'm not going to do it, I'm not going to do it," and we obsess about it. This fixation can actually lead us back to the very thing we are trying to avoid. Just as lifting my eyes beyond the rock wall allowed me to maneuver my bike safely, your vision of something better in your life will help you avoid unnecessary focus on the mistake. Part of the repentance process is turning your gaze upward, forsaking the sin, and moving to something better. For those of you who don't believe you can eliminate a particular activity from your life, remember that "all things are possible to him that believeth" (Mark 9:23). But you have to believe in him, and have a vision for what is possible.

Elder David A. Bednar teaches:

> The gospel of Jesus Christ encompasses much more than avoiding, overcoming, and being cleansed from sin and the bad influences in our lives; it also essentially entails doing good, being good, and becoming better. Repenting of our sins and seeking forgiveness are spiritually necessary, and we must always do so. But remission of sin is not the only or even the ultimate purpose of the gospel. To have our hearts changed by the Holy Spirit such that "we have no more disposition to do evil, but to do good continually" (Mosiah 5:2), as did King Benjamin's people, is the covenant responsibility we have accepted. This mighty change is not simply the result of working harder or developing greater individual discipline. Rather, it is the consequence of a fundamental change in our desires, our motives, and our natures made possible through the Atonement of Christ the Lord. Our spiritual purpose is to overcome both sin and the desire to sin, both the taint and the tyranny of sin.[15]

Why do we sin? We all share the universal dilemma of trying to become spiritual men or women in the context of the natural world (see Mosiah 3:19). We are physical, mental, emotional, social, and spiritual beings. Sometimes unmet needs in one area of our lives will lead us to transgress in other areas. For example, if you are lacking sleep or making it by on Twinkies and cupcakes for dinner, it may have an influence on your spiritual strength. If you make the determination to exercise four times per week, but constantly violate that commitment to yourself, it may influence your strength and resolve as you strive to live close to the Spirit. Finding a way to fill the unmet needs in each dimension of life can help you lift your sights from the immediate problem and gain a perspective on and appreciation for a better way.

We all have many things we need to accomplish. We live in a world of deadlines, a world that values and requires accomplishment, and we often neglect the very thing that will help propel our success—ourselves. Do you ever just take time to renew yourself? Do you take time for thoughtful introspection, to build relationships with the important people in your life, to improve your physical health, or to improve your relationship with your Heavenly Father beyond your standard routine? Think about the following suggestions for developing balance in each of the areas listed above in your own life:

- **Physical.** Maintain proper diet and exercise. Drink a lot of water, and get sufficient sleep (7–8 hours). Don't oversleep.
- **Mental.** Learn something new every day. Don't stagnate. Ponder and wonder. Read a good book, and have stimulating discussion. Emerson, when he met a friend, asked, "What has become clear to you since we last met?" Practice that policy.
- **Social and emotional.** Give love and receive love, reach out to others, and realize that you are not perfect. Be able to identify and articulate your emotions. Repressed emotions can be manifest in many different ways, including physically, mentally, and spiritually. Spend regular time with family and friends.
- **Spiritual.** Have a hunger for Christ. Get away from mechanical scripture reading and rote prayer and pray and study with intent and faith.

John Wanamaker said, "People who cannot find time for recreation are obliged sooner or later to find time for illness."[16] This is not just about relaxation. It is about renewal, and about refilling our physical, mental, emotional, and spiritual reserves, so that our capacity to contribute grows.

B. C. Forbes offers this insight:

"The true purpose of recreation should not be merely to amuse, not merely to afford pleasure, not merely to 'kill time,' but to increase fitness, enhance our usefulness, spur achievement. Any form of recreation that impairs either our physical or mental efficiency does not recreate. Real recreation inspires aspiration."[17]

It might be helpful to make four assumptions as you develop your saw-sharpening plan: (1) Assume you have just had triple bypass surgery. What changes in lifestyle are appropriate? Live accordingly. (2) Assume that the half-life of your knowledge is two years, requiring you to constantly upgrade your understanding. Live accordingly. (3) Assume that everything you say about another can be overheard by that person. Live accordingly. (4) Assume you are going to have a personal interview with the Lord once each month. Live accordingly.[18] Here are a few ideas to consider as you make your own plans for personal renewal.

Physical. "Whenever I feel like exercising, I lie down until the feeling goes away." Have you ever responded that way? Or maybe a more appropriate question, have you ever not responded that way? Why do we take time out of our lives to generate the pain that comes with exercise? We sweat and stretch and exhaust ourselves. So what's the point? We know, of course, that physical exercise, and all the pain that comes with it, actually makes us feel better. But the benefits go far beyond our physical health. Being in shape positively impacts our mental and emotional health as well. Even a *little* work in this area will make a remarkable difference in your life. Consider making some specific fitness goals that include aerobic and resistance training, adequate rest, and proper hydration.

A few years ago I set a goal to successfully complete a marathon. I wasn't too concerned with my ultimate time—I just wanted to make it through alive. To do this would require about a year's worth of effort as I knew I couldn't fake being in shape. I had to alter my diet and put in the miles every week. It forced me to make some changes in my life. I enlisted the help of my angel sister and another friend to train with me and become my support structure. The experience was incredible. The impact for me personally went far beyond simply being in shape. It sharpened my mental acuity and helped me connect socially and emotionally with my sister and friend. I even felt spiritual growth, as I took the opportunity to ponder important things while running hour after hour.

Write down one specific thing you will begin doing now to improve your life in the physical dimension: _____

_____

Mental. Mark Twain once said, "The man who does not read good books has no advantage over the man who can't read them." If you are out of this habit, take time to rediscover the joy of reading a really good book. Develop a lifelong love for learning and challenge yourself to learn new things and to study beyond your particular field. Develop the habit of reading the newspaper and other periodicals. Write letters to others and write in your journal. Often the process of writing, though difficult, clarifies and codifies your thinking on a particular subject. Participate in music, either by playing, composing, or listening. Study math or grammar, learn a new language, or research history.

Write down one specific thing you will begin doing now to renew your life in the mental dimension: _____

Social. Many people have regular physical and mental exercise programs. Having a consistent process for developing your social and emotional dimension is equally important. Remember, relationship-building generally won't happen unless you plan for it, and if you ignore the key relationships in your life, they tend to atrophy. Make a plan to work on your relationships. Consider a goal of connecting with a least one person each week through some act of kindness. Perhaps it is a small gesture, or gift with a note or letter, telling him you are thinking of him. In our world of email, text-messaging, and other forms of instant communication, we seem to have lost the art of the personal note or letter.

Write down one specific thing you will begin doing now to renew your life in the social dimension: _____

Spiritual. We spend a lot of time talking and thinking about sharpening our "spiritual saws" in the Church. Much of this book is dedicated to that objective. So how do you do it? The "Sunday School" answers apply here. You know the basic blocking and tackling for developing spiritual growth. You know that the single most important determinant of a person staying active in the Church from his youth into adulthood is the personal religious experiences he has. These experiences are gifts that come as we work to earn them. We have discussed the power of daily prayer, fasting, service, and scripture study. As you make your plan in this area, you might also consider other things that bring a sense of meaning to your life, including time spent in nature, the gathering and pondering of great quotes, listening to inspirational music, and reading biographies of great people.

Write down one specific thing that you will begin doing now to renew your life spiritually. _____

Remember this admonition from Charles Steizle: "If you sit still long enough, you'll never get up again. If you never lift your arm, you'll soon be unable to raise it at all. If you remain in darkness and never use your eyes, you'll soon become blind. It is the law in the mental world, if you never exercise your brain—never read, study, or talk to anyone, never permit anyone to talk with you, your mind will become blank . . . the body and mind and spirit are kept alive through constant constructive use."[19]

As you engage in the repentance process, consider utilizing the following worksheet, entitled "Personal Scorecard." If you are working with your bishop in connection with this process, you may want to share this scorecard with him as a part of your accountability.

The first step in the scorecard process is to identify some specific goals representing things you would like to do or feel. Pick a point three to six months in the future, and ask yourself, "In the best possible world, what would I like to have accomplished in this time frame? And how do I want to feel?" Write the answers to these questions under the "Goals—Start" section. Don't overdo it. Identifying too many goals is no more effective than having no goals. Examples of these goals could include "Return to the temple," or "Feel connected to my Heavenly Father." Stick to three or four.

Now identify some specific actions in your life that do not support your new goals—behavior that you want to eliminate from your life. Identify a few goals representing these activities and write them in the space labeled, "Goals—Stop."

Once you have clearly established goals in both sections, take each goal and ask yourself, "If I want to accomplish this goal, what is the one behavior that I must begin doing today that will have the greatest impact on my success?" Write that behavior next to the goal in the "Actions" section.

You should have at least one action for each goal, though some goals might share an action. Examples for actions may include, "Daily scripture study for 30 minutes;" "Daily personal prayer, on my knees, and out loud;" "Remove Internet connection from the bedroom;" and so forth.

You will see check boxes that will help you account to yourself and others on these activities. Under the "Support" section, state specifically to whom you will be accountable. You might identify a bishop, stake president, roommate, friend, or family member. I suggest holding a weekly accountability meeting with your chosen support person.

Personal Scorecard

Goals—Start	Actions	S	M	T	W	T	F	S	Support
Goals—Stop									

What Are the Results of Repentance?

The following scriptures summarize the outcomes of the repentance process. These outcomes include a remission of your sins, confidence in your relationship with God, increased guidance from your Heavenly Father, the companionship of the Holy Ghost, and peace of conscience. Think of Alma's experience, who, by his own admission, was the vilest of sinners, yet went on to become a powerful missionary, leader, and prophet. He describes this transformation, first as a sinful man: "Oh, thought I, that I could be banished and become extinct both soul and body, that I might not be brought to stand in the presence of God, to be judged of my deeds . . . for three days and for three nights was I racked, even with the pains of a damned soul" (Alma 36: 15–16). Then, upon the recollection of Jesus and the power of the Atonement, Alma expresses: "Oh, what joy, and what marvelous light I did behold; yea my soul was filled with joy as exceeding as was my pain! . . . There can be nothing so exquisite and sweet as was my joy" (Alma 36:20–21).

Scripture	Summary
Alma 12:34	The Lord will give us a remission of our sins and bring us into His rest.
D&C 84:61	The Lord will forgive us and expects us to remain steadfast, prayerful, and to bear testimony.
D&C 121:45–46	Our confidence with God will become strong, our understanding of doctrine will grow, the Holy Ghost will be our constant companion, and we shall have everlasting dominion.
Isaiah 58:9	When we call upon the Lord, He will answer.
Isaiah 58:11	The Lord will guide us continually, prosper us, and bless us in every way.
Mosiah 4:3	Repentance will fill us with joy and bring peace of conscience.

In the introduction to this book I shared the analogy of an airplane being off course by just one degree and the impact that has on its final destination. Here is one more analogy from Stephen R. Covey. As each flight takes off, a detailed flight plan is logged. Covey wrote:

> [The pilots] know exactly where they're going and start off in accordance with their plan. But during the flight, wind, rain, turbulence, air traffic, human error, and other factors act upon [the] plane. They move it slightly in different directions so that most of the time [the] plane is not even on the prescribed flight path! Throughout the entire trip, there are slight deviations from the flight plan. Weather systems or unusually heavy air traffic may even cause major deviations. But barring anything too major, the plane will arrive at its destination.[20]

So it is with our lives. We will all make mistakes every day that pull us off our individual flight plans. Repentance is available through the Atonement of Jesus Christ and is the process of course-correction. This will eventually bring us to our ultimate desired destination—eternal life. While browsing the newspaper, I came across an obituary that highlights the results of the repentance process. With permission from the family, I have provided a portion of it below.

SCOTT DOUGLAS MORGAN "OUR SCROOGE"

Scott Douglas Morgan passed away Oct. 6, 2007. He loved music and acting and performed in theatres throughout the valley for over 30 years. His favorite role was of Ebenezer Scrooge—a role that changed his life. After graduating from Granger High School and serving an LDS mission in Paris, France, Scott drifted from his standards. During this period, he struggled with addiction and also contracted HIV and AIDS, diseases which he survived for 21 years. In 1997, Scott was cast as the understudy for Scrooge in Hale Centre Theatre's "A Christmas Carol." During his first performance, Scott's life profoundly changed. "I will have Christmas in my heart and try to keep it all the year. I shall live in the past, the present and the future, the Spirits of all three shall strive within me and I will not shut out the lessons they teach." This was the beginning of an amazing transformation. Scott began a difficult repentance process during which he courted Tammy Eves, a long-time friend and fellow actor in HCT's "Fiddler on The Roof." On closing night of the show, Scott proposed to Tammy in front of a sold-out crowd. The two were married on stage Sept. 24, 1999, and were later sealed in the Salt Lake Temple on Aug. 30, 2002. Scott and Tammy shared the stage together for the last time in Dec. 2006. Scott served in several church callings, most recently on the high council of the Midvale North Stake. He had an incredible testimony of the Atonement and was never afraid to share it. One of Scott's mottos was "It's all about choice." He wanted everybody to have the hope that a child can change.[21]

DEALING WITH LIFE'S TRIALS

When we came to this earth, we knew there would be hard times. We knew we would wrestle with discouragement, feel the pressures of expectation and accomplishment, and be tempted by physical appetites. We also knew we would make mistakes. Job, who knew a little about trial, reminds us that despite the trials and challenges and pains and persecutions we knew we would face, we "shouted for joy" at the opportunity to come to earth, gain a body, and experience mortality (see Job 38:7).

I've noticed over the last few years a preponderance of books and pamphlets containing what are referred to as daily reflections, daily meditations, or daily prayers. These are intended to provide nuggets of wisdom, and while some are pure fluff, others are quite inspiring. Many of these are written for the general public, while others target certain groups, including men who love to golf, women who do too much, and of course, for those who want to be highly effective. A friend of mine gave me a copy of a wonderful little volume entitled, *Meditations for Miserable People.* I hope she gave it to me because she thought I would find it funny, and not because she thinks I am a miserable person. Either way, it contains its own brilliant nuggets of wisdom, including, "to bring harmony into my relationships with others I must first realize that their lives are much better than mine."[22] Clearly the author has either a very warped sense of humor or he lacks perspective and doubts his self-worth and divine nature.

Teaching about the Atonement, and specifically how we can become better disciples, King Benjamin said, "For the natural man is an enemy to God, and has been from the fall of Adam, and will be, forever and ever, unless he yields to the enticings of the Holy Spirit, and putteth off the natural man and becometh a saint through the Atonement of Christ the Lord, and becometh as a child, submissive, meek, humble, patient, full of love, willing to submit to all things which the Lord seeth fit to inflict upon him, even as a child doth submit to his father" (Mosiah 3:19).

A requirement for discipleship is found in the last part of this scripture: being "willing to submit to all things." The sorrow that comes with sin is avoidable, and the Atonement provides a way for each of us to overcome this sorrow. But what of the hardship and trial that just comes as part of life, even when one is living righteously? What happens when trials occur due to circumstances beyond our control? How does one come to terms with this? And what can one learn when this happens? C. S. Lewis taught:

> Imagine yourself as a living house. God comes in to rebuild that house. At first, perhaps, you can understand what He is doing. He is getting the drains right and stopping the leaks in the roof and so on: you knew that those jobs needed doing and so you are not surprised. But presently he starts knocking the house about in a way that hurts abominably and does not seem to make sense. What on earth is He up to? The explanation is that He is building quite a different house from the one you thought of—throwing out a new wing here, putting on an

extra floor there, running up towers, making courtyards. You thought you were going to be made into a decent little cottage: but He is building a palace. He intends to come and live in it Himself.[23]

One of my favorite stories of the Savior is the account of his feeding the five thousand and the events surrounding that miracle. Jesus had just learned of the terrible fate of John the Baptist, performed the great miracle of the loaves and the fishes, and sent the disciples into a boat and told them he would join them later. He then went off in solitude to pray. While the disciples were on board their ship, the winds gathered strength and "the ship was . . . tossed with waves" (Matthew 14:24). They battled the rough sea, rowing furiously into the wind for hours.

While there are multiple accounts of this, author Michael Wilcox points out a key distinction between Mark's version and the others:

> Mark relates that Jesus "saw them toiling in rowing" (Mark 6:48). They did not know that He was aware of their danger. They didn't realize He was up on the hill looking down watching them. They only knew that they had rowed a long time, the wind remaining contrary, that they were exhausted, and that they needed help.[24]

Finally help comes to the troubled disciples.

> About the fourth watch of the night he cometh unto them, walking upon the sea, . . . [and] they . . . saw him, and were troubled. And immediately he talked with them, and saith unto them, Be of good cheer: it is I; be not afraid. And he went up unto them into the ship; and the wind ceased (Mark 6:48-51).[25]

Now understand the context—the fourth watch comes between 3:00 AM and 6:00 AM Thus they had battled the storm most of the night. Again quoting Michael Wilcox:

> I have a feeling that the Apostles, if they could have chosen, would have had the Lord come in an earlier watch. I put it to you, as I frequently put it to myself—when I toil in rowing against the wind, when the sea rises and I'm frightened and when it's dark and the storm keeps blowing and I want help—I want Him to come in the first watch.
>
> When we advance into the second watch and he doesn't come, a certain cold fear often begins to spread through us as the wind's velocity does not diminish. As we move into the third watch we may be tempted to make some foolish assumptions that are very dangerous and foolish to make. "God is not listening to me." "He doesn't care."

Or, more dangerous yet, "He is not there." At times the universe can seem so very empty—all that dark space filled with cold stars. Or very common to Latter-day Saints, we assume, "I'm not worthy." "He's not listening." "He doesn't care." "No one is there to respond." Because if He were there and if He were listening or if I were worthy, He would certainly come.

When you feel somewhat desperate, when it seems like your prayers aren't answered and the winds still blow, take comfort in the knowledge the He is on the hillside watching. Remember, you might not know that He's watching as you struggle in the boat, but He is on the hillside watching and He will come.[26]

Imagine yourselves as Moses, the leader of hundreds of thousands of people, with all their attendant issues and challenges, their pleadings, hunger, whining, disputes, illnesses, frustrations, and everything else that comes with leading a group of people. After weathering (surviving) the plagues and the vicissitudes of the exodus from Egypt, and before that the separation from Pharaoh's court, the years in the desert, and after remarkable dedication, sacrifice, effort, and commitment, you find yourself with the armies of Pharaoh in hot pursuit and the panicked cries of your people in your ears.

There is something about trials and deliverance that is a necessary part of our mortal education. Perhaps, as Wallace Goddard writes:

> There is nothing quite so helpful for mortals as total desperation. As long as there is even a sliver of hope that our efforts might remove us from our dilemmas, we are likely to keep floundering along. But when we come up against impossibility, then we may discover the Power. It certainly was true for Moses. . . . Of course, faith is always much easier in retrospect; from our historical vantage point it seems obvious what Moses needed to do—especially if you have seen the Cecil B. de Mille version of the parting of the Red Sea.
>
> But when Moses came face to face with utter hopelessness, he did not have the benefit of "The Bible" in movie form. He knew he was hopelessly over his head. It is when our own efforts cannot possibly save us that we are most likely to turn wholeheartedly to God. If we have faith.
>
> How did Moses feel? Was he serene in the foreknowledge of God's plan? Was he spared some soul-searching pressure because of that knowledge? My suspicion is that he, like all of us, was required to lean on faith for support.

> "And Moses said unto the people, Fear ye not, stand still, and see
> the salvation of the Lord, which he will shew to you today . . . the Lord
> shall fight for you, and ye shall hold your peace" (Exodus 14:15–16).
> Based on decades of wilderness tutoring Moses knew that God would
> deliver them, but did he know just how God would do it? Did he
> wonder if an earthquake would swallow Pharaoh's army? Did he hope
> for lightening to frighten them? Or maybe heavenly chariots to chase
> off the armies of Pharaoh? Or did he already know that God would
> part the Red Sea?
>
> It seems that it was only AFTER Moses had exercised and
> announced his faith that the answer was revealed: "And the Lord said
> unto Moses, Wherefore criest thou unto me? Speak unto the children
> of Israel, that they go forward: But lift thou up thy rod, and stretch out
> thine hand over the sea, and divide it: and the children of Israel shall go
> on dry ground through the midst of the sea (Exodus 14:15–16).[27]

Another example: After his conversion through the efforts and courage of the prophet Abinadi, Alma fled wicked King Noah and his evil
priests. Abandoning a life of privilege and power to preach the good news
of Jesus, Alma and his people establish a community of believers dedicated to the Lord, watching over one another, and nourishing one another
"with things pertaining to righteousness." Soon the people of Alma "began
to prosper exceedingly in the land" (Mosiah 23:18–19). Because of their
obedience, they were blessed. *However, obedience to God's commandments
does not mean a life without trials.* Alma's story continues: "Nevertheless
the Lord seeth fit to chasten his people; yea, he trieth their patience and
their faith." And if we are true to the faith, the Lord promises: "Nevertheless—whosoever putteth his trust in him the same shall be lifted up at the
last day. Yea, and thus it was with this people" (Mosiah 23:21–22).

Alma and his people would eventually be placed into bondage, per-
secuted, and ultimately threatened by death if they were caught praying.
Yet, somehow, some way, their faith and patience endured. About their
trials the Lord whispered:

> I will . . . ease the burdens which are put upon your shoulders,
> that even you cannot feel them upon your backs, even while you are
> in bondage; and this will I do that ye may stand as witnesses for me
> hereafter, and that ye may know for a surety that I, the Lord God, do
> visit my people in their afflictions.
>
> And now it came to pass that the burdens which were laid upon
> Alma and his brethren were made light; yea, the Lord did strengthen

them that they could bear up their burdens with ease, and they did submit cheerfully and with patience to all the will of the Lord. (Mosiah 24:14–15)

I aspire to the perspective Alma and his people achieve in this story. Looking back in time, it appears so simple: all you have to do is keep the commandments, stay the course, and eventually all will be well. It sounds so easy. But in the heat of the battle, without total perspective, the harsh realities of life hit with the force of a locomotive. What seems so simple becomes far more complex.

Haley, 27, shared:

When I am faced with challenges that seem insurmountable, I try to look at the situation realistically and tell myself, "I'm sure somebody else has it worse than I do." But in the end what really gets me through is getting down on my knees and telling my Heavenly Father that I can't do this alone, that I need help. I cast my burden on Him and ask for counsel. This usually involved a few tears and a slice of humble pie. I realize my dependence on the Lord, then get up from my knees and get to work. Wallowing never solved anything. So after a half-gallon of ice cream, a few chick-flicks and a night of tears, the sun comes out and a new day dawns, with new challenges and new hopes.

Life is not designed to be without stumbling-blocks. The pathway to happiness is certain, but not always clear, and certainly not easy. Decisions, challenges, and frustrations loom ahead of all of us. In the opening line of his book, *The Road Less Traveled*, Scott Peck provides this blinding flash of the obvious: "Life is difficult."[28]

Alma and his people were eventually delivered, united with other believers, and had all their blessings restored. And they lived happily ever after, except that their trials—as well as their triumphs—were not over. A few years later Alma's own son and namesake left the Church with a focused and dedicated agenda devoted to destroying it before he ultimately returned to lead it. The point of this illustration is that while life is hard, and though we may have the sure knowledge that trials will rage, we also have the promise that God will never abandon us. Do the following quotes resemble your experience?

How do I deal with disappointment? In stride, after crying.

—Tracy, 24

Honestly, the only way for me to deal with personal disappointment

161

is to remember my inherent worth as a child of God, and to remember the promise that the Lord will not ever let us face a trial without giving us a way to overcome that trial. We cannot fail if we are coupled with the Savior, and His saving power.

—Robbie, 29

I just keep fighting and never give up.

—Jacob, 23

It is easy to be faithful when things are going well. We are tested at times to see if we will remain true to the faith even when things are difficult. Despite the difficulty, I try and remember that if I remain faithful, then rest and relief will come. Again it goes back to staying faithful in the little things. Stay true to the basics and you will see the hand of God in your life.

—Curtis, 27

Sometimes the lessons of adversity seem to have no logic whatsoever. In a stake conference address in the Southern California area, Sister Christie Frandsen shared this insight:

We like to think of the Gospel as being simple. We're accustomed to quoting fragments of scripture taken out of context—a phrase here, a verse there, words that say something appropriate to the subject at hand and tie things up in a neat little package. Someone said, and I believe it is sadly true, that for many of us the scriptures are nothing more than a great quote book! Of course, we have to do it that way: we simply don't have the time to talk about everything at once and explore contexts and how different principles relate to each other. Sometimes, though, I worry that our understanding of the Gospel and our relationship with the Lord is too simplistic and one dimensional. The gospel, the scriptures, and God's dealings with us are complex, deep, sometimes even contradictory and paradoxical. For example, listen to the following:

- "Men are that they might have joy" (2 Nephi 2:25).
- "Man is born unto trouble, as the sparks fly upward" (Job 5:7).
- "Happy is the man that findeth wisdom, and the man that getteth understanding" (Proverbs 3:13).
- "In much wisdom is much grief: and he that increaseth knowledge increaseth sorrow" (Ecclesiastes 1:18).
- "But if from thence thou shalt seek the Lord thy God, thou shalt find him, if thou seek him with all thy heart and with all thy soul. When thou art in tribulation, and all these things are come upon thee, . . . if thou turn to the Lord thy God, and shalt be obedient

to his voice; He will not forsake thee" (Deuteronomy 4:29–31).

- "My God, my God, why has thou forsaken me? Why art thou so far from helping me, and far from the words of my roaring cries? O my God, I cry in the daytime, but thou hearest not; and in the night season, but thou art silent" (Psalms 22:1–2).

These obvious contradictions can be pretty troubling to some people. If we live long enough, we find diverse views and contradictory fragments not only in scripture, but in life.[29]

Elder Bruce C. Hafen writes:

Someone once said you can't visually tell the difference between a strand of cobweb and a strand of powerful cable—until stress is put on the strand. Our testimonies are that way, and for most of us, the days of stress for our testimonies have already begun. It may not be the death of a loved one. We might not yet have been asked to give up something that is really precious to us by and by. Our current stress is more likely to come in the form of overpowering temptations, which show us that a shallow acceptance of the gospel does not have the power to cope with the full fury of the powers of darkness. Perhaps there is a mission call to a place of illness and disappointment, when we had planned on a mission to a place of unbounded opportunity. Or perhaps there are too many questions to which our limited knowledge simply has no answer, and those who claim to know more than we do taunt us with what appears to be a persuasive certainty.

When those times come, our testimonies must be more than cobweb strands of fair-weather faith. They need to be like strands of cable, powerful enough to resist the [fiery darts] of him who would destroy us. In our days of stress and trouble, we must be built "upon the rock of our Redeemer, who is Christ, the Son of God, . . . that when the devil shall send forth his mighty winds, yea, his shafts in the whirlwind, . . . and his mighty storm shall beat upon you, it shall have no power over you, . . . because of the rock upon which ye are built" (Helaman 5:12).[30]

We will not be asked to "run faster than [we have] strength" (Mosiah 4:27), but we will be asked to run, and we will be pushed to the limit in doing so. I take great comfort in Peter's example, when, as the disciples were on the Sea of Galilee one tempestuous evening, they witnessed Jesus walking on water toward their boat. Some of the disciples were fearful, and wondered aloud if they were witnessing a spirit. Peter, however, recognizing the Savior and fueled by his growing faith in the Lord, requested permission to join Jesus and walk on the water. His first effort was successful. But then the boisterous wind incited doubt and insecurity within Peter, and with fear overtaking him, he began to sink. He cried out, "Lord, save me." We should never forget Jesus' reaction, because it has application to each of us in our individual situations: "And *immediately* Jesus stretched forth his hand, and caught him" (Matthew 14:30–31, emphasis added).

Like Peter, we may find ourselves in positions where we are asked to do hard things, otherwise known as opportunities for personal growth and development. These experiences are part of the plan and will test our mettle, but we won't be left alone. And we won't be asked to endure that which is beyond our ability to endure.

One woman wrote me about her process for gaining perspective:

> When I focus on others' needs, mine don't seem so bad. We all have hard times when we feel we can't sink any lower. This is when we need to look for someone to serve. When Christ was suffering the most for us, He was serving us. He called out to forgive the soldiers and for John to take care of His mother. Christ was always thinking of others, even in the most agonizing, trying times of His mortal life. Service is a great suave for any aliment.

We may face impossible tasks. God knows what this mortality entails, and failure is allowed, but failure should teach us rather than defeat us. Our moral agency includes our response to failure as well as triumph. Many of God's children, in far-flung places and abject poverty, have limited choices. Only their response to their limitations defines them.

My wife's uncle Craig, with whom I was very close, was 52 years old and serving in the bishopric of his South Jordan, Utah ward. While presiding at a baptism in a chapel, and without any warning or symptoms, he collapsed on the stand and began to have massive seizures. Because of the shock of the seizures on his system, he stopped breathing. Thankfully, a trauma nurse was in the congregation, and she, along with other members of the ward, attended to him while someone called 911.

This man was in incredible physical condition. He had recently and very successfully competed in a national fitness program. When he arrived at the hospital, he was still having seizures, and because of their strength, the hospital had to induce paralysis in order to complete their tests. The test results were not promising. The initial CT scan showed a large mass in brain. An MRI showed more tragic detail: he had multiple tumors, one inoperable. The family agreed with the doctors that the best course of action was to have emergency brain surgery to remove as much of the cancer as possible, which would also allow a biopsy on the tissue to determine the severity of the tumors, as well as indicate the most advantageous intervention.

As with previous tests, the results from the biopsy brought the worst possible news. The tumor was graded as the most severe kind, fast growing and debilitating. The long-term prognosis was not good: possibly months, most likely weeks.

Of course we were all devastated. We loved Craig, and it was so difficult to imagine him being absent from our lives. Craig and I loved to talk about BYU football and basketball. He told me how excited he was for August 28, the day BYU kicked off the football season. Now, however, when we mentioned dates for the future, we were left wondering where he would be. I was troubled and perplexed as to why this had to happen. Craig played such a prominent role in our lives, and especially in the lives of his immediate family. His youngest son was leaving for the Carlsbad California Mission right at this time. He left with little assurance that his father would be there when he returned.

I had a most interesting conversation with Craig during this time. We had a family celebration with all the aunts, uncles, and cousins. Despite the aggregation of people, the squealing of children, the food preparation, and all the other stuff that always accompanies family reunions, I had a few quiet moments with him. He opened his heart to me as he shared what he had been feeling since his cancer was discovered. He said for several years he felt that the Lord had forgotten him. He cried as he told me he had never felt the experience of having the Savior's arms around him, and he had worried for years that his prayers were ineffective. He then wept as he shared how grateful he was for the experience of his cancer. He said he had never felt the Lord's love as he had in recent days and weeks, and literally felt "embraced in the arms of the Lord's love." Craig mentioned how grateful he was for his family and that he was able to share this experience with them and for the positive impact this had had on them. He expressed deep gratitude for the miracles he had witnessed with his family as a result of this experience, and though his tumors still remained, so much had happened—including direct answers to prayers—there was now no doubt that the Lord knew him, loved him, and was directing the affairs of his life.

I left our discussion with a deep reverence for Craig and his goodness, and a profound appreciation for his perspective. I couldn't help but think of Alma's penetrating testimony of the Savior, that "he shall go forth, suffering pains and afflictions and temptations of every kind; and this that the word might be fulfilled which saith he will take upon him the pains and the sicknesses of his people. And he will take upon him death, that he may loose the bands of death which bind his people; and he will take upon him their infirmities, that his bowels may be filled with mercy, according to the flesh, that he may know according to the flesh how to succor his people according to their infirmities" (Alma 7:11–12).

He knows the depths of our needs, the desires of our hearts, and the lessons we need to learn (see Mosiah 14), and He knows that each of us will at some moment face the urge to plead, "Remove this cup from me" (Luke 22:42). I hope you can maintain a sense of perspective and understanding when life presents challenges and burdens. Please understand that you are not alone. Be patient, but be persistent in all your efforts to bring the power of the Atonement in your life. As you do this and exercise faith, the Lord will never forsake you.

Notes

1. Jenkins Lloyd Jones, *Deseret News*, 12 June 1973, A4.

2. Jonathan Fietzer, "The Bricklayer: Trying to do the Job Alone," 29 December 2008, retrieved 3 January 2009, www.jonathanfietzer. net/2008/12/the-bricklayer-trying-to-do-the-job-alone/.

3. Quoted in "Benjamin Franklin," *Washington Times,* 20 Dec 2001, C10.

4. "Heaven's Peace: The Piano Master," Jan 2007, retrieved 15 July 2007, http://heavenspeace.com/pianomaster.php

5. Ezra Taft Benson, "Jesus Christ and Expectations," *New Era,* May 1975.

6. Quoted in Jerre Patzer, *The Road Ahead* (New York: Pacific Press, 2003), 98–99.

7. C.S. Lewis, *Mere Christianity* (New York: Harper Collins, 2001), 201.

8. Joseph Smith, *Teachings of the Prophet Joseph Smith* (Salt Lake City: Shadow Mountain, 1977), 358.

9. Blaine Lee, *The Power Principle* (New York: Simon and Schuster, 1998), 31.

10. Joseph B. Wirthlin, "Concern for the One," *Ensign*, May 2008.

11. Kenneth L. Higbee, "Forgetting Those Things Which are Left Behind," *Ensign,* Sept. 1972, 83.

12. Unpublished story by Ken Martin, Taylor, Arizona.

13. Thomas S. Monson, "Decisions Determine Destiny," BYU Devotional, 6 Nov. 2005.

14. L. Whitney Clayton, "Blessed Are All the Pure in Heart," *Ensign*, Nov. 2007, 51–53.

15. David A. Bednar, "Clean Hands and a Pure Heart," *Ensign*, Nov. 2007, 80–83.

16. Edward C. Goodman and Ted Goodman, *The Forbes Book of Business Quotations* (New York: Black Dog & Leventhal Publishers, 1997), 505.

17. Edward C. Goodman, Ted Goodman. *The Forbes Book of Business Quotations* (New York: Black Dog & Leventhal Publishers, 1997), 503.

18. Stephen R. Covey, *The 8th Habit* (New York: Simon and Schuster, 2004), 58.

19. Quoted in Spencer W. Kimball, *The Miracle of Forgiveness* (Salt Lake City: Bookcraft, 1969).

20. Stephen R. Covey, *The 7 Habits of Highly Effective Families* (New York: MacMillan, 1997), 9.

21. "Obituary: Scott Douglas Morgan," *Deseret News* 11 October 2007.

22. Dan Goodman, *Meditations for Miserable People* (New York: St. Martin's Press, 1995), 3.

23. C.S. Lewis, *The Complete Signature C.S. Lewis Classics* (New York: Harper Collins, 2002),108.

24. Michael Wilcox, *When Prayers Unanswered* (Salt Lake City: Deseret Book, 2006), 8.

25. Ibid., 9

26. Ibid., 9–10.

27. H. Wallace Goddard, "Marriage and the Parting of the Red Sea," *Meridian Magazine*.

28. Scott Peck, *The Road Less Traveled* (New York: Simon and Schuster, 2002), 15.

29. Christie Frandsen, shared in a talk given 11 June 1995 in the La Crescenta, La Crescenta, California.

30. Bruce C. Hafen, "If with All Your Hearts Ye Truly Seek Me," *Ensign*, Oct. 1984, 71.

7

ANXIOUS TO BE ENGAGED—IT'S *a* GOOD *Cause*

The Marriage Choice

There are few things in the world which give a man such courage as the faith of a noble companion.[1]

—Ezra Taft Benson

Let's talk about the process of getting married and the joys and blessings result. While serving as a bishop of a single adult ward, I could always predict the reactions I would receive when I introduced this topic—specifically the need for the great young people of my ward to date if they ever hoped to marry. Inevitably, the topic was met with audible groans, eye-rolling, and some snickers and jokes. But behind these immediate reactions, I found a genuine desire on the part of both the men and the women to achieve this important goal. In a survey to young adults, I asked, "What are your primary fears about the future?" Interestingly, 75 percent of respondents mentioned fear regarding marriage as their top concern. Here are some of their responses:

Choosing an eternal companion, since I will spend an eternity with this person, is a big concern. It is important that I don't settle or compromise.

—Phil, 24

I've been fairly confident about most decisions I have made. The only decision that makes me pause is whom to marry.

—Russell, 27

Marriage makes me nervous . . . not because I am afraid of it, but because I fear the other person will not be sure about me.

—Rick, 26

It's a big decision, and making sure it's the right one is the scariest thing. There is so much emphasis from Church leaders about marriage being the most important decision one will ever have to make. It makes sense because *it is* the most important decision and nobody can make it but you. So it's hard.

—Connie, 25

I like a lot of people, but loving them enough to sacrifice my independence takes a lot of love.

—Heidi, 21

I have made the choice to marry despite significant reasons to be disenchanted with marriage. I refuse to let the frustration of dating or even the heartache of a failed marriage rob me of my hope that I can one day enjoy a happy, stable, and meaningful eternal marriage. I don't yet know with whom I'll build this marriage, but I have made the choice to marry nonetheless. Whether realized in this life or the next (and I sincerely hope it is in this life), the choice to marry is ultimately mine.

—Kurt, 25

I was in love once but it didn't work out. So now my concern is this: it was a miracle that I got to feel that way once, but how will I ever get to feel that way again and have that person reciprocate? I don't want to feel the pain of losing love again, but I do want to feel the joy that families bring. What do I have to do to have a normal family/loving experience in my life? I'm concerned that I won't. If that is the case, then so be it and I will press forward happily in faith, but it would be so nice.

—Dave, 25

I have a lot of concerns about marriage. First, how I know whom to marry. It will be hard for me to know for sure. After that comes the rest of eternity to actually be married. I hope that I'm preparing enough, that I'll have patience and charity, that I'll be totally devoted to my husband, and that he'll be devoted to me. I think about keeping the love alive when we've been married a long time and have children and careers to worry about.

—Katie, 19

Obviously most young people in the Church have the righteous desire to marry. Unfortunately, not everyone has the same desire to date. Or maybe they have the desire, but they are encumbered with self-doubts, or bad experiences from the past. I frequently encountered a sense of concern and a feeling of "will it ever happen to me?" Not surprisingly, we discussed it often as a ward. Like my objective then, my intent now is not to beat you over the head about dating—you get your share of that. Rather, I desire to convey a sense of hope, and provide some practical advice.

My friend Stacie, 20, said the following:

"The number one decision that scares me is whom to marry and when to marry. This decision affects not only you, but all your children for eternity. Depending on whom you marry, the course of your life changes. This is a scary decision to make."

About this exciting topic, President Kimball declared, "Marriage is perhaps the most vital of all the decisions and has the most far-reaching effects, for is has to do not only with immediate happiness, but also with eternal joys. It affects not only the two people involved, but their families and particularly their children and their children's children down through the many generations."[2]

To add a little more pressure for those who are struggling with the marriage dilemma, President Kimball added these profound thoughts:

> The greatest single factor affecting where you are going to be tomorrow, your activity, your attitudes, your eventual destiny is the one decision you will make that moonlit night when you ask that individual to be your companion for life. That's the most important decision of your entire life! It isn't where you are going to school, or what lessons you are going to study, or what your major is, or how you are going to make your living. These, though important, are incidental and nothing compared with the important decision that you make when you ask someone to be your companion for eternity. The question, "Whom shall I marry?" is an important one to ask, for the proper answer to this question brings a proper answer to many others. If you marry the proper "whom" and if you marry in the proper "where," then you will have an infinitely better chance of happiness throughout all eternity.[3]

I recently had a work assignment with an organization based on the East Coast where none of my colleagues were LDS. During this assignment I often found myself in the most interesting conversations. One topic that came up often is how young Mormons are when they marry. From their perspective, anyone who gets married before the age of thirty was considered very young. Thomas Holman, a professor of marriage, family and human development, shares this interesting bit of research about that issue:

> Years of research suggest that marriage has the fewest risks of later problems when people marry in their twenties. Marrying in your teens or into your thirties simply increases the risk factors associated with poorer marital quality and stability. Pres. Harold B. Lee emphasized this point to the young brethren of the Church: "Now don't misunderstand me. I am not trying to urge you younger men to marry too early. I think therein is one of the hazards of today's living. We don't want a young man to think of marriage until he is able to take care of a family [and] to be independent. He must make sure that he has found the girl of his choice, they have gone together long enough that they know each other, and that they know each other's faults and they still love each other . . . Please don't misunderstand what we are saying; but, brethren, think more seriously about the obligations of marriage for those who bear the holy priesthood at a time when marriage should be the expectation of every man who understands [his] responsibility.[4]

In assembling this chapter, I gathered some research and organized several focus groups; some with children, some with men, and some with women. Interestingly, a common theme among the research emerged, a theme perhaps most appropriate to the brethren of the Church. This theme is captured in one of my favorite quotes, an ancient Chinese proverb, which is: "You can stand for a long time with your mouth open before a roast duck will fly in." In other words, you have to do something about it if you want it. Here is a synopsis of my non-scientific yet very enlightening research—but first, read some humorous perspectives on love from the rising generation.

1. **How do you decide whom to marry?**
   - You've got to find somebody who likes the same stuff. Like if you like sports, she should like it that you like sports, and she should keep the chips and dip coming. (Alan, age 10)
   - No person really decides before they grow up who they're going to marry. God decided it all way before, and you get to find out later who you're stuck with. (Karen, age 10)

2. **What is the right age to get married?**
   - Twenty-three is the best age because you know the person forever by then. (Camille, age 10)

- No age is good to get married at. You got to be a fool to get married. (Freddie, age 6)

3. **How can a stranger tell if two people are married?**
   - You might have to guess, based on whether they seem to be yelling at the same kids. (Derek, age 8)

4. **What do you think your mom and dad have in common?**
   - Both don't want any more kids. (Lori, age 8)

5. **What do most people do on a date?**
   - Dates are for having fun, and people should use them to get to know each other. Even boys have something to say if you listen long enough. (Lynette, age 8)
   - On the first date, they just tell each other lies, and that usually gets them interested enough to go for a second date. (Martin, age 10)

6. **What would you do on a first date that is turning sour?**
   - I'd run home and play dead. The next day I would call all the newspapers and make sure they write about me in the dead columns. (Craig, age 9)

7. **When is it okay to kiss someone?**
   - When they're rich. (Pam, age 7)
   - The law says you have to be eighteen, so I wouldn't want to mess with that. (Curt, age 7)
   - The rule goes like this: if you kiss someone, then you should marry them and have kids with them. It's the right thing to do. (Howard, age 8)

8. **Is it better to be single or married?**
   - It's better for girls to be single, but not for boys. Boys need someone to clean up after them. (Anita, age 9)

9. **How would the world be if people didn't get married?**
   - There sure would be a lot of kids to explain, wouldn't there? (Kelvin, age 8)

10. **How would you make a marriage work?**
    - Tell your wife she looks pretty even if she looks like a truck. (Ricky, age 10)[5]

I polled approximately 100 single young men and women between the ages of 18 and 30 to get their perspective on dating, love, and the decision to marry. The survey revealed that expensive, over-the-top dates are neither necessary nor expected—time spent together is more important. And despite shifting societal trends, LDS young women still expect young men to take the lead in asking for the date. That said, young men almost universally appreciated some initiative from the women.

Below are the summary highlights of this research, segmenting the responses men from the women.

Question	Men	Women
How far in advance should a person ask for a date?	Two or three days	Three or four days
How do you let someone know you would like to go out with them?	Show extra interest in them and get to know them.	Flirt shamelessly, answer the phone if they call, stand close to them, smile and laugh a lot, and invite them to group activities.
How do you want someone else to let you know they want to go out with you?	Flirt.	Just tell me! Ask me out!
Do you enjoy expensive or inexpensive dates?	Inexpensive dates.	Inexpensive. I hate it when a guy I hardly know spends a lot of money on me.
What keeps you from asking someone you like to go on a date?	I am afraid they don't want to go out with me.	It's the guys' responsibility to do the asking.
Are most of your dates good listeners?	Yes.	Not usually.
Who should take the lead on a date?	Guys.	Guys.

Question	Men	Women
What is important to you in a future spouse?	They have similar goals.	I am interested in seeing how he treats others; I want him to honor his priesthood; and I want to know his goals for the future.
What relationship games occur in dating that you hate?	Pretending to be interested.	Not being straightforward. Also, just hanging out and never actually asking me out—be up front with me!
What first attracts you to another person?	Fun personality.	Physical appearance, confidence kindness, good hygiene, smile, and manners.

In addition to the data from young single adults, I gathered feedback from several couples, some recently married and some married for many years. Here is a synopsis of their advice for women:

Tell the Lord you are ready for marriage—make it a matter of prayer. Work to make yourself an attractive person. You don't have to be a fashion model, but your clothing, your grooming, and a little makeup do make a difference. As President Hinckley counseled, pay a little attention to your appearance.[6]

If you don't know what to do, ask a roommate, a friend, or even your bishop's wife—I'm certain she will be happy to help. Be open to blind dates. In my family, my parents and several siblings met their spouses through a blind date, so it *can* work out. Serve others at every opportunity. Develop social awareness and be genuinely interested in the other person. Have good breath—this goes for the brethren as well. Study the gospel and discuss it. Each of you has a remarkable quality of goodness that is very attractive—cultivate this. Be kind. Live in such a way that others know that for you, living the gospel is a joy, not a burden.

Men, your list is similar. The women I talked with urged you to have a sense of humor and don't take yourselves too seriously. At the same time, be firm in your commitment to the Gospel. Choose now to always be worthy of a temple recommend. Go to ward and stake activities. Be trustworthy. Take advantage of every opportunity to serve and fulfill your priesthood responsibilities. This includes doing your home teaching each month, regardless of how busy your schedule seems. These habits and commitments are important to your future spouse. Your future wife and children will seek priesthood blessings from you in times of need. Live now to be worthy of that incredible privilege. Be kind. Again, live in such a way that others know that for you, living the gospel is a joy and not a burden. In short, be worthy of your future eternal companion. She, along with your future children, are counting on your preparation. Do those things, both large and small, that will establish firm footings for future happiness.

Now a word to both men and women on appearance. This is delicate topic, but one that has significant leverage in the process of dating and courtship. As sensitive as the subject is, I believe it is important to address it. I have heard some say, referring to their lack of desire to dress up, be fashionable, or attempt to look attractive: "I am not that way . . . Those I date (or want to date) should like me for who I am, and I shouldn't have to hassle with making myself up." Don't buy that argument. Your appearance *does* matter.

Some, particularly young women, may feel they aren't attractive, so why bother with the effort to improve appearance? Again, that is a faulty thinking. Everyone needs to put forth their best effort, to be the best they can be. When you take the time to improve your physical appearance, it will increase your self-esteem. I have seen wonderfully talented, gifted, and potentially beautiful young adults sabotage themselves because they don't see themselves living up to a certain physical ideal. So they go in the opposite direction. They become as quirky and extreme in their dress and behavior as they possibly can. They let that become their identity. They hide behind a false persona because they think they can't be anything else.

Let me be crystal clear on this point: I am not saying that everyone needs to conform to the same physical type, because they don't. No one should feel they need to look like the next fashion model. The portrayal in fashion magazines of what women and men should look like is, in my opinion, extremely unhealthy and unrealistic. But you need to be your best self, whatever that is. Put a little bit of effort and thought into the clothing you wear and, for the young women, the makeup you use.

There is a popular show on cable television that highlights both men and women who have been nominated by friends and loved ones to improve their look. Participants on this show typically have low opinions about their physical appearance. The producers of the show don't offer the participants cosmetic surgery, expensive beauty treatments, dermatology visits, or LASIK surgery. Instead, participants receive coaching about the clothing that highlights their body types. They are encouraged to purge their grunge attire—including the old pair of sweats that they have been wearing for five years. They receive advice on how to cut and style their hair, and, for the women, how to apply sensible makeup. The participants emerge from this experience having amazing transformations, and they gain a better understanding of what looks good. More important, they feel differently and see themselves differently.

Ultimately, this transformation is not just about dating and finding someone to marry. This is about esteem. It is as applicable to someone who is married as it is to the person who is not in a relationship. It is about figuring out what is the most complimentary and sensible way to present yourself. It is about becoming the best version of yourself.

I saw this transformation firsthand with one young woman who was naturally very beautiful, but didn't see that reality when she looked in the mirror. She didn't know what to do to change, but she was open to and sought assistance from her mother and aunts. She had always been kind, good, and likable. She had many wonderful talents and abilities, but no one really knew it. She was shy and allowed her personality to languish in the shadows. So her mother and her aunts gave her a "day of beauty." They did her hair and coached her on the type of clothing and makeup she should wear to accentuate her natural gifts. This experience didn't change her into a glamour queen; however, she emerged with a better perspective of what she had to offer, the result was spectacular. While this was not done explicitly as a way of attracting attention and recognition from young men, it did have that effect. Interestingly, it also encouraged additional positive behavior and improved confidence.

Of course your appearance need not become the most important thing in your life, because it isn't. But it is an important component, and often, it is the first thing others notice.

I am sure I am not referring to all of you, but over the years I have encountered some individuals, mostly men, who are seeking perfection, or at least someone who is as perfect as they think they are. Please understand this truth about marriage: whoever you marry will not be exactly the same person in two years or five years down the road. When you are courting and engaged, and even for the first eight to twelve months of marriage, you don't know each other's worst habits and idiosyncrasies. But you will come to know them. My wife might have thought she was marrying a nine or a ten, and after a few months she discovered she married a two or a three. Thankfully, the gospel provides the opportunity for couples to work toward perfection and get through the rough spots together. So instead trying to find perfection, find a good person whom you love, who has a good and giving heart, who is committed to working together with you in the gospel.

Consider the following wisdom from the poet Shel Silverstein:

If you want to marry me, here's what you'll have to do:
You must learn how to make a perfect chicken-dumpling stew
And you must sew my holey socks,
And soothe my troubled mind,
And develop the knack for scratching my back,
And keep my shoes spotlessly shined.
And while I rest you must rake up the leaves,
And when it is hailing and snowing
You must shovel the walk . . . and be still when I talk,
And—hey—where are you going?[7]

On this point, Elder Richard G. Scott admonished, "I suggest that you not ignore many possible candidates who are still developing these attributes, seeking the one who is perfected in them. You will likely not find that perfect person, and if you did, there would certainly be no interest in you. These attributes are best polished *together* as husband and wife."[8]

Bruce Chadwick offers this insight:

Those who are married will agree that [a] Cinderella mentality of "if I marry the right person, we will live happily ever after" fails to prepare couples for married life. When problems arise in a marriage—and they will arise—a husband or wife is tempted to think, "Oh no, I married the wrong person because I am not happy ever after." Nonsense! Good marriages are created after you get up from your knees at the altar of the temple. Strong marriages emerge out of helping each other obtain [an] education, struggling financially, dealing with sickness, and coping with the shock produced by the birth of [the] first child. Life changes and moves ahead in many unanticipated ways. Changing jobs, moving to a different city, raising teenagers, caring for an aged parent, retirement, and similar activities and events are what produce eternal marriages. Overcoming these problems as a team—helping and supporting each other along the way—are what produce a happy marriage.[9]

And Brad, 24, advises:

I think that many times people think that a happy marriage has no conflicts, but I think that a happy marriage has two people that know how to resolve conflicts. Two people that really love each other and realize that being right isn't what matters and that there doesn't always have to be one person who is right. A happy marriage is one where both people sacrifice, but don't realize that they are making sacrifices. To them, they are just doing something to help the person that they love. Happiness doesn't come from the size of the ring that the girl gets, it comes from the girl and the guy realizing that their spouse would do anything for them, no matter the consequence.

What happens if you do all in your power for the opportunity for marriage, but it never happens? Given the doctrine of eternal marriage and the essential role it plays in our ultimate progression, how do you come to terms with your position? We may not feel prepared with an answer for why some will go through life without ever finding a spouse. It is in the hands of a loving Heavenly Father who will answer the question. Julie Beck, General Relief Society President said:

It reminds me of an experience my husband had while playing on a high school basketball team. The players had prepared well and traveled to the gymnasium of their rival team. They were physically and mentally ready to beat their opponents. They were in the locker room, and the coach had just finished his pep talk. They were bursting with energy and confidence as they ran for the door that led onto the playing floor. It was locked! The ballplayers plowed into each other against the door, and their energy went flat in the locker room before the game ever started.

Sometimes I think that is what happens to you when we talk to you about marriage and family. We encourage you to get excited about the possibilities, but in reality you may feel you are pushing against a locked door. You do not need to live a life of waiting and wondering. You do not need to lose the momentum and enthusiasm that you now have and that the Lord needs from you in order to build His kingdom.[10]

President Howard W. Hunter councils: "No blessing, including that of eternal marriage and an eternal family, will be denied to any worthy individual. While it may take somewhat longer, perhaps even beyond this mortal life for some to achieve this blessing, it will not be denied."[11]

Elder Bruce C. Hafen adds this insight regarding the timing of marriage: "If you seek . . . to do [the Lord's] will, all the rest will take care of itself. Never forget that all things work together for good to them who love God (see Romans 8:28). Your time for marriage may not come until the autumn of your life and then, in Elder Packer's phrase: 'be more precious for the waiting.' Even if your time should not come in this life, the promises of eternal love are still yours in the Lord's view of time if only you are faithful."[12]

In its early years, the Church experienced periods of financial distress. At a point of significant financial hardship, the Lord issued a revelation to the Prophet Joseph Smith declaring that the Saints were to get out of debt. The only problem was that difficult economic conditions existed, jobs were scarce or non-existent, and pressure and persecution of Church members seemed ubiquitous. In this difficult and seemingly impossible scenario, the Lord issued a formula for accomplishing the difficult or even the impossible. This formula applies even when the goal is marriage. Listen closely to his promise, and as you consider your desires for marriage, know the Lord is prepared to assist you in all your righteous efforts.

"And it is my will that you shall humble yourselves before me, and obtain this blessing by your diligence and humility and the prayer of faith. And inasmuch as you are diligent and humble, and exercise the prayer of faith, behold, I will soften the hearts of those to whom you are in debt, until I shall send means unto you for your deliverance" (D&C 104:79–80).

You will note this formula mirrors the formula in D&C 90:24 discussed in chapter one. Again, here are the steps to the formula: be humble, exercise the prayer of faith, and then be diligent, doing everything in your power to do your part. Let's look more closely at each of the elements of the formula.

Be humble. This means putting the Lord first in thought and action, truly seeking to do His will. Don't resent the admonition to marry. It is a commandment, and represents the highest ordinance you will receive in this life. It is one of the primary reasons we came to earth. Some of you may struggle with a fear of marriage, and sometimes you have good reason. One woman, 24, wrote to me from Hong Kong and said, "I am really concerned about having a family like the one in which I grew up. I have no desire to get married." Some young adults have been fortunate enough to have grown up in loving environments and stable families with two doting parents. Others have not been as lucky. You may have witnessed abuse or other extreme dysfunction, but remember, while you may be conditioned by your environment it does not ultimately determine your future marriage. You are a product of your choices. When a couple invites the Lord into their partnership, it helps smooth jagged edges and more fully develop Christlike attributes. Simply put, a righteous marriage should be the desire of your heart, and you should be actively pursuing it. Take comfort in the Lord's declaration: "Be thou humble, and the Lord thy God shall lead thee by the hand and give thee answers to thy prayers" (D&C 112:10).

Exercise the prayer of faith. I understand that a decision as significant as marriage, with all its eternal consequences, can be daunting. Take hope from the scriptures. After forty years of wandering, the children of Israel were prepared to enter the promised land, and Moses had passed the torch of leadership to Joshua, and Jehovah was prepared to provide a miracle to "impress upon the children of Israel that Joshua was the new prophet and to test their courage one last time."[13] Bruce Chadwick offers this insight:

> Joshua had the camp of Israel move close to the river and asked each man and woman, "sanctify yourselves" (Joshua 3:5). In this day that would mean to wash your clothes, turn off trashy television, catch up on your tithing, read the scriptures, and say your prayers. These activities would encourage the Spirit to dwell with you. In the morning the children of Israel were not left as spectators high on the riverbanks when it was time to part the waters. Rather, 12 men carried the Ark of the Covenant to the water's edge. Then, as the Lord explained, "And it shall come to pass, as soon as the soles of the feet of the priests that bear the ark of the Lord, the Lord of all the earth, shall rest in the waters of Jordan, that the waters of Jordan shall be cut off from the waters that come down from above; and they shall stand upon an heap" (Joshua 3:13).

It took faith and courage for those 12 men and the children of Israel who followed to step off the bank into the swirling waters of the spring runoff. As the water covered the soles of their feet, the miracle then happened, and the waters were stopped.

So it may be with you in your quest for an eternal partner or for an eternal relationship. We cannot sit in our apartments, we cannot spend long hours at work, we cannot endlessly play video games and wait for the Lord to bring a spouse to the altar for us.[14]

Make your goal a matter of daily prayer. Seek to understand Heavenly Father's will for your life, and have faith in His promises. Stay positive. Be a disciple of Christ. Consider the stirring advice from Elder Holland:

> In Mormon's and Paul's final witnesses, they declare that "charity [or pure love] never faileth" (Moroni 7:46; 1 Corinthians 13:8). It is there through thick and thin. It endures through darkest sorrow and into the light. It never fails. So Christ loved us, and that is how He hoped we would love each other. In a final injunction to all his disciples for all time, He said, "A new commandments I give unto you. That ye love one another *as I have loved you*" (John 13:34, emphasis added). Of course such Christlike staying power in romance and marriage requires more than any of us really have. It requires something more, an endowment from heaven. Remember Mormon's promise, that such love—the love we each yearn for and cling to—is "bestowed" upon "true followers of Christ."
>
> You want capability, safety, and security in dating and romance, in married life and eternity? Be a true disciple of Jesus. Be a genuine, committed, word-and-deed Latter-day Saint. Believe that your faith has *everything* to do with your romance, because it does. You separate dating from discipleship at your peril. Or, to phrase that more positively, Jesus Christ, the Light of the World, is the only lamp by which you can successfully see the path of love and happiness for you *and* for your sweetheart.[15]

Be diligent. As stated earlier, there is no need to rush into a decision. Don't be foolish simply for the sake of getting married. Stephen R. Covey offers this dating and marriage advice specifically to returning missionaries:

> I do not believe any time limit can or should be given to returning missionaries as to when they should get married. It depends too much on the people involved and their degree of maturity. . . . Trust in God

and act on true principles. Be patient. Don't expect perfection over-night. Be honest and have sincere dating and courtship relationships. Make your courtship a spiritual one. Pray with each other. Before marriage go to the temple several times, if this is possible.[16]

Being diligent means doing everything in your power to accomplish the goal. Take a minute to be introspective—are you really doing every-thing in your power to obey the commandment to marry? Elder Dallin H. Oaks addressed this theme with the young single adults of the Church. He reminded them (you) that the average age at marriage for LDS couple has increased over the last several years. As a result, the numbers of chil-dren born to LDS couples has decreased dramatically. Dating has been largely replaced with "hanging out." This trend is a cause for concern among the leaders of the Church. To the men, Elder Oaks stated:

"Men, if you have returned from your mission and you are still fol-lowing the boy-girl patterns you were counseled to follow when you were 15, it is time for you to grow up. Gather your courage and look for some-one to pair off with . . . it's marriage time. That is what the Lord intends for his young sons and daughters."[17]

To the women, Elder Oaks was equally clear. He said:

"Young women, resist too much hanging out, and encourage dates that are simple, inexpensive, and frequent. Don't make it easy for young men to hang out in a setting where you women provide the food. Don't subsidize the freeloaders. An occasional group activity is okay, but when you see men who make hanging out their primary interaction with the opposite sex, I think you should lock the pantry and bolt the front door."[18]

I am grateful for the decision I made more than twenty years ago when I asked my beautiful sweetheart to be my wife. While I have made some poor decisions in my life, as we all do from time to time, I have done some good things. On rare occasions, I have even done some great things, and asking her to marry me tops the list. I first met Michele in the second grade. Her last name was Garbett, and I remember calling her Michele Garbage. I also called her "hairy arms" because, well, she had hairy arms. Seven-year-old boys can be so funny!

As we grew older, I began to see her in a little different light. We dated in high school, and though I frequently questioned why she would want to be seen with me, I was happy nonetheless. However, we didn't write much while I was on my mission, so when I returned, I wasn't sure what to expect. But the sparks were still there, and the pieces began to fall into place. Pretty fast actually. I distinctly remember the feelings of peace we felt as we knelt together to ask the Lord for his confirmation of our decision to marry. It was a different feeling than I had experienced before. I was not anxious, nervous, or confused. There were no lightening bolts or angels with trumpets. It was just peace.

While we were engaged, I worried about my lack of financial preparation for marriage and limited college education, which led to occasional feelings of uncertainty or doubt: Was this the one? Was I just being emotionally retarded? Was I moving too fast? When I had these feelings, I would drop to my knees, and again the Lord would overwhelm me with feelings of peace and assurance that He knew me, He knew us, and that our decision was right. I love the Lord's words to Oliver Cowdery in Doctrine and Covenants section 6: "Verily, verily I say unto you, if you desire a further witness, cast your mind upon the night that you cried unto me in your heart. . . . Did I not speak peace to your mind concerning the matter? What greater witness can you have than from God?" (D&C 6:22–23).

I cannot adequately explain the emotions I felt as we knelt across the altar in the Salt Lake Temple when, hand-in-hand, we heard those most beautiful words of the sealing ceremony. It was both sacred and stunning, awesome and overwhelming. Over the years, my love and admiration for my wife has only deepened. She is the love of my life. I echo the words King Arthur spoke about his wife when I think of mine: "If I could choose from every woman who breathes on this earth, the face I would most love, the smile, the touch, the voice, the heart, the laugh, the soul itself, every detail and feature to the smallest strand of hair—they would be [Michele's]."[19]

I like to envision our fiftieth wedding anniversary. I will be bald, and she will be shorter—but we will still be good-looking. Our children and grandchildren will surround us. We will tell stories of the "old days." We will have weathered the storms of adversity and sickness and experienced both great sorrow and profound joy. Most important, we will have experienced all these things *together*.

Those are the blessings that await you. It is true that marriage is filled with challenge and struggle and difficulty. Ask any person that is married. However, it also brings greater happiness and joy and fulfillment than you have ever experienced. It is the Lord's way. Make Him your partner as you pursue the path to marriage. He will remove obstacles in your way, present opportunities, and give you courage. And make the firm decision that He will be the most important part of your relationship after you marry. If you do this, greater blessings than you can imagine await you. Remember that He knows you, He loves you, and He seeks every good thing for you. As you do your part with a prayerful heart, with faith and diligence and humility, He will direct your paths.

Notes

1. Sheri L. Dew, *Ezra Taft Benson: A Biography* (Salt Lake City: Deseret Book, 1987), 80.

2. Spencer W. Kimball, "Oneness in Marriage," *Ensign*, Mar. 1977, 3–4.

3. Spencer W. Kimball, *Teachings of Spencer W. Kimball,* (Salt Lake City: Bookcraft, 1995), 301.

4. Thomas Holman, "The Right Person, the Right Place, the Right Time: Guidelines for Wisely Choosing a Spouse," BYU Devotional, 1 August 2000.

5. Things People Said: Kids' Ideas about Love, 3 March 2006, http://www.rinkworks.com/said/kidlove.shtml.

6. Gordon B. Hinckley, "Your Greatest Challenge, Mother," *Ensign*, Nov. 2000, 97

7. Shel Silverstein, *Where the Sidewalk Ends* (New York: Harper Collins, 1974).

8. Richard G. Scott, "Receive the Temple Blessings," *Ensign*, May 1999, 25.

9. Bruce A. Chadwick, "Hanging Out, Hooking Up, and Celestial Marriage," BYU Devotional, 7 May 2002.

10. Julie Beck, "Unlocking the Door to the Blessings of Abraham." CES Fireside for Young Adults, 2 March 2008.

11. Howard W. Hunter, "The Church Is for All People," *Ensign*, Jun. 1989, 75.

12. Bruce C. Hafen, "The Gospel and Romantic Love," *New Era*, Feb. 2002, 10.

13. Chadwick, "Hanging Out, Hooking Up, and Celestial Marriage."

14. Ibid.

15. Jeffrey R. Holland. "How do I Love Thee?" BYU Devotional, 15 February 2000.

16. Stephen R. Covey, *Spiritual Roots of Human Relations* (Salt Lake City: Deseret Book Company, 1970), 334.

17. Dallin H. Oaks, "Steady Dedication of a Lifetime," CES Fireside for Young Adults, 1 May 2005.

18. Ibid.

19. Scene 25, Camelot, (DVD), Directed by Moss Hart, Warner Brothers, 1967.

8

ONe BY ONe

He answers privately, Reaches my reaching
In my Gethsemane, Savior and Friend.
Gentle the peace he finds for my beseeching.
Constant he is and kind, Love without end.[1]

—Emma Lou Thayne

I am intrigued by the cosmos and the unfathomable extent of time and space. It all reminds me of the Psalmist's poignant contemplation: "When I consider the heavens, the work of thy fingers, the moon and the stars, which thou hast ordained; What is man, that thou art mindful of him? And the son of man, that thou visitest him? . . . O Lord our Lord, how excellent is thy name in all the earth!" (Psalms 8:3–4, 9).

I read a news report in which scientists estimate that there are at least seventy sextillion stars in the heavens. Seventy sextillion—that's a seventy with twenty-two zeros! In fact, it is about ten times as many stars as grains of sand on all the world's beaches. I am not sure how these scientists determine their numbers—those figures are created by people far more intelligent than I—but the expanse of it all is mind-boggling. The report also noted that there are likely many more stars; this is just the number visible within the range of modern telescopes. Our universe is so large that light from the other side of the universe has not yet reached us.[2]

As you ponder this, try this bit of interesting research. Do a Google search on "Hubble Field," and take a look at the recent pictures from the

Hubble Space Telescope. You will access the deepest pictures ever taken in space. These are fascinating and spectacularly beautiful images that show hundreds of tiny dots of light. Each dot or spiral is itself a galaxy containing billions of stars. Scientists have counted more than fifteen hundred galaxies in the Deep Field Image. More startling, however, is that this image covers only the portion of the sky equal to a grain of sand held at arm's length.

In the Book of Moses, we read of Enoch's interview with the Lord after he was caught up into His presence:

> And it came to pass that the God of heaven looked upon the residue of the people, and he wept; and Enoch bore record of it, saying: How is it that the heavens weep, and shed forth their tears as the rain upon the mountains?
>
> And Enoch said unto the Lord: How is it that thou canst weep, seeing thou are holy, and from all eternity to all eternity?
>
> And were it possible that man could number the particles of the earth, yea, millions of earths like this, it would not be a beginning to the number of thy creations; and thy curtains are stretched out still; and yet thou art there and thy bosom is there; and also thou art just; thou art merciful and kind forever;
>
> And thou hast taken Zion to thine own bosom, from all thy creations, from all eternity to all eternity; and naught but peace, justice, and truth is the habitation of thy throne; and mercy shall go before thy face and have no end; how is it that thou canst weep?" (Moses 7: 28–31)

The Lord's answer to Enoch's question sheds tremendous light on His love for His children.

> The Lord said unto Enoch: Behold these thy brethren; they are the workmanship of mine own hands, and I gave unto them their knowledge, in the day I created them; and in the Garden of Eden, gave I unto man his agency;
>
> And unto thy brethren have I said, and also given commandment, that they should love one another, and that they should choose me, their Father; but behold, they are without affection, and they hate their own blood. (Moses 7: 32–33)

If it were possible that we could number all the particles of both this earth and millions of earths like it, it would not even be a beginning to the number of God's creations.

Now go with me to the new world where the Savior appears to the Nephites in the land Bountiful. When juxtaposed with Enoch's vision, this wonderful vignette demonstrates the intimate nature of the Lord's love, and both the infinite and the personal aspect of the Atonement. Remember the scene: the Lamanites and Nephites had experienced the terrible destruction associated with the Lord's crucifixion. Entire cities had been destroyed either by fire, by earthquake, or by being swallowed up in the depths of the sea. But the righteous in the Land Bountiful and other locations survived. The people first hear a voice "as if it came out of heaven." They describe it as neither harsh nor loud, yet "it did pierce them that did hear it to the center, insomuch that there was no part of their frame that it did not cause to quake; yea it did pierce them to the very soul, and did cause their hearts to burn" (3 Nephi 11:3).

Three times the voice is heard, and on the third time, the Nephites finally understand: this is the voice of the Father. They then witness the glorious descension of the Son of God, clothed in white. After Jesus declares Himself to the people of Bountiful, they fall to the earth, overcome by the Spirit. Jesus then does something that for me, as I read the account, is one of the great illustrations of His love. He invites each of the twenty-five hundred people of Bountiful to approach him and to "thrust their hands into his side [and] . . . feel the prints of the nails in his hand and in his feet; and this they did do, going forth *one by one* until they had *all* gone forth" (3 Nephi 11:15, emphasis added). Only after they have this experience and personally feel of His love for each of them, individually, does He teach them.

The image of "one by one" reminds us that he knows us one by one—despite the vastness of His creations and the expanse of His heavens, whose greatness and glory is ever-increasing as His curtains are being "stretched out still" (Moses 7:30). He knows us *individually* and *personally*. If, in this Land Bountiful experience, each person, including the transition time required to move from person to person, were to take just ten seconds with the Savior, this would have required almost seven hours to complete! And this is precisely what occurred.

Like the people in the land Bountiful, Moses learned the nature of the Lord's individual love for His children when he was transfigured before the Lord and was given the opportunity to glimpse the greatness of God's creations. He beheld "worlds without number," (see Moses 1:33) and saw Adam and the inhabitants of this earth and other worlds. The Lord tells him, "But an account of this earth, and the inhabitants thereof, give I unto you. For behold, there are many worlds that have passed away by the word of my power. And there are many that now stand, and innumerable are they unto man; but *all things are numbered unto me, for they are mine and I know them*" (Moses 1:35, emphasis added). We cannot comprehend how this happens, but with all God's creations, we are numbered and known. I truly stand all amazed.

I learned of the reality of this powerful principle early in my mission. I had been in the great Pennsylvania Philadelphia Mission all of three months and my companion had been out two months. We were traveling to a very important meeting at a distant church located in an area unknown to us. While we were on the Pennsylvania Turnpike we heard some strange noises emanating from our car's engine, and soon smoke began to pour from under the hood. Nervous that we might have serious car trouble that would prevent us from keeping our appointment, we pulled the car over and together we prayed that the Lord would bless our car and enable it to get us to our meeting. With sincere humility we reminded the Lord of the importance of this meeting to the work we were doing and that we were on His errand. We asked once more that He would intervene in our behalf, and we set out on our way again with shaky faith and a prayer in our hearts. Just minutes after that, our engine abruptly stalled and we were forced to coast our car to the side of the road, feeling depressed and abandoned. We wondered aloud why our prayers had not been heard. Not knowing what else to do, we set out on foot, unfamiliar with our surroundings, and very discouraged.

However, God does answer the prayers of his missionaries. After we walked only thirty yards or so, a decrepit, copper-colored station wagon pulled in front of us. The back of it was missing, protected only by a sheet of plastic. A scruffy-looking man with wild hair and a goatee got out and approached us. We were not sure if we should speak to him or run. Then he asked us, "Are you the Mormon Elders?" We said we were. He asked if we were having car trouble, which we acknowledged. He asked us where we were going. We told him we had a very important meeting at a certain church, still some way off. He then smiled as he informed us that he was a member of the Church and was employed as the custodian of the very building where we had our meeting! He told us that as he was leaving his home that morning he felt prompted to delay for a few minutes, not knowing why. Upon meeting us, we both realized that our prayer had been heard, that his delay caused his travel to coincide exactly with our car breaking down.

We were reminded again that God does know us and He provides miracles in our lives. Because of his ability to listen to the Spirit, our new friend was able to deliver us on time for our meeting, and he then spent the remainder of the day fixing our car and helping us on our way.

Such is the nature of God's love for His children. At the conclusion of a very long but beautiful and transcendent day in the land Bountiful, the Savior was ready to ascend back to the presence of His Father. The multitude, again overcome and in tears, entreated Him to stay. Jesus had compassion on the people, honored their request, and healed their sick. He then offered a miraculous prayer for his children:

"The eye hath never seen, neither hath the ear heard, before, so great and marvelous things as we saw and heard Jesus speak unto the Father; And no tongue can speak . . . neither can the hearts of men conceive so great and marvelous things as we both saw and heard Jesus speak; and no one can conceive of the joy which filled our souls at the time we heard him pray for us unto the Father" (3 Nephi 17: 16–17).

Jesus, emotions tender, then wept with the multitude before he called for the children, and again, He took them *one by one*, blessed them and prayed unto the Father for them. "And they saw the heavens open, and they saw angels descending out of the heaven as if it were in the midst of fire; and they came down and encircled those little ones about . . . with fire; and the angels did minister unto them" (3 Nephi 11:21, 24).

On Memorial Day a few years ago, my family and I decided to take our boat out for a little fun in the sun. We had planned on leaving at 10:30 AM. As I was attempting to hitch up the boat to my truck that morning, I was having a great deal of trouble getting the hitch to engage. I couldn't understand why, as this was something I had done a hundred times before. It literally took me forty-five minutes to get the boat hooked up. By this time, I was angry and impatient (does this surprise anyone?). We hurriedly loaded the kids up, gassed up the boat, and made it to the marina. I had Michele back the boat trailer into the water, but as I attempted to start the boat, I ran into more trouble. This time the engine would not turn over. I tried and tried to get it going, but all I was doing was wearing the battery down, and it eventually died. I asked a man who was loading his boat next to mine if I could get a jump. He said yes, but that was unsuccessful. Then he told me he was a boat mechanic, and was certified to work on my very engine. Fortuitously, he had all the necessary tools in the back of his truck. As he looked at my engine, he discovered the fuel line was disconnected. He fixed us up, gave us a jump (which worked this time), and we were finally on our way after literally hours of delay.

Several times during this experience, I felt like giving up and going home. Sometimes family fun is not much fun—at least it wasn't for me that day. But after we got going, we came to understand why we were delayed.

I was pulling my young son and daughter in the tube behind the boat, and noticed something funny in the distance, toward the middle of the lake. It looked like birds perched on the water, but not exactly. I chose to take a closer look. The closer I got, the more unusual it seemed. Finally, we were close enough to recognize what was in the water: three people, waving their arms and shouting, with no boat in sight. As I approached the first person, a woman, I asked if she was okay. She replied frantically that she was not, that her two-year-old daughter was missing with their boat, and that her five-year-old daughter and husband who were in the water also needed help. We quickly got her aboard, and then picked up her five-year-old daughter and headed for her husband, who was about 150 yards away. Just as we approached him, he slipped under water, unable to hold on any longer. I reached down and grabbed him and literally had to pull him aboard, as his strength was entirely sapped. He flopped upside down on our back seat and we had to lift him back up. All he could do was lie there; he had no strength to talk, and barely had strength to breathe. He had blood coming from his mouth, and after a time he was able to make it to the side of the boat where he vomited. My children's eyes were as wide as saucers. Had we been there just fifteen seconds later, he would not have made it. As we looked back on our experiences of the morning, we realized that had we not had the trouble with the hitch and the engine, we would not have been in the right place at the right time. Furthermore, had the man who helped us not been certified to work on our exact engine and been able to diagnose the trouble, with the training and tools to repair the engine at the launch ramp, that family would have suffered an unspeakable tragedy.

We learned from the woman what had happened. The family was on the Lake celebrating the five-year-old's birthday. The dad was pulling the mom and birthday girl on an air mattress behind the boat, when the mattress flipped and tangled in the rope. The dad, who was with his two-year-old daughter (but who was not wearing a life jacket), panicked and jumped in to save his wife and daughter, but failed to disengage the boat's engine. As he jumped in, the boat continued on with the two-year-old still on board. The boat and the two-year-old kept going on, and the family was stranded. They were stuck for over forty-five minutes, and the dad had to tread water. I asked the woman if she knew where the boat was and she replied she didn't, as her glasses were on the boat and she couldn't see.

After we got everyone on board, we began our search for the boat. I asked my kids to pray that we would find the boat and the girl, which they immediately did. I was grateful they knew what to do, and I felt comfort and strength in their simple faith. Miraculously, and as a specific answer to their prayers, we drove directly to the boat. (Utah Lake is huge, and the boat could have been almost anywhere, including crashed against the shore or into another boat.) It was only going about fifteen miles per hour. I had Michele take the controls of our boat and move up next to the wayward craft, which I boarded, and then disengaged the engine. The two-year-old was relieved and somewhat confused, as she didn't know where her mother and father had gone and why they had left.

Our entire family was deeply humbled at the timing of the situation. I came away confident that the Lord had directed us on their behalf, and I was grateful we had been able to be His instruments that day. Thankfully, all ended well and everyone was safe. I share this story to emphasize this point: the Lord knows each of you and your individual situations. He knows of your struggles, your self-doubts, your challenges and your temptations. It is not a mistake or coincidence that you are on the earth at this time. There are great things in store for each of you, and despite the difficulty and pressure you face daily, there is much happiness, fulfillment, and success that awaits. And He is willing and anxious to help you as you strive to do His will.

Always remember: He atoned for your sins. Repentance is real and available to each of us. Just do it. And remember He also suffered "pains and afflictions and temptations of every kind; and this that the word might be fulfilled which saith he will take upon him the pains and the sicknesses of his people. And he will take upon him death, that he may loose the bands of death which bind his people; and he will take upon him their infirmities, that his bowels may be filled with mercy, according to the flesh, that he may know according to the flesh how to succor his people according to their infirmities" (Alma 7:11–12).

Just like He watched over the family in the water that day, He is watching over you. He will send you His angels and others to assist you in your trials. You are not alone in this journey. There are legions that cheer for you and pray for you and work for you, both on this side of the veil and beyond.

Joseph Smith taught: "Happiness is the object and design of our existence; and will be the end thereof, if we pursue the path that leads to it; and this path is virtue, uprightness, faithfulness, holiness, and keeping all the commandments of God."[3] Clearly, the key to happiness in this life is obedience. As we are obedient, we will feel the Spirit, and if we feel the Spirit, we will be happy. When I am obedient, I feel the Spirit. When I feel the Spirit, I have more love for my wife, more love and patience for my children, more insight at my job, and greater charity for my fellow man. I testify that as you are obedient, you will feel the Spirit guiding and directing and protecting you in all your efforts.

I love the words of the ancient prophet: "They that be with us are more than they that be with them" (2 Kings 6:16). The Lord promises that as we do our part, He will go before our face, He will be on our right hand and on our left, that His Spirit shall be in our hearts, and He will send His angels round about us to bear us up (see D&C 84:88). I am grateful for the life and sacrifice of the Son of God, even Jesus Christ.

I am grateful for the lowly manger, the Garden of Gethsemane, His condescension below all things, the thorns in His side, the nails in His hands, and the ultimate and infinite sacrifice for me and for my family and for you and your families. I know He knows me. I know He knows my frailties and failures. I testify that He rejoices in our success over temptation and yet His "hand is stretched out still" (see 2 Nephi 15:25) when we fall. I know that He lived in mortality and lives in eternity. As I contemplate the grace and grandeur of His divine gift, "I marvel that He would descend from his throne divine to rescue a soul so rebellious and proud as mine."[4]

Because of His condescension below all things, He has the power to help and heal and save, for He has been there. When we are racked with sin, when we are destitute or ill, when we suffer unspeakable pain, when we are misjudged or torn by others, He will relate to us in His own divine way. When our family is ripped by strife, we must remember "the Lord in his condescension unto the children of men hath visited men in so much mercy, why should [our] heart[s] weep?" (2 Nephi 4:26). As Charles H. Gabriel wrote, so I declare: "I think of his hands pierced and bleeding to pay the debt! Such mercy, such love, and devotion can I forget? No, no I will praise and adore at the mercy seat, until at the glorified throne I kneel at his feet."[5]

Notes

1. "Where Can I Turn for Peace," *Hymns*, no. 129.

2. "Star Survey reaches 70 Sextillion," 22 July 2003, CNN.com/2003/ TECH/space/07/22/stars.survey/index.html.

3. Joseph Smith, *Teachings of the Prophet Joseph Smith* (Salt Lake City: Shadow Mountain, 1977), 255

4. "I Stand All Amazed," *Hymns*, no. 191.

5. Ibid.

ABOUT THE AUTHOR

A native of Utah's Wasatch Front, Shawn D. Moon has traveled the globe mostly for his professional career, but occasionally he travels to simply satisfy the urge to see beyond the present moment and local scenery. Accompanying him to many of the far-flung places is Michele, Shawn's wife, whom he met in the second grade. Sometime between recess and high school graduation they fell in love and, following Shawn's service in the Pennsylvania Philadelphia Mission—but before graduation from Brigham Young University—they were married. After a few moves, including time in Washington D.C., they eventually settled in Lindon, Utah, on the slope of a picturesque mountain where they, with their four bright, well-favored children enjoy music, theater, sporting events, and frequent visits from elk and deer herds that regularly ravage their lawn, trees, and garden, supplying motivation for constant vigil and healthy, strenuous activity.